LONG LEASE!

The Story of Slough Estates
1920 - 1991

By MICHAEL CASSELL

A Pencorp Book
in the Pencorp Management Series

Published by:
Pencorp Books
Beagle House
80 Hill Top
London NW11 6EE
Tel: 081-458 9343
Fax: 081-455 7828

ISBN: 1 870092 02 3

Set in 9 1/2 pt Garamond and printed by Biddles Ltd., Walnut Tree House,
Woodbridge Park, Guildford, Surrey GU1 1DA.

Designed by The Production House, London

CONTENTS

ACKNOWLEDGEMENTS

THANK goodness for long memories. The story of Slough Estates stretches back more than 70 years and my task in chronicling one of Britain's most remarkable property stories was made so much easier - and more interesting - with the help of people who, between them, could recall almost the entire period in question.

Companies are inanimate entities. They are only brought alive by the characters who populate them and the events which surround, and sometimes overtake, them. In the case of Slough Estates there are many who have helped the business on its way since the 1920s and who were more than happy to recall and reminisce.

All those who were asked to play a part in telling the tale - from within the company and without - responded readily and enthusiastically, for which I express my gratitude. Without them, the task would have been impossibly difficult.

The assistance of John Isherwood, whose knowledge of many aspects of the earliest days of the Slough Estate proved invaluable, and of Richard Peskett, a bottomless mine of information on the early days of road transport, made my task so much easier. Isobel Thompson, the curator of Slough Musuem, also gave expert and invaluable guidance.

My thanks also to the Slough Estate directors, past and present, and to the large number of current and former employees of the company drawn from every level of the business who helped paint the picture. Without exception they made clear their respect and affection for the company which had played a part in their lives.

I must also thank Peter Hardy and Roger Moore of S.G. Warburg Securities for helping me understand and portray the business as it confronts the last decade of the century in which it was born.

I would particularly like to thank Brigadier Neville White for co-ordinating the project within the company, ever-ready to answer increasingly urgent inquiries at startling speed. Thanks also to Arnold Kransdorff, my editor and publisher, always on hand when necessary.

Above all, I must pay tribute to Austin Wormleighton, my researcher, whose enthusiasm, diligence and painstaking hard work put my own contribution firmly in its place.

Michael Cassell,
Clunton,
Shropshire.
March 1991.

PREFACE

TAKE A pinch of free-wheeling entrepreneurial spirit, a nose for a deal and an eye for an opportunity and the story of Slough Estates quickly begins to take shape.

It is a story with an unlikely beginning in the second decade of this century, about pioneering, far-sightedness, cool heads, perseverance, and a carefully calculated determination to succeed.

It is a story which began at the height of a bloody war and which quickly became enveloped in a national controversy over the mismanagement and waste of scarce public resources. Winston Churchill, no less, would play a role in the row which ultimately led to the creation of a business born in a muddy field and destined to spread around the world.

Government embarrassment over its involvement in a huge mechanical repair depot to the west of London, conceived in time of war but hardly underway when hostilities ended, offered a once-in-a-lifetime opportunity to Noel Mobbs, a clever businessman who knew a thing or two about motor vehicles.

With a group of wealthy colleagues he bought a 600-acre site at Slough, known locally as "The Dump," started repairing the lines of rotting and cannibalised vehicles and selling them off. When that ended and he was left with vacant land, he began to develop a centre for industrial production, the likes of which had not been seen before.

The business survived the Great Depression and the bombers of the Second World War and, by the 1950s, was beginning to spread its wings abroad. It was becoming one of the largest landlords of industrial property anywhere in the world, its success based on a determination to provide manufacturing accommodation on fair terms and in a way which relieved its tenants of huge capital expenditure.

The formula was to prove spectacularly successful and almost impervious to the ravages which beset other property development and investment companies. As the big names in British property tumbled out of bed in the early 1970s, Slough Estates went from strength-to-strength.

Despite the highly disruptive ups and downs of repeated economic cycles and increasingly draconian attempts by government to manipulate the property industry's activities, the group has prospered, its profits rising annually for more than four decades. In a business where companies came and went, people made fortunes and lost them, Slough Estates remained sound, solid and consistent.

The group's very predictability is a source of regular criticism. It is accused of being boring in what is a very racy business. Its answer always lies in yet another remarkable corporate performance.

For years almost wholly dependent on the industrial market - the "Cinderella" of the property world - the group has gradually begun to diversify into other types of property investment and into some non-property activities. Even so, it has remained overwhelmingly an industrial property company doing what it know best.

Throughout its history the descendants of Noel Mobbs have played a pivotal role in the fortunes of the business. His son and his grandson have chaired a steadily expanding empire which, despite its size, still retains something of the air of a family-run organisation.

It has championed the concept of professional property ownership, tried to protect the best interests of its shareholders and seeked to push back the influence of what it sees as interfering bureaucrats ready to stifle the spirit of free enterprise.

By the start of the 1990s Slough Estates was the fourth largest publicly-quoted property company in Britain and probably the largest owner of industrial property in the world. With businesses in the United States, Canada, Australia and across Europe, where more expansion beckons, its international assets exceed £2 billion.

The group has 70 years of history behind it and considers that it is well placed to cope with whatever lies ahead. In property, the future can end tomorrow. Slough Estates intends to be around a lot longer than that.

1

WHITE ELEPHANT

IN THE AUTUMN of 1917, as the smoke lifted from the battlefields of Passchendaele to reveal another one quarter of a million British injured and dead, the War Office in Whitehall was confronted with more than one set of ghastly statistics.

With the Great War widely expected to have lasted only a few months entering its fourth year, concern at home about the efficiency and effectiveness of His Majesty's fighting forces in Europe reached fresh heights. In the opinion of some, several aspects of the military effort were little short of a shambles.

The casualty lists themselves were horrific enough. It was less than a year since the battle of the Somme had claimed nearly 20,000 British lives in a single day.

Each new despatch from the Western Front brought news of more fatalities. The daily hospital trains arriving at Victoria and Charing Cross paid testimony to the carnage across the Channel.

Despite huge military setbacks the morale of the troops had never actually broken. The British "Tommy" grumbled, swore, ate his bully beef, drank his tea and slogged on. He faced mutilation or death from rifle and machine gun fire, mortar bombs, shells and mustard gas.

At Passchendaele there was a new horror. Torrential rain had turned the battlefield into a swamp. Soldiers drowned in water-filled shell-holes, weakened by conflict and sucked down by clinging mud. To keep up their spirits they sang "Roses are blooming in Picardy" and "Pack up your troubles in your old kitbag." They prayed that, if they were to be injured, they would be wounded just sufficiently to get sent back to "Blighty."

Back home confidence was low. The introduction of conscription in 1916 had impressed on the population the scale of the crisis the nation faced. If they needed further evidence, the pubs were no longer open from 6 am until midnight for fear that the war effort would be conducted in a haze of alcohol.

Londoners began to take shelter in underground stations from Zeppelin and aeroplane raids, while the intensification of the German U-boat blockade meant the introduction of food rationing. There were strikes by a fledgling Labour movement beginning to flex its muscles, angered by the use of semi-skilled and female labour to do jobs previously undertaken by skilled workmen who had been called up.

The disastrous events on the Somme and the general deterioration in the military situation had led, at the end of 1916, to the replacement of the Asquith administration by another wartime coalition, this time led by Lloyd George, who had been Secretary of State for War since the death, six months earlier, of Lord Kitchener. He had at once formed a small war cabinet to inject a badly-needed element of co-ordination and decisiveness into the conduct of the war.

In the War Office there was also a new determination to come to grips with an increasing crisis involving the provision and maintenance of transport on the battlefields of Europe. There were those who felt that the logistics of warfare had too often been overlooked in favour of battle strategy.

While the government placed great emphasis on the need for arms production, some high-ranking officials believed that the mechanical transport fleet used to move troops and weapons in the field was being neglected - with potentially disastrous consequences.

One such critic was Major General Sir Alban Crofton Atkins, Director of Supplies and Transport at the War Office. Crofton Atkins, a tough-talking no-nonsense army man had, together with some of his colleagues, become increasingly alarmed at the way in which the British military's transportation needs were being handled.

Though manufacturers had mounted a herculean wartime effort to supply vehicles in the volumes required, they had remained severely handicapped throughout the war by labour problems and raw material shortages. Many of them were simply instructed to abandon their normal manufacturing activities and turn their hand to the production of armaments and aero engines.

The Great War had, almost overnight, revolutionised the use of mechanical transport. The army's interest in mechanical, as opposed to horse, transport had been awakened by the use in 1899 of steam traction engines to haul heavy guns during the Boer War. Trials had been started at Aldershot in 1901 but their unreliability remained a prime concern. Many senior soldiers believed nothing could ever take the place of the horse.

By 1910 the vehicle numbering system introduced by the Army Service Corps had reached 27. When Germany declared war on France on

August 1, 1914 the War Office had 47 motor lorries in use and could call on 700 other vehicles owned by civilians. Many of them were motor buses, quickly adapted to operate as lorries. The first convoys made an extraordinary sight, an eccentric mix of brewers' drays, grocers' vans and coal delivery lorries on their way to war.

Vehicle manufacturers responded well to the challenge, to the extent that by the summer of 1915 they were meeting the demands placed upon them by the army. Supply, however, was rapidly outstripped by the military's rapidly growing appetite for additional vehicles and American manufacturers were called in to help. Names like Packard and Studebaker began to appear on radiator grilles alongside the more familiar emblems of manufacturers like Albion, Daimler, Wolseley and Triumph.

By 1917 Crofton Atkins was convinced that the position could be significantly relieved if an extensive repair and maintenance operation could be established to lengthen the active life of those vehicles which the manufacturers managed to provide.

Though it still appeared a long way off, he also believed that the end of the war would leave behind an enormous accumulation of vehicles in varying states of repair, the majority of which would need to be overhauled if they were to be sold. The alternative would be to dispose of them at scrap value, raising the prospect of a scandalous waste of taxpayers' money.

The existing arrangements, to Crofton Atkins at least, appeared ill thought-out and woefully inadequate. There were a number of spare parts stores scattered throughout London, one at Liverpool and another at Avonmouth.

As for repair shops, activities were centred on the London General Omnibus Company garage at Camberwell and nearby Grove Park, from which various sub-depots were contracted to help if the workload required. They housed parts estimated to be worth £8 million, some of which lay exposed in the street. By the summer of 1917 there were moves to obtain a larger workshop in Battersea, south London.

Crofton Atkins was particularly concerned at reports of large numbers of vehicles lying by the roadside in France, left to rot because of the absence of any proper arrangements to have them repatriated for repair. To him, the evidence was overwhelming. Quite apart from the wanton waste involved, he believed that, without a central repair depot, the success of Britain's military operations was in grave danger.

It was in October that he was presented with a solution. Six months earlier, on May 4, he had welcomed Andrew Weir, a wealthy Scottish shipowner, to his new post as Surveyor-General of Supply at the War Office. The two men were of like minds on the issue.

Crofton Atkins had already started an internal search for buildings in which repair activities and parts storage could be centralised. He had employed a former member of staff at Harrods, now with an officer's commission, to locate suitable storage premises. Both men had agitated for the repair shop and stores warehouse but met a wall of resistance.

Weir's arrival gave Crofton Atkins an influential ally and he further pressed his case. In a memorandum on the issue, he wrote: "From the military point of view, as well as from the economic standpoint, it is urgently necessary to develop our repairing resources at home. The possible output of new vehicles from home factories, plus what we can obtain from America, is wholly insufficient to meet the demands of the armies in the field. In the future we shall be compelled to rely very largely on repaired vehicles."

The army by now required the delivery of 350 new vehicles a week; at their most productive, the manufacturers could not manage more than 275.

The new Surveyor-General responded by establishing an independent committee to inquire into and report back on the mechanical transport situation in England.

To the committee he appointed just two people, Bertram Jones and Arthur Bennett, civilian businessmen who were unknown in Whitehall. As Weir later recalled: "I did not know them. I had never seen them. But we were obsessed then by the idea of businessmen assisting government."

There were, nevertheless, immediate suspicions in some quarters that Weir had deliberately chosen people sympathetic to the case for centralised operations. What precise qualifications they had for the task in hand was never made clear.

Their deliberations did not take long. On July 21 they recommended the immediate provision of a single vehicle repair operation. No time, they urged, should be lost.

They painted a picture of poor organisation and unnecessary duplication of manpower and costs. Irreplaceable parts were stored in a range of buildings vulnerable to enemy action. In addition, hundreds of people and man-hours were swallowed up in transporting vehicles parts around the country to various depots.

The inquiry found that the repair facilities were incapable of tackling the volume of necessary repair jobs and warned of the possibility that the entire mechanical transport operation was in danger of breaking down. Because it had struggled valiantly against all the odds to provide a service in the past, it would not necessarily be able to continue to do so.

To drive home their warning, the two men pointed out that a total of 2,540 lorries and 1,486 cars already awaited urgent repair work either in domestic workshops or on the other side of the Channel. Another 1,800 motorcycles were also in need of attention.

They claimed a central depot would save handling expenses of at least £60,000 a year, that wage costs would be significantly reduced and the greater utilisation of second-hand parts could save nearly £500,000 a year. Heavy losses arising from the deterioration of vehicles left out in the open could also be eliminated.

The report emphasised the need to have in place an extensive repair facility once the war ended and vehicles began returning from overseas. The authors added: "It is impossible to contemplate with equanimity the enormous loss that would arise were a sudden termination of the war to find the situation as it is at present."

The conclusions were music to the ears of Andrew Weir. Within weeks Lord Derby, Secretary of State for War, agreed to the establishment of the Mechanical Transport Board charged with responsibility for drawing up plans and estimates for a new depot.

The War Office had not been idle, having already organised a search for a site which had to be within 40 miles of London. It would, preferably, be to the west because of the reduced risk of air raids and also close to a railway link.

Led by Colonel H. F. Cobb, a London surveyor and chief valuer to the Directorate of Lands for the War Office, inquiries were made throughout the area. Several estate agents, including Knight Frank and Rutley, Daniel Smith and Drivers Jonas were called in to help locate the land.

By the time Lord Derby announced his initiative a site had been found by officers of the staff of the War Office mechanical transport department. It was at Cippenham, once the site of a palace for Saxon and Norman kings, and close to Slough, a country town in Buckinghamshire with fewer than 15,000 inhabitants. Its roots dated back at least to the 13th Century.

Best known as the place where Sir William Herschel, King's Astronomer to George 111, "looked further into space than ever human being did before me," the town was also noted for being the birthplace of the world-famous Elliman's Embrocation, an unlikely blend of vinegar, turpentine and egg white sold the world over as a medicament for humans and horses alike. In the 15th Century the town had possessed a kiln used to supply the bricks for the building of Eton College. The 17th Century saw Slough sporting several fine coaching inns offering temporary refuge for the passengers of the 80 coaches a day which passed through.

By the 18th Century the town's biggest claim to fame was its highly productive nurseries, home to Cox's Orange Pippin apples and the famous Mrs Sinkins Pinks.

The War Office was less interested in Slough's history and floribunda than in its location, less than one hour's drive west of central London on the main road to Bath and the west country. Other sites had also been examined as far afield as Aylesbury, Basingstoke, Dunstable and Sunningdale. A number of locations around the capital, at Wembley, Hayes, Perivale and Harrow Weald, had also been considered.

But, in the opinion of the War Office, none fitted the bill as well as Cippenham Court Farm, comprising 668 acres of the finest corn-producing land in the Home Counties. It was located close to Brunel's Great Western Railway, which had been opened in 1838 despite initial and vehement opposition from Eton College. The Grand Junction Canal, an important commercial artery, was less than two miles away.

The farm, one of five which would be affected by any proposed development, had a long history of winning prizes for the quality and volume of its crop output, including a 25-guinea cup presented by a suitably impressed Prince Consort.

Now Cippenham Court was run by Ernest Headington. Like his father before him, he was a tenant who worked the land as though it was his own. His landlord, however, was to be made an offer of £60 an acre which he would not be able to refuse.

To the War Office the farm, together with smaller parcels of adjoining land, offered the only feasible opportunity to establish a depot ultimately capable of repairing 100 lorries, 100 cars and 130 motorcycles each week. Plans included the construction of 400 homes to house some of the 3,000 men who were expected to work at the depot, though it was not clear if the government or Slough Urban District Council would build them.

The Financial Adviser to the War Office was told the repair shops could be built for an estimated £990,000, a figure which would almost exactly double within a year. Advice on design and layout of the complex was provided by Lieutenant Colonel John Napier, an engineer who, before the war, had been managing director of the Arrol-Johnston Motor Car Company.

To the scheme's supporters, however, a total cost approaching £2 million would still seem an acceptable sum given the £40 million-a-year expenditure on military motor transport and the potential estimated saving of £1.5 million annually in keeping on the road vehicles which would otherwise have been immobilised.

Despite the urgency surrounding the issue, the project became bogged down in bureaucracy. It was another six months before the War Office was ready to discuss its plan with the Food Production Department headed by Lord Lee of Fareham.

Not surprisingly the Department was furious at the prospect of the loss of such valuable land at a time when the nation was being urged to produce as much corn as possible. Lord Lee also suspected that he was being "steamrollered" by a War Office which had already made up its mind to accept the proposal. He called for more time to consider alternatives.

The Department's objections meant the proposal was referred to the War Cabinet, which was understandably anxious to avoid damaging agricultural production but which appreciated the need for early action to provide proper support services for the nation's military machine.

There were other critics as well, including the Board of Agriculture, while the select committee on national expenditure counselled caution about progressing with such an ambitious plan.

A powerful individual opponent was Lord Desborough, who had lived at nearby Taplow Court all his life. A former MP for the area, he had even presented prizes for the best red wheat to Cippenham Court Farm in his capacity as president of the South Buckinghamshire Agricultural Society.

Not only did Lord Desborough object to the ruination of valuable agricultural land, he believed the concept of a centralised depot was wrong and needlessly extravagant. He persistently claimed that the private sector could, in any case, prove itself well capable of providing the required repair facilities. His objections would resurface at a later date to prolong the controversy surrounding the proposals.

For a while the War Cabinet sat on the fence, apparently unwilling to take a decision which was certain to prove unpopular with some. At one stage it appeared ministers might back the Food Production Department.

The corn gives way to contractors - 1918, two years before Noel Mobbs and his colleagues acquired the site from the War Office. The land was previously a farm which was located close to Brunel's Great Western Railway and the Grand Junction Canal.

In April, 1918 the Treasury gave its approval to the plans but the following month the cabinet referred them back to the War Office to enable alternative sites to be reconsidered. One was at Baldock in Hertfordshire but this proved even more productive in agricultural terms than the land at Slough.

On May 23 the Cippenham scheme was put to the War Cabinet as the only one of 11 original alternatives which made sense. Approval was finally forthcoming. The next day Ernest Headington and other local farmers were given notice to quit their land and Weir was finally able to get on with the job.

The German advance on the Channel ports, following their breakthrough at Cambrai, had by now forced the British army to abandon repair depots at Bergues and St. Omer, while a large spare parts depot at Calais had been burned down. Secret plans to shut down up to half the French-based depots and to repatriate the operations were in hand.

"The Dump" at the time of the Armistice in 1918. In those days the land around Slough was best known for its fruit and in particular Cox's Orange Pippin apples and the famous Mrs Sinkins Pinks.

Crofton Atkins later admitted that the War Office was a trifle "jumpy" about German progress. He would reveal that the army was preparing a general offensive for the early summer of 1919 "based almost entirely on mechanical effort." The Slough depot was intended to be an important part of the war effort in 1919.

An original boundary post marking the extent of the 600-acre estate.

So anxious was Weir to get on with the depot that he wanted to avoid using the Royal Engineers to carry out building work and to seek a civil contractor. He was over-ruled and the military moved in on June 11 to start initial ground work. No sooner was work underway than the project came under renewed fire, this time from the motor manufacturers.

In July a formal offer on behalf of 11 manufacturers was

submitted by the Association of British and Motor Allied Manufacturers, representing more than 95 per cent of the industry, to the House of Commons Select Committee on National Expenditure. The industry, alarmed at the potential loss of business arising from the establishment of

Cannibalised chassis in a sea of mud. The original vehicle was one of thousands built for war use. When Germany declared war on France in 1914 the War Office had just 47 motor lorries in full-time use.

a vast government-owned vehicle repair business which could ultimately supply the post-war private market, came up with an alternative.

It was willing to undertake repairs on 250 army vehicles a week on condition that government-owned spare parts were made available and that loan finance of up to £250,000, along with 1,000 skilled men, were

Laying the foundations - 1918. The land was bought for £60 an acre.

also provided. The plan, under which profits on the work would be fixed by agreement with the government, was at once rejected by the War Office.

Although work at Slough had barely started, Weir was already making it clear that he was unhappy with the rate of progress being made by the Royal Engineers, who were hampered by serious material and equipment shortages. Just as the German army began showing unexpected signs of collapse and hopes of an end to the war gathered momentum, he resurrected his plans to find a private contractor to take over.

Dispensing with the normal formality of seeking competitive tenders for the project, he approached Sir Robert McAlpine, the well-respected builder, to see if he would consider handling the project.

The war was, indeed, quickly reaching a victorious conclusion but Weir's determination to see through a project which be considered to be no less important to a peacetime economy did not weaken. By the time the Armistice was signed on November 11, 1918 the War Office was ready to strike a deal with McAlpine before any other contractor had even seen the site.

In Weir's eyes Sir Robert was simply "the best man for the job." As important was the fact that he was in possession of the men and materials necessary to make an immediate start. The builder's eagerness to help out even led Weir to believe that "he would do it for nothing if we asked him."

Rotting on the Rhine. Some of the vehicles abandoned abroad at the end of hostilities.

No such request was made and under the terms of an original contract set down in a personal letter, the job was to be carried out at cost. The terms were later changed to enable a Treasury standing committee to fix the final remuneration.

The end of hostilities meant troops began pouring back from Europe to what Lloyd George had promised would be "homes fit for heroes." Three quarters of a million British men would never be returning while the final weeks of 1918 saw the repatriation of some of the last of 1.6 million fighting men who had come home bearing wounds inflicted in the war to end all wars. Peace was unconditionally welcomed after four years of tragedy, hardship and deprivation.

Against this background a question mark now hung over a project which had been conceived in the dark days of war.

By the end of 1918 very little on site progress had been made and work had only just started on the first buildings. The critics who had originally raised doubts about the need for a motor repair depot on such a huge scale were again in full cry.

Before the year was out newspaper headlines began to refer to the mechanical transport depot at Slough as a white elephant. To some it seemed the vast project had fallen victim to events even before the first vehicle for repair had been transported down the Bath Road.

2

SCANDAL ON THE DUMP

ONE CERTAIN sign that life in Britain was slowly beginning to get back to normal was the return of horse-racing around the country. At Kempton Park, however, punters waiting to put sixpence each way on a promising filly would have to be patient.

Even before the end of the war the racecourse, close to the River Thames at Hampton, had been put to use as a mobilisation depot for army vehicles being transported to and from the European theatre of war. Peace saw the arrival of huge numbers of battle-weary vehicles at the course, chosen for its open spaces and because its perimeter fence supposedly helped to ensure security for army stock worth many millions of pounds.

By the end of 1918 there were 16,000 vehicles standing idle at Kempton. The long lines of rotting and dismembered mechanical paraphernalia helped bear out the War Office's contention that a repair depot would be needed as badly after the war as it had been during hostilities. They made a depressing sight.

Almost at once a decision was taken to sell off to the public as many of the unwanted cars and parts as the public was prepared to buy. By applying to the Director of Mechanical Transport at 6, St. James's Square, London, interested parties could obtain a list of cars for sale and an introductory letter allowing access to the racecourse.

Entering by Number Four gate, the inquisitive visitor would first notice an old army lorry body which had been converted into a site office to handle the sale of vehicles. A corporal in high rubber boots would escort buyers along the ranks of vehicles often lying in ankle-deep mud.

As one potential purchaser recalled: "To pick out a vehicle was almost a game of blind man's bluff. If one's fancy was taken by any vehicle, the procedure was to tender for it by making a bid. I could hardly help remarking how much simpler it would have been if the authorities had in their own mind valued the vehicles and placed a price upon each one, leaving it to the public either to pay the price or make a counter offer."

Around the cars lay broken axles, dented radiators, crankshafts, connecting rods and the odd complete but disembodied engine. Between each row of vehicles a space was reserved for Holt caterpillar tractors to haul their rotting loads through the quagmire.

A visiting journalist sniffed scandal and reported to his readers: "It is not my place to instruct, but I feel that the way these vehicles, which have cost scores of thousands of pounds, are allowed to rot by neglect is a very serious one. I tremble to think what the fate of the more up-to-date vehicles will be when they return. Because of the absence of spare parts, many vehicles are gradually deteriorating to become eventually valueless scrap-iron."

Kempton Park was not alone. As the army's fighting machine was demobilised, surplus vehicle parks sprang up like daffodils in Spring.

In Cumberland Market, close to Regents Park in London, army cars of all shapes and sizes awaited attention from a garage wholly unable to cope with the volume of repair work. Rumours spread that other repair depots had such little work on their hands that otherwise idle mechanics were simply dismantling vehicles and then putting them back together again.

Some of the vehicles parked in the market - the Lancia saloons costing £800 or more when new, the six-cylinder Wolseleys and the less powerful Clement-Talbots - had apparently seen only a few months' service. Even so, they were in an appalling state of decay. Corroded with rust from hub to hood, their upholstery collecting pools of water, children had made the vehicles their playground, removing any bit of brasswork that had not been stripped off for safe keeping.

On examination it would quickly become clear that water had penetrated into the vehicle engines. Unworn tyres had deflated and perished. Brand new AEC lorries shared the same fate. Bureaucracy dictated that, before any vehicle was sold, it first had to be transported to Kempton.

A national scandal. The Slough "white elephant."

The cause was at once taken up by the national Press. The Globe castigated the army and complained no-one was lifting a finger to stop the scandal. The Times said the vehicles rotting in Cumberland Market were valuable only as firewood while the Sunday Times said the real problem was finding the department with authority to sell vehicles that dealers were ready to buy.

A leader column in the newspaper complained: "Dealers were referred to one branch of the Ministry of Munitions, from that to the Admiralty, which referred them back to another branch of the Ministry, which pleaded that it was without authority from the Admiralty to do anything with the cars." The additional involvement of the Surplus Government Disposal Board and the Surplus Government Property Disposal Advisory Board meant the potential for "red tape" appeared endless.

The War Office was only too well aware of what was happening. The answer had to be to make rapid progress with its plans for a central repair depot.

A week after the signing of the Armistice - which had prompted Jimmy Gunn, a well-known financier, to throw a party for the depot's "high command" at his stylish riverside home near Bray - the Mechanical Transport Board met in London. On the agenda was one item: whether or not to proceed with the Slough project, still in the very early stages of development.

A camp for 200 Royal Engineers had been built and another camp for up to 1,000 site workmen had almost been completed alongside the Farnham Road. Separate, basic accommodation had also been built for up to 2,500 prisoners of war who, it was anticipated, would help build the depot.

The first POWs to arrive had been 300 Austrians, who were soon joined by 1,500 Germans. All of them were put to work under the watchful eye of a camp commandant. Their construction skills were highly questionable; the wall of the very first building they erected promptly collapsed, killing one unfortunate who had managed to survive the war unharmed.

The POWs were not to remain at Slough for very long. British

workmen staged a strike, refusing to work alongside the Germans. The prisoners were removed, leaving behind them row upon row of empty huts.

By then a gravel-washing plant and concrete factory were both operational, the beginnings of a permanent railway track were taking shape and depot roads were also being laid. Work on a canteen was underway but none of the repair shop facilities were anywhere near complete.

Among those at the London meeting were Sir John Cowans, the Quartermaster General, Crofton Atkins and the two businessmen originally appointed by Andrew Weir to inquire into the case for a centralised repair operation. Weir, who would shortly be made Minister of Munitions before being created the first Baron Inverforth, also attended.

The meeting was brief and decisive. The Mechanical Transport Board agreed that, despite the end of the war, the repair shops should go ahead in their entirety although it was decided that the amount of storage space originally proposed might now prove excessive.

The decision backed the Select Committee on National Expenditure which had, shortly before the Armistice, endorsed the case for the Slough complex and commended Crofton Atkins for his "foresight and persistency" in pressing for the proposal.

The committee had made it clear that while the depot would prove invaluable during wartime and even during the process of demobilisation, it could not feel justified in backing the project because of post-war considerations alone. The Army Council, according to the committee, should keep a careful watch with a view to restricting the scale of development at Slough if circumstances changed.

The War Office saw things differently. With the conflict over, the British army would still require repair, maintenance and training facilities on a huge scale. In addition, the depot could be used longer-term to co-ordinate the mechanised transport requirements of all departments of government.

The Post Office, for example, was cited as a potential customer, though it had not been consulted by the War Office and at the time possessed only 23 vans and lorries, five cars and 47 motor bicycles. In addition, sales to the private sector would provide a valuable source of income for the government.

Weir enforced his case with War Office estimates which suggested that the Slough depot could achieve profits of £1.75 million in its first three years of operation. The basis for the forecasts was, to say the least, questionable but Weir was a determined man. He was to remark later that he had made up his mind in 1917 about the need for a depot and had never subsequently altered it.

Lord Milner, the Secretary of State for War who was responsible for the expenditure involved, was told by Weir that the War Office was already committed to spending £1.1 million on the project. If work was stopped, savings would amount to only £250,000. The cost of the scheme, he added, had now unfortunately risen to £1.75 million.

Lord Milner backed Weir and Sir Robert McAlpine was told to proceed with haste. At once there were renewed complaints from the motor industry, which continued to claim that a depot would siphon off badly-needed work "rightly belonging" to it. The industry also claimed it would do it more efficiently and economically than any government operation.

By the early months of 1919 the Slough depot was the subject of questions in the Lords and the Commons, with peers and MPs concerned about the mounting cost of the project and the relevance of a scheme conceived during the war.

Winston Churchill, who replaced Lord Milner at the War Office in January 1919, found himself facing angry questions from all sides of the Commons. There were accusations that cars were still being left to rot at Kempton so that they could eventually be moved to Slough, thereby helping to justify its development.

A rebuilt 5-ton chain-driven truck.

MPs demanded to know if the War Office intended to put any of the vehicles up for auction in order to limit the extent of potential government losses on war surplus. Churchill declined to elaborate and in March announced that the Ministry of Supplies was assuming responsibility for the Slough depot.

The government's apparent resolution to press on with the development aroused fresh passion almost daily. The Times thundered: "Why did the government push on with a £2 million pound permanent scheme six weeks after the war ended without any clear idea of what it was needed for and why do they not stop it now?"

"The Motor," which had publicised the motor industry's continuing campaign to stop the government from poaching its post-war business, launched a scathing attack on the Secretary of State for War. "The sooner Mr. Churchill gets a grip of the enormity of the Slough expenditure and the sooner he shows sufficient courage to say 'stop it,' the better it will be for the country. Eventually, the government will have to get rid of the Slough incubus at a loss. Who will subsequently benefit by this persistent perpetration of official stupidity?"

By March 1919, as the controversy continued, around one quarter of the construction work at Slough was complete, with 3,400 men working on the site for up to 48 hours a week. By the end of the year the contracting workforce would rise to more than 5,000. Carpenters and bricklayers were being paid 1s 4d an hour and labourers received 1s 1d hourly. Included on the payroll was "a hale old man of 92" working as a ganger.

Skilled and unskilled workmen were drawn from the locality and from around the region, thousands of them arriving daily by train from London. Until a Great Western Railway terminus was built within the depot for passengers many workers arrived from Paddington or Slough stations at nearby Burnham Beeches and walked up a rough road through security gates into the depot.

Basic accommodation in wooden huts was available for some, though many preferred to travel daily from their homes to take advantage of a very generous 4s a day travelling time allowance.

As they worked on, political pressure continued to mount. On March 28 Lord Desborough won the approval of the Lords to establish a Select Committee to inquire into the Slough project. In the Commons Churchill also backed the move for a full investigation and it was agreed that members of both Houses would sit on the Committee.

It comprised the Earl of Kintore as its chairman, Earl Russell, Lord Clinton, Lord Denman, Lord Faber and five members of the Commons. As they began their hearings the government finally sanctioned the sale by auction of some of its surplus vehicle stock and also began moving vehicles, at the rate of 600 a day, from Kempton to Slough.

Within weeks of the committee convening, vehicle repair work at Slough was underway. Power came from a newly-built station on site following the breakdown of talks with the Slough and Datchet Electrical Lighting Company aimed at securing supplies.

The Slough and Datchet Lighting Company would not offer a fixed price and had suggested a likely tariff of about 1d a unit, which was considered too expensive by the estate's owners. A private power station capable of providing nearly 2,000 kilowatts was built and would soon also be selling surplus power to the electric company.

The depot now comprised rows of large concrete-floored sheds in which the vehicles were either stored or overhauled. One workshop alone covered eight acres and could accommodate 15,000 vehicles, well over half of those awaiting immediate attention. Batches of 10 vehicles of similar make were being pushed through the overhaul shops.

As yet no machine shop had been installed and repair work was carried out from travelling workshop units similar to those used in Europe during the war.

Under the watchful eye of an American production manager, civilian personnel stripped down each chassis, engines were dismantled and new parts fitted as required. After re-assembly, vehicles were given a quick road test before being sprayed from bonnet to back bumper with a somewhat unimaginative but readily available army grey paint.

The vehicles, the majority of which were Peerless cars and AEC lorries, were lined up in a separate shed which acted as a showroom, where members of the public could view them. If the overhauled vehicles were not bought back by the manufacturers for resale, they were sold to the public by private treaty or at auction.

While repair work carried on, so the depot continued to take shape under the direction of Lieutenant Colonel N.M. Hemming, the superintendent engineer in charge of the development. His task was not helped by continual alterations to the details of the project and daily difficulties over finding and retaining the labour force. The job, he said later, was "the worst I have ever had anything to do with."

The select committee moved quickly, meeting eight times in May and taking evidence from a large number of witnesses, including Lord Inverforth, Crofton Atkins and the hard-pressed Colonel Hemming.

Lord Desborough siezed the opportunity to mount an outspoken attack on the government's handling of the entire saga. He delivered a damning indictment, in the form of detailed statement criticising the decision to establish a single central depot and challenging the need for such a complex either in times of war or peace.

Lord Desborough claimed that private vehicle repairers could have done the job better, that the depot was unnecessarily large and extravagant and that, even if a case for it could have been made, the complex had been built in the wrong place. The final cost, he added, was likely to be far in excess of any figure cited by ministers.

He told the committee that further expenditure should be curtailed and the ambitious plans reined back to relate much more closely to the volume of work the depot might, in peacetime, be expected to attract. Some of the depot sheds, he suggested, "would make very good museums."

The select committee reported on July 3, 1919 and it carried a mixed message. It criticised early delays in getting the project off the ground, which it said had led to the waste of large sums of public money. It also stated that the decision to continue with development of the depot after the signing of the Armistice had been taken "without sufficient consideration of the altered conditions and without any trustworthy estimate of the financial results of the undertaking."

The promise of large profits, the committee added, had been too readily accepted by Lord Inverforth.

The peers and MPs agreed he had conceived a plan which he was anxious to promote even as his government responsibilities altered. When the first sod was turned for the Slough complex he had used his position as Surveyor-General of Supply to press the scheme for war purposes; on his appointment as Minister for Munitions he had also not lost a day in adopting and pushing forward the plan.

But the committee also said it was "obviously too late to turn back" and abandon the works. The result was that the nation was now "in possession of an elaborate and costly factory, partially completed." It agreed that the motor industry would not have been capable of handling the projected volume of vehicles planned for repair but doubted whether Slough's role, as originally contemplated, could last for more than three years.

Even so, the report believed that, given a wider responsibility to deal with all forms of government motor transport, the depot could still prove to be a useful national asset.

Lord Inverforth's original decision to hand the building contract to Sir Robert McAlpine was supported but the report said it would have been "desirable" if more usual tendering practices had been adhered to and that alternative bids from other contractors had been considered.

While recording that, at the end of hostilities, Lord Inverforth had been faced with either abandoning the depot or persevering with the project, the committee went on to say that, in its opinion, there had been a third possible choice which had apparently never been considered by the War Office.

While the works had been in their embryo state, it suggested, a possible, private purchaser might have been found. Indeed, the committee had heard that one offer to buy the depot had recently been put forward, though it had not progressed.

The committee concluded by saying that the Slough operation would have no chance of success unless it was run on commercial lines. In three years' time, it believed, the whole issue would have to be re-examined and Slough's future would, again, have to be debated.

By the time the report was published the War Office was issuing figures which only strengthened the hand of the critics. The cost of the depot, it revealed in a parliamentary written answer, had risen to about £1.95 million and was still rising.

Vehicle repair work stepped up throughout the remainder of 1919 and, by the end of the year, the government had included the motor transport depot at Slough on a list of 12 national munitions and other war establishments which it intended to retain "on a permanent basis."

The government's resolve to retain control of a controversial project which many, if not Lord Inverforth, regretted starting was to prove very short-lived.

3

THE DEAL

AS JOINT manager of the Associated Equipment Company - better known as AEC - the largest manufacturer of commercial vehicles in Britain, Sam Wallace knew a thing or two about the rapidly developing motor transport industry. He also knew quite a bit about the Slough repair depot.

Wallace had only arrived in Britain in early 1916 to take up his post with AEC after managing the General Electric Company in the United States. He was a highly competent engineer and had built for himself a reputation as a production man capable of maximising the output of any plant he ran.

During the war he had occasionally been called in by government departments to offer advice on transport issues. He had appeared before the Select Committee investigating Slough, where he had made clear his support for the principle of a central repair depot.

So impressed were those seeking his advice that, by the end of 1919, he found himself on temporary secondment from AEC to manage the Slough operation. While he believed in the concept which had led to the creation of the depot Wallace quickly resolved that its best chance of success lay in its conversion to a privately-run business.

In early 1920 he was ready to act on his plan and began talking to some of his contacts in the motor trade to establish the extent of interest in the idea of making a bid for the Slough complex. His inquiries also led him to the United States in an attempt to include US interests in any bid but, by the time he returned at Easter, he had ruled out the possibility. It was to be a British enterprise.

Although Wallace had motor industry expertise, he was no financier but he knew to whom he should turn. High on his list was Sir Percival Perry, a Bristol-born businessman who had made a fortune in the rapidly developing motor trade and who was held in high esteem by the business community.

Before the war Percival Lea Dewhurst Perry had run the Ford Motor Company's new operations in Britain for Henry Ford from offices in London's Shaftesbury Avenue. The two men had met in 1906 when Perry had gone to the United States to seek financial support for a company which imported American cars and in which he was a shareholder. The business was failing because British customers regarded American cars as "cheap and nasty."

Henry Ford was not interested but the two men established a close friendship which led to Perry working for Ford when, eventually, the American motor manufacturer decided to expand overseas and open up in Britain.

At the time this association caused something of a dilemma for Perry because his boss was a militant pacifist. Wartime meant that the expertise of businessmen was badly needed as part of the national effort to crush the Kaiser, so he sold Ford ambulance chassis to the War Office and worked in the Food Production Department and the Ministry of Munitions. Perry managed, however, to make his wartime contribution - for which he was knighted - without incurring the wrath of his boss.

That manifested itself immediately after the war when it became clear that Ford wanted to run the English company as a branch of Detroit, making his British executives little more than managers. Perry wanted to run his own show.

He resigned in May 1919 to concentrate on developing Motor Organisations, a business he had founded to purchase and sell on the entire surplus stock of US expeditionary force motor transport left in Germany after the war. The deal had been fraught with problems, not least because the 11,000 vehicles purchased had subsequently been overwhelmed with flood water. Perry and his colleagues accused the US authorities of negligence and were forced into lengthy and expensive legal action.

Among those colleagues was Arthur Noel Mobbs, another successful entrepreneur who had recognised the potential for developing businesses associated with the motor car industry. Mobbs had spent some time in Coblenz trying to sort out the mess. It would not be the last time the two men faced a similar problem.

In 1903 25-year-old Noel Mobbs, together with his brother Herbert, had formed the Pytchley Autocar Company to sell private cars. Already a leading figure in the Society of Motor Manufacturers and Traders, he had also founded the Pytchley Hire Purchase Company, the first of its kind to offer easy payments for the purchase of motor cars. The company was eventually renamed the United Motor Finance Corporation and would survive until the 1950s when it was taken over by Mercantile Credit.

To complete his motor business portfolio, Mobbs also ran the Anglo-Saxon Insurance Company.

The automobile business was based in Northampton, home for successive generations of the Mobbs family. It had other garages in Market Harborough and Banbury and had secured a major coup by being appointed as agents for the fast-growing Fiat Company of Turin. Pytchley's other claim to fame would be the invention and development of a sliding roof for motor cars. The "sunshine roof" became immensely popular and the Northampton company reaped the benefit of large royalties as the ingenious device was fitted to several million motor cars.

Sir Percival - later Lord - Perry, the company's first chairman. In tandem with the Slough business he was running his own operation to buy and sell on the entire surplus stock of American expeditionary force motor transport left in Germany after the First World War. The 11,000 vehicles he bought were subsequently flooded and Perry was forced into lengthy and expensive legal action.

Noel's other two brothers, Grailey and Edgar, also played a part in the Pytchley autocar business. Edgar's contribution, however, was to be cruelly cut short.

Before the war Edgar had been capped 11 times playing rugby for England and he answered the 1914 call to arms by writing to a thousand rugby players asking them to join him in enlisting. More than 400 had responded to his rallying cry to be marched by Mobbs from the market square in Northampton to the barracks of the Northamptonshire Regiment, where they formed into the 7th Battalion. They were instantly dubbed the "Mobbs Battalion."

Like his great-great-grandfather and grandfather before him, Mobbs did, indeed, command one of the regiment's battalions. And, like many of his comrades, he was to be killed in action in 1917 on the Menin Road during the third Battle of Ypres. He was commanding the 7th Northamptonshire Battalion. A Mobbs memorial match between the Barbarians and the East Midlands - both of which Edgar had captained - would later be arranged and played annually.

During the war Noel Mobbs had made his own contribution to the national cause. He had been appointed Assistant Director of Food Production at the Ministry of Agriculture and was responsible for the efficient operation of 30,000 tractors imported from the United States. He received the OBE in 1918.

Together, Perry and Mobbs made an impressive team. By February 1920, their interest excited by the potential for Slough so enthusiastically spelled out by Sam Wallace, they decided to make a joint bid for the depot.

They had canvassed many of their business friends to seek financial support for their offer and began negotiations which involved the Ministry of Munitions, the Treasury and the Surplus Government Disposal Board. The government's publicly-stated position on the Slough depot, which was to retain ownership on behalf of the state, might have suggested that any potential buyers faced an uphill struggle.

In reality, ministers were by now hyper-sensitive to the issue of wasted public resources in the wake of the war and heartily sick of the criticism surrounding the government's continuing involvement at Slough. To cap it, Lord Northcliffe, the all-powerful newspaper publisher, had taken a particular interest in the project which he believed characterised the government's muddled thinking and extravagance. His publications made his views well known, making repeated swipes at Lloyd George's administration.

Noel Mobbs, in at the beginning and the first in a line of family chairmen. A leading figure in the Society of Motor Manufacturers and Traders, he founded the Pytchley Hire Purchase Company, the first of its kind to offer easy payments for the purchase of motor cars. The company was eventually renamed the United Motor Finance Corporation and was taken over by Mercantile Credit in the 1950s.

Almost every day the national newspapers carried outraged reports about mountainous dumps of British military equipment littered around Europe. In Belgium and France an estimated £50 million worth of surplus stock was lying unprotected and apparently unwanted. There were accounts of pyramids of tins of pork and beans in Abbeville, mountains of bicycles, paint tins, soap and bedding at Calais and huge stocks of flour, peas and rice at Rouen. The Seine rats, screamed the Press, were growing fat at the expense of the British taxpayer.

Looters were walking away with beds, kitchen ranges, brass lamps, gum boots, trench caps, medicines, wine and pre-war whisky. Often, soldiers with empty rifles faced thieves armed with loaded guns. Lord Inverforth, now head of the Disposal Board, went to France to see for himself. He was not amused.

Things were little better at home, with acres of rusting materials disfiguring the port of Richborough in Kent. To make matters worse, there were repeated allegations that good offers had been made for much of the stock but that they had not been acted upon.

The estate's fire service at action stations in the 1920s.

It was against this background that the government was keen to do a deal over Slough with anyone sufficiently interested. If necessary it was also apparently quite ready to abandon any open tendering process if it meant a speedy sale could be arranged.

Though it was not made public knowledge at the time, the government had actually received a bid of £1 million for the Slough operation from the Great Western Railway. Ford of America, now anxious to establish its manufacturing base in Britain in order to avoid import duties, also made an offer of £3 million. But neither wanted the vehicles and so neither were entertained.

The Slough Trading Company works band - 1920.

Perry and Mobbs were determined that they should be given a better hearing. Given that the government had publicly declared the final capital cost of the depot alone to be £2.55 million, they also knew any deal would cost them a lot more than the offer which had failed.

There would be two elements to any deal which would be struck. Though possible purchasers might have been more interested in simply acquiring the depot buildings, the government was ready to insist that any buyer took the vehicles and parts as well. Any package would also have to include most of the surplus vehicles still left in Europe and beyond.

Negotiations quickly established an agreed price for the depot itself. The site and buildings were now valued at £3.35 million but, when it came to assessing the worth of the vehicles and spare parts, the issue proved more problematical. In short, neither side held a full inventory of the vehicles and parts to be covered by any sale although the numbers were at least clearer in England now that most of the stock had been assembled at Slough.

By the beginning of April, as the discussions continued, Slough held 10,500 lorries (of which 8,500 were derelict), 3,500 cars (including 3,000 derelicts) and 3,600 motorcyles (half of which were not usable). A further 4,000 vehicles of all types were held at other depots. Putting a value on rusting and cannibalised trucks and cars was altogether more problematical.

What the Disposal Board itself would later describe as "a rough and ready" valuation was undertaken by both sides. The approximate number of vehicles was multiplied by a valuation of £150 each and spare parts were thrown in at £800,000. Most astonishingly, while the new owners would own all new government surplus vehicles becoming available over the following two years, only cursory attempts were made to calculate the possible numbers involved.

The real problems arose in assessing the value of those vehicles abroad, many lying in dumps across France but some as far afield as Cairo, Gallipoli and Salonica; even so a figure of 3,000 was suggested and accepted. No average value was attached to them, however.

As one of the negotiators put it: "The idea was impossible. A motor lorry in Mesopotamia was probably not of any great value." The new owners would be left, in any case, to make their own arrangements to repatriate most of the vehicles.

A figure of £3.65 million for vehicles and parts was finally agreed upon, bringing the total value of the sale to £7 million. The figure was colossal and represented one of the largest transfers of assets on record in Britain. It paled into insignificance, however, alongside the £339 million raised by the government in sales of surplus stocks since the war had ended.

It was agreed that the purchase price was to be made on a deferred basis as receipts from sales flowed in; the new owners would also have to pay the government a proportion of the proceeds of all vehicle sales once gross receipts passed £5 million.

As a reciprocal measure, to take effect after two years, one quarter of any deficiency between the £5 million figure and the cash actually raised in sales would be financed by the government. The new owners would also be obliged to carry out any repairs for the government on a cost-plus-10 per cent basis.

The deal was eventually struck on April 9, 1920. Mr Daniel Neylan, finance member of the disposal board, who had been at the centre of negotiations, heaved a sigh of relief: "They think they are getting a fairly good bargain and we also think we have made a fairly good bargain." And James Hope, the junior Munitions Minister, told the Commons: "A chance has occurred of a profitable transaction and I think the government are rightly taking it. There will be some satisfaction at any rate in some quarters of the House because, as a result, there will be one government establishment less. Every individualist should be pleased."

In truth, and with the benefit of hindsight, the new owners had got themselves a bargain although not everyone was quite so happy at the time. The question many people wanted answering was exactly who were the new owners of 1.8 million sq. ft. of covered space - the largest industrial complex under one roof in Britain - and more than 17,000 vehicles along the Bath Road. Sir Frederick Banbury, the chairman of the Select Committee on National Expenditure was to ask: "Who is Sir Percival Perry by the way?"

Despite his business record the government knew that Sir Percival was not in a position to find such vast funds from his own resources but were assured he could secure the sums necessary. His own contribution to the sale, which formed the entire deposit, was £275,000 - a sum subsequently to be largely financed by other partners in the new venture.

Questions were at once asked about the advisability of handing over the ownership of such a strategically important business to a group of unknown businessmen who already had motor industry interests.

The suspicion in some circles was that the motor trade had scooped up what might have become its biggest competitor giving it a stranglehold on all its customers. One MP said the deal represented "a seven-league stride towards the monopoly of motor traction in this country."

When, on April 20, Sir Percival announced that he was forming a new company to own and operate the Slough depot some of the low-profile figures behind the deal emerged into daylight.

Their identities made interesting reading. There were to be six directors of the company, which it was proposed to name Slough Depot Ltd. They included Sir Percival as the first chairman and Commander Redmond McGrath, a tall and well-built man who possessed a booming voice and a finely developed sense of humour.

McGrath hailed from County Clare, had served with the British Army as a subaltern in South Africa and returned to help with the development of tanks during the war. He had worked with Winston Churchill, who had served as First Lord of the Admiralty and, as such, was responsible for work on tanks. McGrath had, accordingly, been given a naval ranking.

A fine polo player and a top rank amateur tennis player, McGrath did not have the benefit of family money but was very able and had first-class contacts and very influential friends. Sir Percival was among them.

The board also included Lieutenant Colonel Brinsley Fitzgerald, who had served in the South African war with the Somerset Yeomanry and spent 12 years as a land agent in his native Ireland before becoming a partner in a London stockbroking firm. The former Guards Officer knew Mobbs and Perry well and his City contacts were expected to prove extremely useful.

Also on the board was the Honourable Lionel Guest, the fourth son of Ivor Bertie Guest, the First Baron Wimborne, whose family name had become incorporated in that of Guest Keen and Nettlefold, the engineering group it helped create. The remaining directors were Major John Sewell Courtauld, the holder of the Military Cross and who would shortly become the Unionist MP for Chichester, and Evelyn Kyrle Smith, a business associate of Perry's who came from a highly respected City banking family.

Redmond McGrath, a founder director acquainted with Sir Percival Perry. He had served with the British Army as a subaltern in South Africa and returned to help with the development of tanks during the war. He worked with Winston Churchill, who had served as First Lord of the Admiralty and, as such, was responsible for work on tanks.

The company's capital was £820,000, funded by individual subscriptions from debenture holders in Motor Organisations. Among those taking a stake were Noel Mobbs, who invested £20,000, Lord Inchape, the shipping magnate, who put in £100,000, Sir Kenneth and Lady Crossley of Crossley Motors, the private motor car manufacturers, and - via Anglo-Canadian Finance - newspaper publisher Lord Beaverbrook. Also on the list was Lord Montagu of Beaulieu, among the first of the British aristocracy to develop a passion for motor cars.

The first meeting of the intended directors took place at 4, Dean Stanley Street, Westminster on April 22. There was a brief discussion of executive responsibilities and it was agreed to start auction sales at Slough, as well as at a sales centre which operated from Earls Court in west London. By the end of the month it was being suggested that, rather than becoming a director, Noel Mobbs should be appointed as technical adviser to the board at a salary of £1,500 a year.

Major Courtauld was given the job of approaching Mobbs with the offer and was authorised to go up to £2,000 if he felt it would help. Mobbs made it clear, however, that he was not interested in accepting such a post and that he expected a directorship. His terms, having been reported back to the board, were duly met and he was appointed director in charge of sales.

The end of April saw the start of an inevitable shake-out in the workforce at Slough. With the payroll approaching 8,000 people - equivalent to nearly half the population of Slough itself - the government announced that it was laying off all workers, permitting the new owners to re-engage those for whom they had jobs.

The decision led to extraordinary scenes at the depot. Uncertainty about how many people would be re-employed led to spontaneous demonstrations, one of which took the form of an early morning mock funeral procession headed by a model white elephant.

The workers, angered at the government's handling of the entire affair and nervous about their future employment prospects. marched to a grass patch outside the general manager's office. There they placed a headstone on the ground and a jazz band played the "Last Post" as they presided over the interment of what everyone now referred to as "The Dump."

The depot was anything but dead, however. On the same day the new owners agreed on measures to reduce the workforce initially by one-third, ending piecework payments and introducing a 40-hour, five-day working week. The concept broke fresh ground in industrial relations and succeeded in boosting productivity. Assurances were given that no-one re-employed would suffer loss of earnings.

Female labour was to be kept to a minimum, usually restricted to typing and filing jobs, and every endeavour was made to ensure the two sexes remained segregated during their working day.

Morale at the depot was understandably low as large numbers of men lost their jobs. While the shake-out proceeded Harry Morey, a blue-eyed, curly-haired Irishman, emerged as one of several workers who quickly became firebrands.

Always ready to step forward to air the grievances of his mates, Morey belonged to the Associated Society of Engineers at a time when trade unions were still finding their feet. A deep-thinking socialist always concerned to protect the limited rights of workers, he found himself being pushed to the forefront by the upheaval at the depot. Each morning, as the sackings continued, he lined up his colleagues in the maintenance shop to carry out a roll-call. As the numbers fell daily, he warned: "Beware all you men with bald heads. They're sacking all the old 'uns first."

On May 13 the directors decided to change their mind about the company name. Slough Depot Ltd was, instead, to be the Slough Trading Company Ltd, thereby providing the first public indication that the owners might harbour wider ambitions for their new business. Talks now also began with the Great Western Railway to pave the way for a direct rail link into the depot.

By the end of the month, with the Press suggesting that the government might, in the event, have done rather well out of the deal, the new company was formally registered. On May 27, the day in question, the board met briefly at Dean Stanley Street to confirm the board of directors and to appoint Charles Giller as its first secretary.

Sir Percival had one other item to report. He had been approached by a one J.B. McLean, the representative of an anonymous business syndicate who "were desirous of buying out the company at a profit." An appointment had been arranged as he believed it might be profitable to the company "to treat with Mr. McLean's syndicate."

But Perry had to tell his new colleagues that Maclean and his friends had failed to turn up. If there had been any second thoughts by Perry or his colleagues about pursuing the project, the prospect of selling out or bringing in others had not materialised.

As the company was registered the trade newspaper Motor News painted a bleak outlook for Sir Percival and his friends. "It will be something of a miracle if they succeed in converting Slough into a money earning concern," it forecast.

The Slough Trading Company had been born but there were many who were not prepared to guess how long it could survive.

4

THE ESTATE IS BORN

THERE was no time to lose if the new owners of the Slough depot were to succeed in proving their detractors wrong.

The strategy was to sell off without delay those vehicles for whom ready purchasers could be found whilst cannibalising the other cars and lorries for parts which could be reassembled as complete, saleable vehicles. The management reckoned that it could construct about 10,000 sound units from those it held in England.

At the same time there was an urgent need to begin to organise those company assets which remained widely-scattered around Europe and beyond.

Some of the ex-servicemen anxious to find work discovered that their knowledge of the whereabouts of army vehicles made them particularly useful. They were recruited without delay to help locate and organise vehicles stocks on the Continent. Those which were not to be sold off to local buyers would continue to be repatriated for repair through the port of Richborough.

During the first year of trading some salesmen employed by The Motor Organisations, Perry's other principal business interest, would help sell Slough vehicles while the company would appoint its own agent to negotiate sales to the Russian government.

With a European sales manager appointed, surplus vehicles were quickly sold in Spain and disposals were stepped up in France. The first moves were made to form a company in India for disposing of any vehicles left in Asia and a sales department was opened in Cairo. The board also set up a separate UK agency to handle the sale of tyres.

Perry's American connections and the company's stock of US vehicles also nominated the United States as a possible market. An associate company to mastermind sales was established, although the venture would prove short-lived.

There would be other setbacks. A fire at a depot in Baghdad cost the company £500,000 in lost vehicles; those that survived would subsequently be ruined by floods. The directors also found themselves in the early stages of what would prove to be marathon saga of litigation with the government over more flood-damaged vehicles left stranded in France.

During the original negotiations to buy the government's stock of surplus vehicles the company had voiced suspicions that those in France were parked on land liable to flood. The suggestion having been roundly denied by the War Office, the land in question fell victim to floods.

"One careless owner" - one of many wartime casualties which were repatriated, repaired and sold on. The company's worldwide inventory topped 25,000 trucks, cars and motor cycles.

The company was furious and searched London for a firm of solicitors prepared to take on a case against the State. All warned against any such action, suggesting that to sue the government was tantamount to suing the Crown.

One firm was not so horrified at the prospect and took up the challenge. Kenneth Brown, Baker Baker, which had a rather colourful reputation for handling divorce cases, eventually won a protracted battle securing a £1 million reduction in the original £7 million sale price.

The firm, eventually to become Turner Kenneth Brown, was retained by a thankful client, marking the beginning of a successful business relationship which would still be flourishing 70 years later.

With Sam Wallace still in charge of depot operations, although he was not an investor or a director, the essential buildings and equipment required to handle the huge volume of vehicles were quickly made operational.

Machine shops, foundries, assembly plant, paint shops and offices were geared up to accommodate the flow of Austin lorries and Peerless five-ton trucks, some still loaded with motorcyles returned from the battlefields of France. Apart from the commercial vehicles there were Daimler, Wolseley and Sunbeam cars as well as rows of battered motorcycles.

One initiative aimed at clearing the backlog entailed an immediate decision to begin auction sales. The first was held on May 19, comprising 200 assorted vehicles, 40 lots of spares and one hundred Douglas motorcycles.

Police on duty at the Bath Road main gate as a convoy of rebuilt lorries leaves for road trials.

Though the company readily admitted that none of the items for sale was a "runner," large crowds gathered. Among the stars of the show were a Daimler limousine without its magneto and a Wolseley Landaulet which realised 300 guineas.

Henry Morey and children - a champion of workers' rights at the time the new owners had to trim the work force. He warned: "Beware all you men with bald heads. They're sacking all the old 'uns first."

Generally, however, the lines of rotting, dismembered vehicles looked depressingly familiar. One motoring correspondent present observed that every vehicle appeared to be have been "scrounged." Another was equally critical, reporting that there seemed to be "no machines which really represented valuable property."

Even so, the day's sale realised over £30,000 for the company, confirming that there was a lively demand for vehicles no longer required by His Majesty's armed forces but keenly sought after by a public whose imagination had been fired by the chance of personal motor transport for all.

There were to be a few further auction sales but by the end of June the company's newly formed sales committee had decided that auctions should temporarily cease and that all vehicles would be individually priced and then advertised. Trade buyers would get a 10 per cent discount and there would also be price reductions for customers buying several vehicles.

Given the early evidence of success in using auctions to reduce the stockpile of vehicles the change of policy puzzled some observers. The sales also raised some eyebrows among other members of the motor trade who had not forgotten earlier protests that the activities at Slough were undermining the prospects for motor manufacturers and dealers.

Slough Trading Company had no wish to alienate its motor trade colleagues and Noel Mobbs made a short public statement explaining that the decision had been taken "in order to stabilise the commercial motor industry." Weekly sales of spare parts and vehicle bodies continued.

As the depot workload stepped up, so the management looked for ways of improving efficiency and output. The result was higher productivity but a steady fall in the huge workforce. Even so, the company was faced with the problem of securing enough accommodation for its employees in an area which was quite incapable of providing enough affordable housing.

The go-ahead was given for the construction of 10 cottages to house foremen and work also began on the construction of nearly 200 semi-detached houses. At the same time the board agreed to pay £6,523 for a number of former army huts which had not been included in the original sale. They were, the company announced, to be turned into proper dwelling places.

In the event the huts were to become the hub of what developed into an extraordinary community of workers drawn from all over the country by the lure of paid employment. They were to become not only workmates but neighbours in what quickly became dubbed Timbertown.

By the mid-summer of 1920, with Sir Percival Perry in the United States and Noel Mobbs briefly assuming his executive duties, the company's development committee prepared proposals intended to make better use of some of the acreage of land under its control.

Almost from the outset the potential of the land for alternative uses other than as a vast vehicle park and repair shop had not been far from the minds of its new owners. Everyone realised that depot activities directly emanating from the aftermath of the war would be relatively short-lived; the more efficient it was, the faster its workload would shrink. An alternative function for Slough would have to be found.

Some, like Perry, believed any diversification was likely to keep the depot actively engaged in the motor vehicle business. There was, for example, a suggestion that the company should undertake the construction of charabanc bodies, while some directors envisaged the depot taking on a more general motor repair and maintenance role for vehicle operators and even private car owners. Some in the trade even believed the company was preparing to manufacture its own family car.

But people like Mobbs began to think in terms of a much wider role for the Slough complex.

It was undeniable that Slough was somewhat out on a limb, well away from the more obvious centres of business activity. But it also had the benefit of being away from the congestion of London and could be put to a variety of purposes in what was expected to be a rapidly developing post-war economy.

The shortage of industrial accommodation in the more traditional business centres only gave added weight to the suggestion that companies might be prepared to try somewhere new - provided they were offered something attractive.

In fact pressures in favour of a move away from London were building up. The capital was increasingly regarded as hopelessly choked and filthy. The lure of new rural townships like Letchworth Garden City were proving irresistible and rapidly improving transport systems were giving birth to the possibility of commuting from home to workplace.

Britain's population faced a revolution in life style and working conditions and those who seized the hour might be able to take full advantage of the population's aspirations.

At around this time, in July, the company received a tentative inquiry from a local business asking whether it would be possible to lease a one-and- a-quarter acre site on which it could erect a factory. The suggestion at once encouraged the company to prepare a scale of rental charges based on figures for each square foot taken.

The company decided that it would entertain the leasing of selected sections of its land for 999 years at an annual ground rent of £75. In selected cases, it agreed, the first year's ground rent might be remitted.

At first no rentals were fixed on the basis that it was impossible to guess what prospective tenants might pay. It was thought around 3d a square foot might be achieved. In order to test the water, the directors earmarked £50,000 to construct a number of buildings which it would advertise as available to let.

As a further inducement to potential customers the company decided that it would make advances to occupiers of up to 85 per cent of total building costs, to be repaid at 7.5 per cent interest in instalments over 10 years.

From now on Slough Trading Company advertisements listing the latest menu of available vehicles would also carry a footnote to the effect that space at Slough - "with the benefit of excellent communications" - was now available for commercial purposes.

By the autumn of 1920 the workforce engaged on vehicle repair activity was declining and there were fresh rumours that work was running out so quickly that the depot would have to be at least temporarily shut down.

With workers demanding to know their future, one of the first editions of the company's own magazine attempted to put an end to the gossip and to raise morale. An anonymous editorial, referring to suggestions of closure, complained: "Could anything be more absurd? Do you imagine that the directors of this company purchased the depot for the sheer delight of spending money and losing it? Really, they must be given credit for a little more business acumen and commonsense."

But the same article - sandwiched between warnings not to lose personal identity badges costing 2s 6d each and a prize-winning suggestion for substituting electric for acetylene in ambulance headlights - carried a clear warning about overall employment prospects. The company, it revealed, envisaged a permanent workforce of no more than 2,000 people, only one quarter of the total which had for a brief period been employed.

However, in an attempt to cushion the impact, it was emphasised that other businesses would be developing and expanding on site, offering the chance of jobs for many of those no longer required by the depot. The company magazine editorial concluded in contrived bemusement: "It seems a pity that the discharge of a few employees should create an atmosphere of insecurity among the remainder. When reorganisation takes place it is obvious that discharges must occur. On the other hand, engagements also rise."

There would be tough competition for any vacancies, however. Unemployed girls from South Wales would, by the year-end, be arriving in search of work and happy to be earning 25s a week or less. They would be followed by many more Welsh workers, including redundant miners. Though they were made welcome by the Welsh already there, others saw them as unwelcome immigrants and they were not universally liked around the depot. Timbertown became known as New South Wales.

Jim Rule, who worked for more than one employer on the estate, remembers: "The Welsh worked for 6d an hour; they would do anything to snatch our jobs and then, having got them, would create merry hell until they got the full rate of pay."

Autumn 1920 saw the first formal tenancy deals agreed.

Crossley Motors, one of the depot shareholders, had already leased a small space in the existing buildings to repair army surplus motorcyles. On October 1, the board approved the letting of floorspace to the proprietor of a small ball bearing manufacturing company. A week later it endorsed another letting, this time to the Perfection Enamelling Painting Company, a coachwork specialist employed at Slough to help restore vehicles. The business took over the old army stables and would spend countless hours trying to rid the building of the smell of mule urine.

"Timbertown" huts. The encampment soon became known as New South Wales because of the influx of Welsh workers looking for employment.

Other companies would now quickly follow, some of them destined to become household names in the years ahead. The Gillette Razor Company, makers of the world-famous safety razor, took some of the existing space and prepared for production in only three weeks. The Mentholatum Company moved in to produce its famous healing cream for everything from colds and burns to catarrh and influenza.

There was even to be a cattle market complete with sales ring in one corner of the estate, operated by Pedigree Stock Sales. Among other tenants to move in while the 1920's were still young would be Johnson and Johnson, the American surgical dressing manufacturer, while the Hygienic Ice Company took a 14-year lease on the old washing shed at £1,200 a year.

Hygienic trucks would trundle backwards and forwards delivering blocks of ice to businesses and hospitals. As a popular sideline, it sold "velvet" ice cream. Customers included estate workers. A telephone call from nearby Windsor Castle to supply ice for a party took driver Fred Sheppard on the first of many visits to the royal residence. Four monarchs would get their supplies of ice from the building regarded by locals as a giant refrigerator.

Other arrivals included Life Saver Sweets - "The Sweet Without a Personal Touch" - on a 21-year lease and an annual rental of £725, and St Helens Cable and Rubber, manufacturers of the famous "Everlastic" inner tube, insulating tapes and hot water bottles which later moved its entire staff from Warrington to the south.

As the very first businesses arrived Perry presented his board with a detailed plan of the Slough estate spreading from the Farnham Road in the east to Burnham Lane in the west and bordered to the south by the Bath Road.

The railway, which carved a path right across the estate, now offered two connections to the site, one solely for workman's trains - the return fare to Paddington was 1s 2d - and the other providing extensive sidings for goods traffic. For those still wary of steam transport and unable to afford the bus, there were plenty of storage racks for bicycles.

Almost from the start, the railway was put in the hands of George Lines, whose surname aptly reflected his natural affinity with the railway. He would stay with the company, at one stage managing one of the group's estates, until his retirement in 1959. His son Jerry would also become an employee.

Sir Percival's map came complete with suggested street names like Bedford Avenue, Buckingham Avenue, Northampton Avenue and Sheffield Road. The avenues ran from east to west and the roads from north to south; those to the north of the estate were christened with the names of northern towns while those to the south received the names of southern locations. To make the St. Helens' workers feel more at home the landlord named one of the housing estate streets Warrington Avenue.

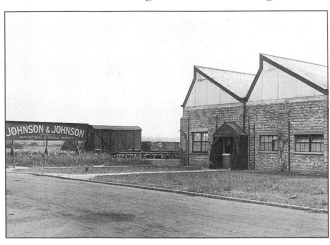

The Johnson and Johnson sheds in Fairlie Road. The company moved on to the estate in the early 1920s.

Almost without anyone fully realising it, as the depot carried on with its daily job of breathing new life into war-battered vehicles, the seeds of a new concept in the provision of industrial workspace were being born alongside rotting chassis and mountains of rusting parts.

The board authorised expenditure of £50,000 on the construction of new buildings to let, to be constructed by its own workforce. A West End publicity agency was instructed to compile a brochure explaining exactly what was meant by a trading estate and extolling the virtues of the one taking shape at Slough.

The idea of a large-scale industrial estate providing a range of utility and support services was not entirely new, although there was only one established industrial centre which, so far, fitted the description.

Trafford Park Estates had first been incorporated as long ago as 1896, charged with the construction and management of an estate offering "works, warehouses and manufactories" to businesses in the Manchester area. The estate had proved successful and, by the turn of the century, what was about to become the Trafford Park Company was winning parliamentary consent for greater powers to develop the complex properly.

So far, however, Trafford Park's example had not been followed up on anything like a similar scale anywhere else. The directors of the Slough Trading Company intended to be the first and a somewhat utilitarian brochure did its best to help them convey their pioneering message.

The estate, it explained carefully, was an industrial centre "of the most approved modern type" which would be almost impossible to better. Around 100 acres had by now been developed and the lucky occupiers-to-be were told that "every effort in science and industry has been brought to bear upon the estate to provide the tenants with every convenience that a city can offer and all the advantages, in low rates, healthy atmosphere etc that are obtained in the heart of the country."

The prospective customer was enticed by the availability of good communications and offered a choice of plain one-storey buildings "excellently designed for works of various descriptions" and some even "furnished with cranes, loading platforms and other advantages." Many had fans for ventilation and heating appliances could be arranged.

However lyrical the publicity material, the accompanying photographs made it clear that customers were being offered little more than a choice of sound but very basic sheds. Even so, many businesses, particularly small operations with big ambitions, were being offered a refreshing change from the old, cramped and inefficient factories of the pre-war years.

The first buildings, to be designed by the company's own architects, would at first be kept to the north of the railway. Bill Price, the first surveyor, would identify a site, put down a marker and merely pace out the dimensions. They were later confirmed with a tape measure and usually found to be uncannily accurate.

Water was readily obtainable from an artesian well on site, which yielded a chemically pure supply at the rate of 30,000 gallons an hour and could be purchased at 8d for every 1,000 gallons. The power station provided electric energy, lighting and compressed air for a standard charge of £6 a year; six-tenths of a penny was added for every unit of electricity consumed.

There was also a supply of steam which was rushed to factories under a pressure of 200 pounds per square inch via underground ducts, some of them wide enough to contain three men walking abreast.

To add to the estate's attractions, there would be a town gas supply, sewerage and drainage systems. Proper drainage, however, would not be provided quite as easily as it was pledged and waterlogged land would provoke complaints for years to come. Plans were also in hand to provide centralised services such as an employment department, a canteen, restaurant, a resident fire brigade and police officer.

It would not be easy going for the fledgling industrial estate, however, and the depot's principal business would remain centred on the vehicle repair business for a little while yet.

The end of 1920 saw Sir Percival Perry, who was planning on adding the responsibilities of managing director to his chairmanship, examining trading figures which appeared to fully justify the original gamble.

Though he emphasised that, from the outset, conditions had proved very difficult, he revealed that total gross sales of vehicles and parts had, in little more than seven months, exceeded £5 million. The figure triggered that part of the sale agreement which obliged the company to remit some of its revenues to the government.

The absence of any accurate stocktaking figures meant that, at this stage, further details of the company's performance were scant. There was no profit and loss account and only a hint of good financial results ahead. The directors appeared confident enough to announce that the depot workforce would receive a Christmas bonus of one quarter of one week's wages.

But the brief post-war boom was nearly at an end and no-one really knew whether they would even have their jobs, let alone a bonus, in another 12 months' time.

If economic depression was on the horizon, the directors and workers of the Slough Trading Estate and of the small but growing number of companies which had already opted for the bracing air and wide open spaces of Slough were first going to celebrate.

5

AN UNLIKELY GOLDMINE

THE NEXT 12 months were, indeed, to see the beginning of a period of deepening economic crisis and social division. Important markets had been lost to competitors during the war and high prices made many British goods uncompetitive.

Motor car production was only one of the new industries being developed. Electrical and chemical products were also evolving, although most British companies were unable to compete with the Americans and some Continental manufacturers.

The Slough Trading Company had problems of its own. While its battle for compensation over the vehicles flooded in France continued, its eagerness to get on and develop an industrial estate was being being hampered by the continuing failure of the government to convey the freehold of the Slough site to the new owners.

The problems were essentially bureaucratic but the delays would drag on throughout 1921 and well beyond. The official documentation transferring the freehold from the government to the company would not actually be signed until December 1927. Until then, the onward sale of freehold building plots would be impossible. In the event they would never take place.

The company, nevertheless, proceeded with its development plans, choosing not to contemplate the repercussions of any breakdown in the agreement and to put the matter down to procrastination in Whitehall.

Confident in their strategy, the directors were also examining the possibility of extending the Grand Junction Canal from the west into the heart of the estate. The idea had become a live issue following an offer from an expanding manufacturing company to relocate to Slough. The move, however, was conditional upon the canal link being provided.

The district council also showed an interest in the project, making possible an injection of public funds.

To the estate owners the canal would not only add another valuable transport link for businesses; it would provide a useful way of transporting coal to the power station.

Wary of the potential cost of building a link of nearly two miles, the company nevertheless decided to proceed and lawyers drafted the Slough Trading Company Canal Bill for presentation to parliament. Authority to construct the canal extension was enshrined in the ensuing Act and the company began buying the necessary land at £500 an acre. The initiative ultimately died, however, when the company decided it would be simpler and cheaper to make better use of the rail link.

Bill Price, the first Estate surveyor. He was succeeded by Cliff Richardson who worked for the civil engineers Sir Alexander Gibb and Partners.

The vehicle repair and sale business, meanwhile, remained buoyant despite the wider problems with the economy. Throughout the year the company would offer "exceptional opportunities in motor vehicles." Daimler charabancs sold for £805 and Peerless lorries for £350, with every vehicle carrying a six month guarantee. In 1921 the number of vehicle sales from Slough would exceed the combined output of all the UK commercial motor manufacturers.

With the volume of vehicles for repair on the inevitable decline, the company started to look for other ways of putting its trading skills to good use. It decided, however, that as a matter of principle it would not invest in any subsidiary undertakings.

It discovered that, apart from unwanted vehicles, the government also possessed large numbers of wartime vessels which were no longer required. They did have a scrap value, however.

The board decided to repeat the purchase-and-resale philosophy it had adopted for motor vehicles and in talks with the Admiralty offered to buy a number of ships at £1 19s a ton. The plan was to sell them on for breaking at £2 3s 6d a ton to the former enemy, in the guise of a

German consortium by the name of Reichstreuhandgesellschaft.

Redmond McGrath was given responsibility for clinching the deal. He was now prospering in the City where Guinness Mahon, the merchant bankers, offered him the use of a desk from which to conduct his private business. His board colleagues at Slough voted a special payment of £25,200 for his services in securing the business although the payment was never made because the sale eventually fell through.

By way of compensation the company went on to purchase a consignment of unwanted tanks for which it paid £21 each. If there were no tracks attached, it paid only £18. They were sold on for scrap.

By the end of 1921 the company was able to report a profit in the previous 12 months of more than £651,000. The result had been achieved against a harsh economic background which Perry described as the "darkest depression in modern times."

In fact the entire sales operation at Slough had been shut down. Responsibility for sales was entrusted to Slough Lorries and Components, which had itself bought a large number of vehicles from the depot, where it also occupied floorspace.

There had been other moves to reduce costs; redundancies continued, including 20 of the estate's own police force and nine of its

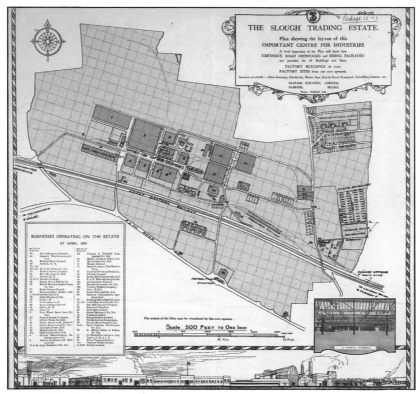

Plan of Slough Trading Estate circa 1927 - it was being billed as "an important centre for industries."

firemen. The board also decided to put up for sale its Dean Stanley Street offices and opened its main office on the estate. Number 27, Bedford Avenue was a dingy single-storey building with a brass name-plate by the front door bearing the company's name.

It would take five years to find a buyer for the London property. The building was eventually sold for £9,000 - the price originally offered at auction and rejected by the directors.

Back at Slough, the estate was taking on the appearance of a community. The beginning of 1922 saw the opening of the Peerless restaurant on the estate, its operation handed over to an outside operator on a three-year lease starting at £500 a year. For many years the restaurant would form a popular meeting place where estate workers could be served meals "to suit all pockets" by uniformed waitresses. Some of the wooden trestle tables had crisp white tablecloths while others were left bare. Despite its claims, the restaurant - which would also become a venue for boxing evenings - was too pricy to be used regularly by many estate workers for whom wages had to stretch a long way.

Though some executive ranks would be lucky enough to occupy the new houses being built in Farnham Road - eight with parlours at £500 each and 40 without for £375 - many more workers had to settle for nearby Timbertown, which was spreading.

The former army huts were now home for a growing number of people, not all of them employed by the Slough Trading Company but most with jobs somewhere on the estate. Though they could not compete with the new brick houses being built, they offered the sort of accommodation for which most of their occupants were very grateful.

Once used to accommodate some of the prisoners of war working at the depot, the huts looked very much like a POW camp, built in rows and standing on concrete blocks above the ground. They were surrounded by a wire fence beyond which stretched farmland.

Each hut had partition walls lined with sheets of asbestos intended to keep in the warmth and to deaden any noise from the neighbours. The innovation was only partially successful.

Irene Harwood and her family was among the first to move in during 1922. Her father, a former blacksmith, chauffeur and regular soldier with the Royal Engineers, had managed to get a job as a vehicle tester at the depot. The daily bicycle ride from Marlow had proved too much for Rupert Harwood - he liked to be called Charlie because he thought his Christian name was too "high faluting" - so he applied for a home in Timbertown. His wife and three children all liked their new home and were particularly pleased that each hut had its own little garden. Previously they had all shared two rooms in a house. According to Irene: "It was sheer luxury having all that space. We had a piano in the front room, which was only brought into use on special occasions."

Some huts, however, had to accommodate more than one family

so that the rent could be split. Inside there was a bathroom, a kitchen and eating area, a sitting room and three bedrooms. For £1 a week rent there was running water, gas lighting and a flush toilet.

But the rooms had no ceilings, which made them bitterly cold in winter. The only heating came from a gas fire in one room, although the gas cooker was invariably left on when the temperature plunged. There were no proper paths around the huts and rain brought thick, cloying mud which stuck to bicycles, shoes and clothes.

After the first winter the tenants would be allowed to have real fires, despite the obvious fire risk. If disaster struck the estate fire brigade was alerted by a steam hooter, the number of hoots determining the rough

The dingy single-storey building which was the first headquarters of Slough Trading Company in Bedford Avenue. The cars belong to the directors.

location of the fire. For a while the brigade's only piece of mobile equipment was an old Lewis machine-gun truck which had seen service in France.

In summer the huts became uncomfortably hot and all the windows, which were on chain hinges and could be completely unhooked, were often removed altogether.

There was a communal laundry and the former army mess became the unofficial social centre, where neighbours gathered for a dance or a sing-song. One special form of entertainment was to watch the daily outings of an experimental racing car as it growled through the estate entrance for a run along the Bath Road. The car, one of Sir Percival's pet projects, was driven by his chauffeur who lay back from the wheel, his head perched on the rear petrol tank as he raced past.

There were no shops in Timbertown but, once a week Darville's grocery in Slough would send a man to take orders. Other shopkeepers followed the grocer's example and, before long, butchers, bakers, greengrocers and newsagents all began deliveries.

For those who wanted to go into Slough there was always the "Lucas Special," a one-ton truck with a canvas roof stretched over metal hoops. It was driven at breakneck speed by Freddy Lucas, a former pilot in the Royal Flying Corps, who charged 6d for the return journey into Slough.

While the occupants of Timbertown went about their business, so the directors of the Slough Trading Company were anxiously examining the prospects for theirs.

Efforts to renew the original contract with the government, giving the company the exclusive rights to purchase all surplus stock, had ended in failure. Perry complained that the terms demanded by the Disposal and Liquidation Commission were totally unacceptable.

Cloche hats and Trilbies. Lunch at the Peerless Restaurant - 1920s-style.

After the previous year's good performance, the business was now heading for a balance sheet loss of nearly £600,000. The values of land, buildings and vehicle stocks all had to be written down and the company faced continuing management and logistical problems in organising the business of vehicle repatriation, repair and sale.

The directors took comfort from the continuing arrival of new tenants on to the estate - the O-Cedar Mop Company was among the latest arrivals - but there was increasing concern about the performance of what remained the core business.

There was evidence that the company was in need of much tighter management and better control systems. It was obvious that dishonesty was commonplace; "private arrangements" meant many sales were transacted at low prices while numerous vehicles and countless parts were simply disappearing.

A police presence on every gate at Slough proved no deterrent and the problem was even worse overseas.

By March 1922 Perry returned after a two-month absence because of ill-health to tell his fellow directors that he was under doctor's orders to take a further prolonged rest. He tendered his resignation as chairman and managing director, though he would go on to serve as deputy chairman until being appointed company president in 1952.

His semi-retirement from business was not to last long, however. In 1928, Henry Ford made one of his rare trips to Europe and offered his former colleague the chairmanship of the Ford Motor Company in the UK. The expansion Perry had wanted to oversee after the war was now being offered him. He accepted and, 10 years later - in recognition of his achievements as a business leader - became Baron Perry of Stock Harvard.

But back in 1922, while Perry was making arrangements to seek peace and quiet on Herm in the Channel Islands, his colleagues met on March 16 and elected Noel Mobbs as chairman. The directors agreed that, as Mobbs was also about to take on the responsibilities, if not the title, of managing director, he should be paid a salary sufficient to leave him with an income, after tax, of £10,000 per annum. His existing director's fees were then added to the total. By any standards Mobbs was being paid well. He was, in return, expected to produce results.

Like Perry, Mobbs was his own man. Intimidatingly tall with a penetrating look to his eye, he at once commanded the respect of those around him. He did not suffer fools gladly, possessed a fairly short fuse and had an intuitive business sense which had helped him prosper.

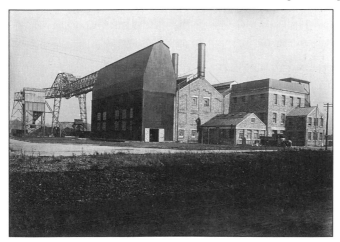

The power station in the early 1920s. Slough Estates is one of the country's last remaining small power generators.

From the day of his appointment as chairman Noel Mobbs was to become the driving force behind the business; he would dominate it for nearly four decades.

In his mid-40's by the time he took the chair, he had developed not only impressive financial skills but a keen sense of social responsibility which was to become the hallmark of his - and his successors' - approach to the role of business in the community.

A keen sportsman, he was a five-handicap golfer, had won several lawn tennis tournaments and had skippered a curling team. His lifelong passion, however, was bridge and he would eventually be elected as chairman of the card committee of the Portland Club, the premier world authority on bridge, and help write new rules for the game. He was also elected president and chairman of the executive committee of the European Bridge League. His ability to think two or three turns ahead was not an asset he reserved just for the card table.

On moving from Northampton, Noel and Frances, his wife, at first chose to live at Gorse Hill, Woking, conveniently next to the local golf club, which spoiled his plans by promptly refusing him membership. The large house had impressive grounds, a swimming pool and a putting course, and it became the setting for some very colourful weekend parties.

Sir Percival, who lived nearby and who was godfather to Gerald, one of Noel's four children, was a regular guest. So, too, was Marcus Colby, who went to Oxford with Richard, another of the sons.

Colby remembers Noel Mobbs as a man "with a big personality and an impressive intellect. In business, he could be pretty hard-nosed. He gave the impression of being able to see straight through walls. Away from business, he was a hell of a big spender. There were extraordinary parties, the sort people talked about and tried to get invited to. There was a lot of bridge and a great deal of betting on just about every sporting event you could imagine."

Colby had good reason to be particularly grateful for one particular party invitation a few years later. He found himself playing bridge with Edsel Ford, then chairman of Ford in America, who informed the eager young stockbroker of his company's plans to seek a flotation for the British business.

He was told to ring Ford's secretary, who would ensure that he received a full allotment of shares on flotation. Colby had no funds, however, but told his employers. They applied for 30,000 shares and saw them yield a huge premium when dealing began. Colby was immediately authorised to deal and set out on a career which would still see him at his desk in the City more than 60 years later.

Now in the chair Noel Mobbs determined to identify and correct some of his company's most obvious weaknesses. There would be a number of new appointments.

In 1923, shortly before the election of the first Labour government under Ramsay MacDonald, the board welcomed a new member. Sir Guy Standing, a wartime naval commander and peacetime financier, who had been advising Mobbs and Perry since the company was formed, was appointed a director. He would remain on the board for just three years, eventually leaving with Lionel Guest, neither of them holding the number of shares required to retain their boardroom seats.

Much more significantly, Mobbs also found himself a new general manager to replace Colonel Marcus Bruce, who had held the job for only 12 months. Edward Dulley was to have a rather more lasting impact on the company.

A Northamptonshire man, he had the added benefit of being the chairman's brother-in-law. Trained as a brewer to join his family's long-established business, he had decided instead to try the motor trade and had got himself a job working in a garage repairing Mercedes, Packard and Berliot motor cars.

He had gone on to manage a small garage in Banbury which became one of the outlets for the Pytchley Autocar Company. Mobbs had been impressed with Dulley's managerial talents and proposed that he should take the general manager's post at an annual salary of £2,000. It was the sort of offer that few could refuse.

Though he was called "Ted," Dulley was not best known for his familiarity or his readiness to strike up friendships. A short round figure who could not have looked more different to Noel Mobbs, he was not always on the best of terms with his chairman.

Sometimes they wrote formally to each other about aspects of business, with Mobbs addressing his general manager as "Dear Sir." Sometimes they would only communicate indirectly, instructing their secretaries to write to each other. But Dulley did not see popularity as a priority; he was primarily interested in getting the business on a sound footing. He was precise, punctilious and there was little that escaped his notice.

Staff whispered as they passed his door. He once reprimanded a clerk who walked past his office whistling, warning him that such behaviour

Ted Dulley, the company's first general manager and brother-in-law to Noel Mobbs, who had been impressed with his talents while managing one of the outlets for the chairman's Pytchley Autocar Company. The two men had a very formal, if not abrasive, relationship.

endangered his career with the company. The clerk was undaunted, explaining that he worked for another company which had taken space in the building.

Dulley banned scruffy people from the company's offices and outlawed any activities at work which were not directly related to that of the company. Believing that departure was disloyal, he laid down a policy that anyone who left the company would not be re-employed. He would later make an intimidating Justice of the Peace, an assiduous Buckinghamshire Alderman and become, like his chairman, a High Sheriff of the County.

When it was time to go home he would sweep everything off the top off his desk into an open drawer, lock it and go home. Only then would others relax.

Slough Trading Company was having to watch the pennies and no-one was better qualified for the job than Dulley. Depot workers could recite his favourite phrase before he said it: "I'm here to make money for the company, not to spend it." Once he spilled a cup of tea down his trousers and was angry because someone had sent his complete suit to the cleaners and not just the stained trousers.

The general manager scrutinised weekly labour cost sheets, spotting the red entries which denoted overtime and demanding to know if it had been necessary. Dulley was precisely what the company needed. If he could appear mean and small-minded, he also had a clear idea about how the business should be run.

He believed that organisational errors had been made when the company was formed and he was determined to instil discipline where he saw inefficiency and lack of control. Dulley would later be acknowledged as a key figure in ensuring that the Slough Trading Company had a future, a contribution ultimately rewarded with a seat on the board.

His approach to business, however, would never change. For many years he would insist that anyone wanting a new pencil first had to produce their old one to see if it had been worn down sufficiently.

In later life, while he would not permit anyone to ride with him in his Daimler driven by Bert Boore, an estate caretaker, he would insist that company vehicles travelling to other parts of the country were fully occupied; economy was all.

There was to be another addition to the company's staff in 1923. Charles Fairall had been working for the consortium in Germany, trying to sell off stocks of unwanted US motorcyles. Mobbs asked him to return home to take charge of leasing the available floorspace on the estate.

Fairall, a heavy smoker who spoke in clipped tones but possessed a sardonic sense of humour, thought the challenge was worth accepting. It would, at least, get him home. He was solid and entirely dependable and, though he would always maintain a low profile, would become an invaluable link between tenant and landlord. A man with the common touch, he would play a significant role in the development of the business and also eventually take a place on the board.

He also had some of Dulley's traits, including the same parsimonious approach to company funds. Years later he would reprimand a future chairman for buying himself a new chair.

By the time Fairall arrived a significant part of the original floorspace had been taken over by tenants. Around a dozen small factories along the lines originally envisaged and dubbed "bijou" units had also been especially built.

In one such unit a "highly secret" operation had commenced,

much to the puzzlement of the landlord. Only later was it found that the tenant was reclaiming old hats from rubbish tips, inserting the label of a well-known hatter and exporting them to Africa.

For the first time leases for factories and houses were to be offered together. Hygienic Ice and Crane Packing were among the first to sign up, the houses being let at £41 16s a year.

Fairall at once began the task of persuading potential occupiers to join the other pioneer industrialists. He recalled later: "I interviewed most of the leading industrial estate agents and was told their clients would never consider taking factories as far out from London as Slough. They stressed that there was no road lighting, a poor bus service, no theatres or multiple shops. In their opinion, the estate would fail." They would be wrong.

By 1924, as the last vehicles were being repaired and sold by the company, the company prepared to complete its metamorphosis. The US business was finally wound up and the board presented a private Bill to parliament to secure the powers to further develop the estate roads and the other on-site services.

Charles Fairall, who joined the company in 1923 to take charge of leasing the available floorspace on the estate. He played a significant role in the development of the business and eventually become a director.

At the same time, the company finally extricated itself from its long-running battle with the government over compensation for flood-damaged vehicles in France.

The effort to woo new tenants was stepped up. Articles began appearing in the Press identifying the estate as an attractive alternative location. One, in Cassier's Industrial Management, describing it as "London's New Industrial Centre," extolled the virtues of an estate with acres of space, plentiful supplies of energy and 12 miles of internal railway tracks linked to the Great Western Railway.

It went on to list the names of 37 companies who, by the autumn of 1924, had taken space. They included the St. Martin Preserving jam-making business, where vast vats of bubbling sugar filled the air with the aroma of seasonal fruit, the Be-Ze-Be Honey works, the Rheostatic Company, which produced powerful speed control equipment for trams, and the Four Wheel Drive Company, an American business which had grown out of the depot's vehicle repair activities.

They were joined by soap makers, pump manufacturers and wireless apparatus suppliers, all of them lured by the promise of a new start. The Slough estate beckoned: "There is no sign whatever of the smoke and grime and din of London. One works in the healthiest and happiest of surroundings, one's lungs filled with good fresh air."

In May, 1925 the last vehicles had been repaired and sold and, given the end of litigation with the government, the directors were able to disclose losses during the previous year of £291,250. The company's fluctuating performance was apparently continuing, with the board trying to give some overview of progress by pointing out that, from the time the

All Change! Workers arriving at the estate, courtesy of the Great Western Railway.

company had been formed until the end of 1924, it had made a net profit of just £8,750. The preference shareholders were reminded, however, that they had received £300,000 in dividends over the same period.

On August 7, 1925 Royal Assent was given to the Slough Trading Act which gave the company the "green light" to press on with its strategy of converting and building factories for letting. A huge acreage of land, with a current capital value of no more than £1 million, lay waiting to be exploited to the full, an unlikely gold mine awaiting a courageous business prospector.

6

"THE HARDEST WORKING TOWN IN BRITAIN"

THE ARRIVAL of Citroen, the French car makers, in the summer of 1925 gave Slough Trading Company a perfectly-timed boost to its finances and to its morale.

After months of rumour it was confirmed that the car maker had leased the former main workshops on the estate, along with an option on 60 acres of adjoining land for subsequent expansion. Up to 100 workers would be initially employed on a production line at first producing around 30 cars a day.

The plant was officially opened on February 18, 1926 by M. Andre Citroen, a member of the company's founding family, and would become a major car production unit. Citroen would remain on the Estate until February 1966.

In a bid to counteract the continuing economic depression a new Conservative government under Stanley Baldwin had imposed high duties on imported goods in an attempt to boost British manufacturing activity. It was a return to the strategy of Imperial Preference which had first emerged towards the end of the previous century.

Noel Mobbs and his colleagues had been quick to turn the situation to their advantage. In a piece of marketing which would not be out place 65 years later as Britain prepared for the enactment of the European single market, the company spelled out to overseas businesses - with a particular eye on the Americans - the advantages of manufacturing within their target market.

UK production, a Slough brochure stressed, opened up a trading bridge between England and the outlying parts of the British Empire. Not only would manufacturers save custom duties by producing within England, they could have lower distribution costs and benefit from the government's drive to promote UK-manufactured goods abroad.

And if Britain was the "Gateway into the British Empire Markets," where should a manufacturer locate? Where else but Slough.

In a passage which was to become enshrined as a central element in the company's future business philosophy, potential occupiers were told: "It is not necessary for you to sink money in real estate. We find the capital for the building or the site. You conserve a considerable amount of capital for the running of your business." Ownership of a factory, it seemed, was no longer necessarily the most sensible or responsible option.

Businesses interested in hearing more were invited to cable "Sloudeplim, England" or to telephone the estate offices on Slough 240, where their inquiries would be dealt with promptly and politely.

When an interested customer made contact, it was invariably Charles Fairall who would drive to London, pick them up and keep them talking all the way back to Slough in the hope they would not notice the length of the journey. After the estate tour some likely customers would be lavishly entertained, perhaps at Skindles restaurant on the Thames at Maidenhead, before being returned to London in a happier frame of mind; sometimes it would work.

One of the problems was that the visitor would be met by all the noises and disruption of a construction site as land was being cleared and services laid on. Against a background of hooting steam trains, delivery vans chugged along the web of roads now well under construction.

The fire brigade might dash by, pushing aside boys astride yellow bicycles who were employed by Slough Trading Company to take messages to tenants. The so-called "yellow perils" had arrived before the telephones had been installed but would quickly disappear as the marvels of modern communication took over.

But gradually tenants were being attracted. The chance that the estate might fulfil its owner's expectations also lured the major banks - Barclays was first and shared space in the company's own building - into opening branches. The General Post would quickly follow at a rent of £65 a year.

In its first year of trading as a property business Slough Trading Company achieved a net profit of £47,294 17s. The rent roll, most of which was based on what it regarded as long leases, was more than £50,000. In addition, there was an unspecified income from the supply of power, light, steam and water, the distribution of gas and the provision of railway loading facilities.

March 1926 saw the end of Slough Trading Company. In its place arose Slough Estates Ltd, a name intended to better reflect the new activities and point to a brighter future. The directors now had an eye on winning a Stock Exchange quotation, long delayed by the continuing wrangle with the government over flood damage compensation and the transfer of the estate freehold. With both issues settled Laing and Cruickshank, then a small City stockbroking firm, was given the task of preparing the company for market.

The year brought desperate economic trouble on a wider front. Long-running discontent in the mining industry reached a head just weeks after the company's name-change. The general strike, which meant emergency powers for the police and saw troops delivering food in lorry convoys, only added to the problems of a country laid low by recession.

Dial Slough 240 for space.

What was known as the "southward trend of industry," under which new industries were being born in the south and old ones were dying in the north, was helping to shield the southern half of the nation from some of the worst effects of the economic crisis. According to the headlines the north was losing its industrial supremacy.

Hardly surprisingly Slough and some of the estate's tenants could not escape altogether from the slump. When the directors of Hygienic Ice asked for a meeting it was not to seek more space; the company was in serious financial difficulties, owing its landlord nearly £3,000.

In a decision to which the company would again resort in respect of other tenants, it decided not to press for the tenant's liquidation. Hygienic Ice was a valuable customer for electricity and water and its collapse would hardly help the estate convey its message of mounting success. A package of extended credits was agreed and Hygienic Ice stayed in business, though it would not be the last time it was forced to seek financial help from its landlord.

Laing and Cruickshank did its job well, for which it was paid 250 guineas. On July 5, 1927, supported by a modest increase in net profits for 1926, the board of Slough Estates saw dealings begin in 420,000 ordinary £1 shares.

The share flotation caused little excitement in the City; there was no scramble for shares in the fledgling property company based somewhere out in the country which would have attracted still less attention if not for some of the reputable names associated with it.

In a coincidental move which nevertheless seemed quite symbolic, the ugly corrugated iron fence which ringed the entire estate was dismantled. A more discreet wire boundary fence was erected in its place.

On the estate itself, progress continued. By Christmas 1927 the estate had 65 companies operating within its new fence. Black and Decker was making its revolutionary electric-powered drills complete with "pistol grip and trigger switch" while the latest arrival was Aspro, manufacturers of tablets intended to speedily disperse headaches, nerve pains and neuralgia. The brand name had emerged by extracting letters from the company's full title - NicholAS PROducts.

Shortly afterwards High Duty Alloys would move in next door. The engineering company had just been founded by Colonel Wallace Devereux, who quickly earned a reputation for offering the best wages on the estate and who would become an influential and prominent local businessman. Devereux had been a superintendent at the National Aircraft Factory during the war, was in love with aeroplanes and would eventually become a Fellow of the Royal Aeronautical Society. His company was destined for a long and successful future, eventually employing around 12,000 people, many of them at Slough.

It was in 1927 that Slough Estates took another important policy decision. The take-up of floorspace meant that, by now, much of the original depot accommodation had now been filled and the newly built space was also finding tenants.

The board decided that the time was right to begin the development of some units for leasing even before occupiers had been identified. The idea of building for stock was not universally approved but Mobbs and Dulley believed that, provided the new supply was modest, the company could bear the cost of the plan and help attract more businesses to the estate.

There was also some concern that the company was becoming dangerously over-exposed by relying too heavily on large space-takers. Mobbs warned privately that up to 20 per cent of profit expectations lay in individual tenants and that the position was unhealthy. Smaller units and more tenants would limit the risks.

Work began on a number of "off-the-peg" units. The "A" type offered 4,000 sq. ft. of floorspace while the "B" provided twice that floor area. They were aimed at light industry and initially confined to Buckingham and Bedford Avenues. The units were advertised at rents of between 9d and 1s a sq. ft. and quickly proved popular. More would be built in Bedford Avenue.

The board's horizons were far wider, however. Early in 1928 the directors agreed that the company did not necessarily have to content itself with developing the Slough land. If the concept was good enough on the Bath Road, there was no reason why it could not be successfully promoted in other parts of the country.

The thought had been triggered by an unexpected approach from Major Alfred Allnatt, who had converted his small catering company into a contracting business specialising in the construction of manufacturing floorspace. In its earliest days the company had also run holiday camps at Cowes, Rhyl and Dymchurch and organised the catering for major sporting events such as the Richmond Royal Horse Show.

By 1925 the business had found itself providing refreshment services at the Empire Exhibition at Wembley, an extravagant display of pomp and riches designed to demonstrate that the sun was not about to set on the British Empire.

Allnatt bought some buildings and land nearby and turned them into dormitories and dining rooms, largely catering for parties of schoolchildren who came from all over the country to see the Exhibition. After the Exhibition closed in 1925, never to re-open, an inquiry from a whitewood furniture maker about taking some of Major Allnatt's space as a workshop led him to realise that there might, after all, be a use for the accommodation he no longer required.

His cooks, waiters and drivers became bricklayers and carpenters. An industrial building company was born and the resulting Chase Estate at Acton in west London would form the foundations of a thriving business.

Now, Allnatt had approached Noel Mobbs and suggested that the two companies might like to join forces to develop the 81 acres of land he had assembled for industrial development at Acton.

Although the idea was rejected, the directors realised that such projects were not beyond their reach. There were visits to Birmingham to look at possible sites and the directors also travelled to Liverpool to investigate the opportunities for land purchase.

For the immediate future, however, Mobbs and his colleagues were content to concentrate primarily on Slough. There was much to do, not least in sorting out the problems of tenants. The owners of the Peerless restaurant had disclosed that they could not afford to pay for the liquor licence and the board responded by advancing the funds in return for a percentage of the equity in the business.

By the end of 1928 Redmond McGrath had arranged the purchase of the enterprise on behalf of Taylor Walker, the brewery group which he had helped float on the London stock exchange and of which he would become chairman. Work on a new restaurant began and Taylor Walker was also granted an option to build a commercial hotel in Farnham Road, which Dulley believed would be well used by travellers.

An internal debate over a possible name for the new hotel began, with Noel Mobbs rejecting Dulley's suggestion that it should be called the Slough Estates Hotel. Any wrongdoings at the establishment, he warned, would reflect badly on the company. In the event, the hotel was never built.

The company had notched up another year of good profits, arranged to increase its overdraft facility and organised a rights issue, pricing the shares at 30s 6d each.

Out in the wider world the national economic climate was by now reaching blizzard conditions and it was going to take every ounce of skill and ingenuity to maintain early progress on the estate. National unemployment was set to double to 2.5 million - though in Slough it was barely one per cent - and confidence was rapidly draining out of the City.

Nevertheless more housing was triggered on the estate - several thousand would ultimately be built by the company, the council and other developers - and the momentum of development appeared oblivious to the problems beyond the perimeter fence.

A visiting journalist was suitably impressed and reported to his readers in the Daily Star: "The growth of this new industrial centre amazed me. New factories are springing up rapidly and a small town has sprung up to house the big influx of workers. It is not unlikely that this suburb of Slough will, in the course of a few years, become greater than the parent town itself."

The Aspro factory in Buckingham Avenue. One of the early tenants on the estate, the company was also one of the first supporters of Noel Mobbs' community centre.

The company's reputation was meanwhile spreading. Further afield, in Glasgow, the success of Slough's estate was raised in the council chamber by Bailie J. A. D. McLean, who said a far-seeing company had set out to accommodate manufacturers by building "first-class, up-to-date factories, fully equipped with every industrial facility."

He added: "Incredible as it may seem, they can be ready for occupation within eight weeks of the order being placed." Glasgow, he insisted, should take inspiration from the efforts down south and do the same.

In 1929, as Ramsay MacDonald formed a second ill-fated Labour government, The Daily Mail described Slough as "the hardest working town in Britain." There was overtime, instead of short-time; the local labour exchange was portrayed not as a place of hopelessness but as centre of hope.

The chorus of approval grew. The Daily News took a look and concluded: "Candidly, Slough is astonishing." According to the "Evening News: "If "being busy is the secret of happiness then Slough is the happiest town in England." Companies like Citroen, the newspapers marvelled, were actually expanding, with the French car maker still finding a ready market for its Ten Saloon model at £198 each.

The government, too, was by now clearly impressed with progress at the Slough complex and decided to open up on the estate a 400-place training centre for unskilled and unemployed men between the ages of 18 and 32. Ex-servicemen up to the age of 35 could also apply. Apart from unemployment benefit, all trainees would receive a free mid-day meal on weekdays and an additional allowance of 2s 6d.

Not everyone saw Slough in such a rosy light, however. Its interest aroused by "glowing" publicity which gave the impression that the town was "paved with gold," the Slough, Eton and Windsor Observer made its own inquiries. It was not impressed.

The newspaper filled four columns with evidence to support its contention that unemployment was a serious local problem and that the miracle reported in Slough was a mirage. It reported queues of frozen men outside the labour exchange, quoting the secretary of the Slough Young Mens' Christian Association as saying that men had come from all over the country for work which did not exist. It even claimed a bus operator was selling large numbers of one-way tickets back to Wales, their purchasers having "no intention of returning to this land of unfulfilled promise."

But, despite the claims of the local Press, the Slough estate did appear to be escaping the worst of the economic storms which raged overhead. The number of companies on the estate had now reached around 100 and there were an estimated 10,000 people at work, many of them still arriving from Wales and the north.

Building work was stepped up further with around 500 roofers, plumbers, bricklayers, electricians, navvies and chippies employed by the company in the construction of buildings and the provision of site services.

Len Jillians was one of them, an unemployed and unskilled ganger who turned up looking for work and was lucky enough to get it. He was just 18 years old and company rules stated that he would not receive full pay until he was 21. At first he was paid 1s 1d an hour instead of the full rate of 1s 2d an hour but he worked well and, despite company rules, was quickly put on full pay.

"It was a comparatively easy place for a labourer to work," he remembers. "The earth was so easy to dig because it had been prime farmland. That ground must have saved Slough Estates a fortune in labour costs."

Jillians was issued with a pick, a shovel and a grafting tool and put to work helping a gang of about a hundred men to hand dig the first three million gallon reservoir in the north west corner of the estate. As they dug rabbits and hares ran about in the fields which surrounded them. The only mechanical assistance came from a steam crane driven by Bill Knox, a fiery Scot who left no-one in any doubt if he believed they had overfilled his half-ton bucket.

Citroen car bodies on trollies. Moving assembly lines were still a long way off. The company was one of Slough's early tenants.

The earth was then dumped in skips and drawn along rails by horses that were pulling carts all over the estate. Many of them belonged to Ted Collins, who owned a haulage business on the Farnham Road and who hired out his animals and carts for 12s a day. The horses had seen better days and the workmen tried not to overload them.

While some men dug, others laid railway sleepers or helped put down factory floors. If it rained and work was impossible, no-one got paid. Earnings some weeks could be down by three-quarters. Anyone arriving more than three minutes' late for work had 15 minutes' earnings docked from their pay. There would be no tea-breaks until the end of the 1930s but someone was allowed to get beer at 10 o'clock in the morning. A pint of beer and a lump of cheese from the Peerless cost 8d.

All the construction activity was carried out under the watchful eye of Charlie Hockley, the clerk of works, a short and stocky man who wore rimless spectacles over his red face and white moustache. He was always smoking a pipe, was rarely seen without his Trilby hat and invariably carried a rolled umbrella.

He was considered to be something of a tyrant but those who worked under him conceded that he knew the building trade like the back of his hand. He would often watch the men from his office with the help of a pair of binoculars.

Hockley objected to them wearing overcoats when it snowed, arguing that it hampered their ability to work properly; when they were finally issued with "donkey jackets" he insisted they were brightly-coloured so that he could more easily see them working. If he spotted someone "with a straight back," implying that they were not using their shovel, he would sack them. Time was not even allowed for rolling cigarettes.

Those who wanted to ingratiate themselves with the clerk of works would go to the Queen of England public house in Slough, where he was the landlord. They would make sure he saw them.

Despite the harsh regime there was never a shortage of labour on the estate. There was also a constant flow of building materials on to the site.

Bricks arrived by rail and were stockpiled in Buckingham Avenue and Farnham Road. At any one time at least two million were waiting to be used. The bricks were thrown down, several at a time, to be caught by other members of the unloading team. If the foreman spotted fewer than four bricks being handled at once, those responsible would be reprimanded.

The bricks were then run in what were called "crowding barrows" to be stored. Cement arrived by lorry, packed in leaky hessian sacks. By the end of the day those who unloaded them were covered in blinding, burning powder.

Some of the navvies employed to dig the three million gallon reservoir on the north west corner of the estate. Being prime farm land, workers found it easy to dig, saving Slough a fortune in construction costs.

Their labours were certainly contributing to the success of the estate and of its owners. At the end of 1929 the board was able to report a further rise in profits to nearly £90,000. They thanked all those who had helped and voted themselves an annual pay rise of £250, taking their salaries to £950 a year.

As the new decade began and the Labour government stepped up its increasingly unequal struggle against financial crisis, the estate now boasted 123 companies. The streets and avenues had never been busier as the vacant buildings and empty plots were filled.

Side by side, face to face, there were companies making cabinet gramophones, mahogany wireless speakers, mint-flavoured chewing gum, dental supplies, egg cartons, beer crates, sweets, soap, floor polishes, aircraft parts and book matches.

New production processes and new materials were being developed on the estate. There were new textiles and fabrics, like rayon, pharmaceutical products were quickly evolving and Bakelite was being manufactured for use in everything from ashtrays to lamp sockets.

With workers from as far afield as Tyneside, Cumberland and Scotland heading for what was now dubbed "Sunshine Slough," the town had not only become an industrial test-bed but also a human crossroads. In 10 years the consortium's uncertain vision had materialised.

Efforts by the trades unions to set up their involvement in the area made little progress. Given the need for unskilled labour in the emerging mass production industries, the town and the estate had developed something of a reputation for low wages, but at least there was employment. Cheap female labour in particular was always in demand.

The pace of industrial development brought with it new concerns. The encroachment of bricks and mortar into previously unspoiled countryside was watched uneasily by growing numbers of people. According to the New York Herald, such was the spread of commerce in the area that nearby Stoke Poges church, immortalised in Thomas Gray's "Elegy in a Country Churchyard," was itself "in danger of being imprisoned by new buildings."

American interest had been aroused not so much because Gray's resting place was allegedly at risk but because, over the poet's grave, stood a monument to him erected by William Penn, the founder of Pennsylvania, whose own remains were interred a few miles further north at the village of Jordans.

The newspaper reported that a Penn-Gray Society had been formed in order to purchase and preserve the surrounding fields and protect them from the onward march of industry. The church and its surroundings would remain safe and few people would do more to ensure their protection than Noel Mobbs.

The chairman and his wife had moved in 1928 from Woking and paid £30,000 for Stoke Park, once the residence of the Lord Chief Justice of England but by now situated in the grounds of the 36-hole Stoke Poges Golf Club.

He would undertake many of his business responsibilities from the house and would in time be ably assisted by the formidable Kate Garnett, his private secretary. She was a tall well-built woman whose voice exuded authority and who regularly managed to intimidate hapless power station workers who inadvertently parked in her space on the estate.

Her straight-laced composure and woollen socks usually managed to disguise the less austere character underneath. Though few were supposed to know, she loved a flutter on the horses and her racing expertise, not to mention her ability to place discreet bets, was a source of widespread admiration.

Mobbs lived in part of the club house and became Lord of the Manor of Stoke Poges. He would personally mastermind the creation of the Stoke Poges Gardens of Remembrance, opened in 1934, which were eventually extended to cover a 40 acre site alongside the churchyard.

The Gardens, in Mobbs' eyes, provided a dignified solitude and a living tribute to the dead. Groves of silver birch, rose and heath gardens, ponds and waterfalls offered an island of tranquillity and helped to keep progress at bay.

Though events like the weekly cattle market helped Slough maintain its rural atmosphere, the changes taking place in its character were undeniable. A suggestion in The Estates Gazette that, despite the spread of industrial development, Slough could "never lose its countrified charm" was to prove a little wide of the mark.

By the end of 1929 the urban district council was engaged in debate about the need to extend the authority's boundaries into the parishes of Farnham Royal - 312 acres of which were covered by the trading estate - Burnham, Stoke Poges and Langley Marsh. The initiative was based on the need to provide modern sewerage systems in an area of rapid industrial expansion.

All the councils involved gave their agreement and Greater Slough grew overnight from 1,600 acres to 6,082 acres. According to The Estates Gazette: "Within a mile radius of the trading estate there is enough land to accommodate 100,000 people and, if the town is to be enlarged to that extent, the necessity for wise town planning is a matter of extreme importance."

It continued: "Since it appears to be certain that the town will be developed as an industrial centre the problem of town planning assumes, to many people, an appalling nightmare. In all probability, this depressing outlook is due to visualising Slough as a second Black Country. We feel confident, however, that the well-balanced commonsense shown in the construction of the Slough factories will also show in the development of the housing schemes which will be designed to accommodate the workers in those factories. In any event, we do not fear another bout of industrial hooliganism such as we had in the last century."

The arrival of 1930 inspired Slough Estates, which was still achieving a steady level of annual profits of a little under £100,000 a year, to scale fresh heights. With the year only three months old, it gave serious consideration to a proposal to develop an aerodrome on land next to the estate.

The company had already proved that good communications were an excellent selling point and to provide an air link at a time when air transport was becoming increasingly fashionable would complete the picture.

Land adjacent to the estate had already been used by aircraft belonging to the famed Cobham flying circus. Estate workers daring enough to "have a go" could enjoy a quick circuit in an open cockpit for five shillings or pay seven shillings and sixpence for a flight in an enclosed cabin.

The company wanted the aerodrome as close as possible to the estate and began making inquiries about the likely cost of acquiring the necessary land. Believing that the airfield would be essential to the estate's future they were particularly anxious that the company should control it. Land was quickly offered but, at £200 an acre, the board declined.

Stoke Poges Golf Club - for a time the stylish home of Noel Mobbs.

The project, however, was to become hopelessly bogged down in planning problems and by the insistence of Slough council that any airfield should be controlled by the municipality, a proposal which the company eventually came to accept. Land for the project was found at Langley but the idea would be abandoned with the outbreak of war in 1939.

In early 1930 the chances of building an airport was not the only expansionist idea being pushed around the Slough Estates boardroom.

In defiance of the gloomy economic outlook - the newly-published Slough Estate Journal spoke of "the weight of the great depression which lies not only on Slough but all over the country" - the directors decided to buy a development site at Speke in Liverpool and to begin work on a second industrial estate. Once again their plans were to be thwarted, this time by problems over access to the railway. The company's taste for a new venture was not dulled, however.

By 1931, as Ramsey MacDonald struggled unsuccessfully to keep his Labour administration afloat in the face of deepening financial chaos, Slough Estates briefly considered a proposal from Knight Frank and Rutley, the London estate agents, to purchase a site at White City, close to the heart of the capital.

Edward Dulley visited the site and reported back that it appeared "eminently suitable" for factories and warehouses. It was, he concluded, one of the most valuable development sites in London. But the board was not excited and, instead, proceeded to offer £75,000 for a 56-acre site four miles to the south of central Birmingham, occupied by the King's Norton Metal Works.

Given the economic situation the move may have appeared rash but it had been carefully calculated. Birmingham's industrial heart was still pumping and the directors believed that the concept of a modern estate, tailor-made to meet the requirements of companies used to operating in many cases from old, inefficient properties, would win friends in the Second City.

Names like Schweppes were still taking space on the estate but the directors agreed that the time had come to spread the company's geographical and income base.

So the Birmingham Factory Centre was born and building and conversion work began on more than a hundred factories. Progress would initially be slow, although the company placed great faith in the impact of the tariff reforms introduced by Neville Chamberlain, the Chancellor of the Exchequer, and intended to help stem the flood of imported goods and stimulate domestic manufacturing activity.

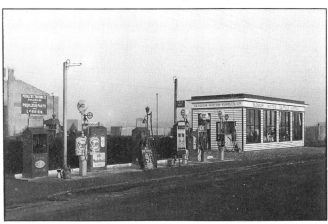

The estate petrol station around 1930. Petrol was 9 1/2 d a gallon.

They did not quickly fulfil the government's ambitions but, within a very short period, Slough was able to report that its rental income from the Birmingham estate - where rents ranged from £28 a year to over £1,000 - was exceeding running costs.

Even so, the company had a worrying number of vacant properties on its hands at Slough and Birmingham. It decided, much to the disapproval of Perry, to implement a scheme under which tenants could arrange loans of up to £3,000 to help tide them over an increasingly difficult trading period. A total of £20,000 was allocated to the plan.

As the Birmingham project got underway the chairman's youngest son joined the company. Gerald, who had been educated at Marlborough

College and Christ Church, Oxford, was the only one of his brothers to join Slough Estates. Richard, his eldest brother, became a barrister and joined the board of United Motor Finance Corporation in 1927, becoming chairman in 1959. Eric would eventually run ML Holdings, a defence contractor which became a tenant at Slough.

Though his father was running the company, 21-year old Gerald was to be put through his paces. A bright and charming young man, he would, in turn, make his own indelible mark on the company and on Slough, though he first faced a long apprenticeship, including a spell managing the Birmingham estate.

There was another recruit in 1931, this time to the board. Cecil Woodbridge had been a local director of Barclays Bank in nearby Windsor since the bank which carried his name had been taken over.

Woodbridge would prove extremely useful in arranging the Slough Estates overdraft facility with Barclays and he would chastise Perry, who was deputy chairman of the National Provincial Bank, for not being able to do the same. The National Provincial is said to have recorded a board minute to the effect that Perry could, indeed, authorise overdraft arrangements for Slough Estates - provided Woodbridge at Barclays had already done so.

Gerald's father, meanwhile, was dipping his toes into the murky waters of politics. The company had welcomed the so-called tariff reforms, expecting them to yield more tenants among overseas-based companies wishing to circumvent the 10 per cent import duties by manufacturing in Britain and, hopefully, at Slough.

As 1932 ended Noel Mobbs - who had now married Helen Cornish following the death of his first wife in 1929 - informed shareholders that the company was failing to attract the numbers of tenants recorded during the late 1920s. He was in fighting mood and his fists were aimed at the government.

Shortly before the chairman made his report to shareholders, the Board of Trade had announced that, in the first year of import duties, 218 foreign companies had set up operations within Britain. Of the total, 27 had chosen the Slough estate, a number which delighted Mobbs. But the chairman's pleasure was clouded by his conviction that, but for the government's unwarranted meddling, the figures would have been a great deal higher.

Firstly he complained that essential foreign personnel who were required temporarily in Britain to train indigenous workers had been refused entry permits. Having discovered that if those with responsibility for training were made directors of their companies they could not be prevented from entering the country, he then made it his business to see that such advice was passed on to interested tenants.

But the chairman saved his most outspoken criticism for what he saw as the Board of Trade's blatant interventionism in deciding how many manufacturers in any one industry should be permitted to establish themselves in Britain. He remarked: "This may be to the interests of the shareholders of the companies in the various industries who would be subject to competition from modern factories at cheap rents with contented labour in ideal surroundings at Slough, but it is very much against the interests of the unemployed and country generally."

Mobbs went on to accuse the Board of Trade of wanting to encourage employment "in the smoky slums in the crowded cities." In a theme to be regularly repeated in years ahead, he warned MacDonald's national government: "You cannot dictate to manufacturers as to where they should have their factories. If you hamper them, they will stay abroad."

He added: "The President of the Board of Trade can no more stop the tide of industry coming to sunlit, open factories in pleasant surroundings than could Canute prevent the tide from advancing up the shores of Dover." He concluded in sombre tones: "Frankly, at the end of the year, I am a disappointed man."

7

MARS BARS AND
AIR RAID SHELTERS

AMONG THE new tenants who had taken space at Slough during 1932 was one young and highly ambitious American businessman who had searched Europe before choosing the estate as his base. He had a team of 12, including himself, a product already proven in the US and a determination to succeed.

His name was Forrest Mars, an energetic 28-year old with a razor-sharp business mind who had not seen eye-to-eye with his confectioner father Frank over the development of the family business. He had decided to see whether he could prove himself in Britain.

"The English," he was told by Philip Wrigley, who had for five years been making chewing gum in Wembley for an appreciative public, "eat a lot of milk chocolate."

Forrest had, one Sunday, found himself upriver on the Thames and liked what he saw. He had been told about nearby Slough and decided to drive down from central London to the estate to have a look. He would remember the journey well, cramped in a sporty MG which swallowed up the miles.

On arrival in the town he went to see James Horlick who, 24 years earlier, had started producing a popular malt food beverage intended to deal with what the company had identified as "night starvation." Horlick told him to go and see Mobbs.

Mars was warmly welcomed and shown a large shed in Dorset Avenue. The roof leaked but it was good enough to begin with and Mars signed a lease. He and Mobbs became immediate friends, the newest tenant being offered personal accommodation at Stoke Park.

Mars intended to produce Milky Way, the chocolate bar created by his father and which had been so successful in America. By the August bank holiday of 1932, less than four months after he had first seen the estate, his factory was ready and Mars Confectionery was underway. Forrest decided, however, on a change of name for his product. The Mars Bar was born.

The bar sold for 2d and sales went well. "Mars are Marvellous" ran the advertisements and the British public seemed to agree. It was to be the start of a success story for Mars which would see it flourish and expand to become the single biggest tenant on the estate and a major force in the local business community. Fifty eight years later the Mars workforce at Slough alone would number more than 2,000.

In its early days the business also quickly diversified into the production of Chappie dog food, which would receive daily supplies of meat and cereals by train. But production of "the dog food the Greyhound Racing Association uses" eventually had to move, forced away by complaints about the odour and the failure to win special planning consent to stay.

The estate now offered an even headier mix of manufacturing smells, from the whiff of rubber from the St. Helens' plant to the scent of perfume from the 4711 cologne factory. Their success was equally diverse.

One new tenant and neighbour of Noel Mobbs was Cyril Griffith, who was running Coopers Mechanical Joints, a business supplying gaskets for the motor car industry. The business had been started in 1907 by Cyril's father, Dr. P.G. Griffith, a physician who had invented a water steriliser and had sought a company through which to market his discovery. He had found Edwin Cooper & Co. in the City, an importing business which had developed into a gasket manufacturer supplying, among others, the Sunbeam Motor Company.

By the early 1930s, by which time Dr. Griffith was chairman, the business had expanded and diversified sufficiently to justify a move to larger premises. It chose Slough and the younger Griffith, having conducted all the negotiations for space in Liverpool Road, became a friend of Mobbs and moved close to him at Stoke Poges.

Another of the estate's natural entrepreneurs, he took a particular pride in claiming his factory was the cleanest and most efficient on the estate. He would tour the plant to ensure every bit of spare copper, brass and steel was re-used. If he spotted waste, he would complain: "That's my spending money lying on the floor." The business would prosper as the principal supplier of gaskets to the motor industry and would stay on the estate for decades to come.

In contrast, others would struggle. By 1933 - the year Gerald Mobbs married Elizabeth, second daughter of Frank Lanchester, one of the founders of the Lanchester Car Company and a close friend of both Sir Percival Perry and Noel Mobbs - Hygienic Ice was again in trouble. Negotiations brought more financial support from its landlord to keep it in business.

Elsewhere, the St. Martins Preserving Company, by now the largest business on the estate, was also in serious difficulties and persuaded Slough Estates to sign guarantees for £110,000 to help keep it in business. Throughout the year, as Mars moved to bigger premises, further help had to be given to the jam makers.

Such assistance from a landlord to a tenant was unusual but the company believed it to be essential if business confidence was to be maintained and the estate's factories were not to empty. Some tenants, however, did lose the unequal fight to stay afloat and several took to selling their tools and equipment out in front of their buildings for 3d and 6d each.

In early 1934 there was a dramatic reminder of just how dire the nation's economy had become. On a bitter night in February, 285 Welsh hunger marchers stopped overnight in the town on their way to Westminster to demand government action to help combat the poverty provoked by mass unemployment. With dole benefit cut back from 26s to 24s for married men and from 17s to 15s for single men, their plight was becoming even more desperate.

The specially-formed Slough Reception Committee organised beds in homes, churches and chapels. Street collections to feed the men had been held but, even so, such was the hospitality that the Committee found itself £2 17s 3d short when the marchers left.

By now Slough itself was beginning to hurt. The Slough Observer spoke of the "desperate poverty" of Timbertown and reported that 30 of its tenants had been taken to court for rent arrears. They were ordered to resume their rent payments - now around 15s a week - and to pay off arrears at 5s a week.

Some of the Timbertown residents claimed they were living in slums and petitioned the Slough Board of Guardians for funds "to keep body and soul together." Sir Alfred Knox, the local Conservative MP who had commanded a White Russian Brigade against the Bolsheviks after the First World War, was asked to help. His response was not best calculated to calm tempers. He told the protestors: "There used to be some wooded huts at Aldershot barracks which were built at the time of the Crimean war. I found them quite comfortable to live in."

Some of the businesses on the estate failed to respond any more constructively and were happy to exploit the unemployment situation. One furniture manufacturer sacked workers earning 7d an hour and then offered to re-employ them for one penny an hour less. With the dole denied to any worker refusing an offer of a job, they had no choice but to accept.

But even as the marchers left, new tenants arrived to defy the economic storm raging around them. The Weston Biscuit Company - owned by the acquisitive Garfield Weston and famous for its "ready to use" cake mixes - moved into a 100,000 sq. ft. factory on Buckingham

Avenue made operational in only three months.

On Ipswich Road a small business making furniture casters was celebrating with champagne its first order for wheels for six dinner trolleys. Flexello had been started by Marcel Menko, who had been born in France of Dutch parents, and a friend. A business education in Manchester had encouraged him to establish his own small company. It had begun life as Suvretta but was soon rechristened Flexello - a combination of "flexible" and "excellent," the two characteristics which the founders believed best suited their new product.

The business occupied a "bijou" factory building and some office space which was so small the staff referred to it as the "watchman's hut." So embarrassed were they by the modest quarters that they removed the company's name from the front wall so that it could not be seen from the railway.

Flexello and Slough Estates would enjoy a close relationship which would eventually see the property company acting as agents for its products in Europe and Canada. A much-enlarged Flexello business would still be a tenant at Slough nearly 60 years later.

While the champagne corks popped in Ipswich Road, Metal Colours was stepping up operations from a 150-ft. long wooden hanger in Oxford Avenue, built by prisoners of war and for years used to house bales of wool.

The company had started out on the estate in 1929 as Kent Nail Works, manufacturing pit prop nails before turning to the manufacture of lead-based paints. It was mainly staffed by Germans, although it was being backed by British financiers, including Lord Astor, who lived at nearby Clivedon. The Germans had perfected a revolutionary process for making white lead, replacing the method which had been used in Britain for centuries.

Metal Colours worked 24-hours a day employing people on three shifts, seven days a week. The pay was £2 11s a week and employees were expected to work hard for it. The materials being used were hazardous and the men were instructed to drink one pint of milk a day in a bid to stay healthy.

Arthur Martin was one of the few non-German employees and remembers that anyone who made a mistake could expect to get slapped around the head, quite literally, by the managing director. "They had not perfected personnel relations to the same extent they had perfected their product," he recalls.

By the autumn of 1933 the Slough Estates Journal was able to report more than 150 companies based on the estate. They included less well-known names like Archbald and Bercovitz, British Chewing Sweets, ExLax, Gutberlett, Kasimar Baumgarten, No-Pe-Lo Potatoes, Ockenfel's, Rocker Blotters, Snoecks, Superflexit, Woodrims and Zwicky.

Some would fail and others would be swallowed up. Some would prove to be the kernel of something much bigger; there was a small undergarment manufacturer, for example, by the name of Berlei.

Slough Estates launched an expensive advertising campaign in the national newspapers. The whole country was to be told that factories, ranging from 1,469 sq. ft. to 150,000 sq. ft. were available to rent at 6d a sq. ft. or as little as £80 a year. Anyone interested had to contact the company's office where "Blackie" Blackman, the lady switchboard operator through whom every call to and from the estate had to go, would be of assistance.

The continuing influx of tenants meant rising demand for power and steam, which was now metered and which, because of its inherent cleanliness, was proving very popular as an energy source for food manufacturers.

One outside customer for electricity from the estate power station was Noel Mobbs, who signed a formal agreement with the company to provide all the power required for Stoke Park. Few of the guests arriving for a weekend party or a no-holds-barred bridge evening would fail to be impressed by the electrically-operated gates which dominated the entrance to the imposing house.

Wally Wallington joined Slough Estates in 1934 to work in the power station along with 200 others. He remembers the continuous railway wagon traffic bringing coal to the power station, just equipped with its first concrete cooling tower. "The coal was tipped into a pit in the yard, which would take about enough to keep us going for six weeks in case of a miners' strike. We never ran out of coal, although it occasionally caught fire and we had to turn the hoses on it."

The directors were in two minds as to whether they should commit further extensive funds to expand the capacity of the power station and asked the local electricity company to make more power available so that they could avoid additional investment. Their request prompted the electricity board to suggest that Slough Estates, which it intimated had no business to be involved in the generation of electric power, should sell its power-making capacity to those whose job it was to supply electricity.

The directors declined, offering instead a deal under which the company retained control of the steam supplies but leased its electricity generating plant to the electricity board. No deal was struck and Slough Estates was to become increasingly committed to supplying power to its tenants, an arrangement which, from time to time, would come under close internal scrutiny.

The company would also have an approach from the local Gas Light and Coke Company to see if it would consider selling its gas distribution apparatus, a proposal which was accepted and eventually would be concluded in 1941 for £57,000.

By 1936, as another national government - this time led by Stanley

Baldwin - struggled to come to grips with persistent unemployment, Noel Mobbs decided to take up a very personal challenge of his own. With the Daily Herald becoming the latest newspaper to query the "Slough miracle," claiming its success was being built on the backs of low-paid labour, he was ready to launch a social initiative which he had been considering for some time.

He had been stung into action by a few impromptu admonishments from the local rector, who had wagged his finger at a slightly startled Mobbs and said: "You know, you ought to be ashamed of yourself; you have all these people walking about in the streets in the evenings and committing crimes and it is all because you do not make any provision for their spare time. If you provided amusement for them in the evenings, this juvenile crime which is so prevalent would cease."

Women workers in the early days at Slough, seated at belt-driven machines produce gaskets.

There were greater fears than the prospect of rising crime among the young. Concern had been growing about the widening gulf between the poor and the well-off and about the repercussions of such manifest inequalities. Some were frightened that Britain could still see the sort of revolution which had overtaken Russia, with Marxism triumphing in the wake of capitalism's failure.

Mobbs had a less lurid imagination but, as a practical step towards encouraging a more cohesive society, he envisaged some form of social centre for the use of a community which now embraced 45,000 people - and not least for the people of Timbertown.

Some of the larger companies, like Aspro, Johnson and Johnson and Black and Decker, were staging occasional dances and there was often a boxing evening at the Peerless. While these companies, and some others, had begun to provide amenities for their own employees Mobbs wanted local industrialists to be "sufficiently broad-minded to come into a scheme by which they provided facilities for the whole community."

The chairman believed, as he told his friends, that an employer had a duty to do something more for its employees than merely pay their wages. He had seen and admired the way in which the Cadbury family had built not only a business but a thriving community at Bournville in Birmingham and saw no reason why the pattern could not be repeated in Slough.

An artist's impression of what would eventually be named Fairlie Road, with an overhead conveyor system running from the Black and Decker factory to the Citroen works.

After talking to his fellow directors, to the council and to some of his tenants, the chairman launched his bid to give Slough a heart. In a letter dated February 6, 1936 Mobbs wrote to dozens of companies asking them to help in "building up a contented, modern town in our neighbourhood."

Another 1935 sketch, of Leigh Road, with the Pytchley Autocar factory on the left.

He complained of a serious lack of facilities for healthy enjoyment in the long winter evenings, the absence of playing fields for use throughout the year and the dearth of what he described as "semi-instructional entertainment."

Mobbs pointed out that the proliferation of housing estates had created new social problems and that the provision of leisure time activities was one of the greatest challenges of the time. Mobbs had correctly identified the fact that, despite the long shadows cast by recession and unemployment, the 1920s and 1930s had witnessed a notable increase in leisure pursuits.

Football and the football pools grew in popularity and cycling was enjoyed by millions. The wireless had brought a revolution in home entertainment and, by the mid-1930s, about 20 million people visited the cinema every week. Girls of all classes walked the streets in "Garbo" coats and waved their hair like Norma Shearer.

Above all, the cheap motor car had arrived. Mass production meant that the number of private vehicles on Britain's roads was heading towards two million, though they remained beyond the reach of most working class families. Millions, however, still had their motor cycles and sidecars.

Leisure activities had achieved a new dimension since the war had ended. A genuine break with Victorian attitudes had been achieved. As the opportunities for relaxation increased, so simple pleasure-seeking by the masses became more acceptable. The weekend of recreation at home or out of doors became more of a reality for the working classes as well as for the middle classes. The Victorian work ethic, which decreed that the working man should work long hours and earn his keep by the sweat on his brow, no longer held true. Times were changing.

Mobbs refuted the suggestion that attempts to encourage relaxation with the provision of sporting and social facilities was the responsibility of local councils alone. He reminded his tenants that factory premises had been de-rated in order to encourage industrial growth, thereby relieving them of making any contribution to Slough's amenities.

He clearly spelled out his philosophy: "Slough is developing as a modern town upon modern lines and it should be run upon modern lines as far as the healthy education and contentment of its inhabitants are concerned. Happy lives, social evenings, keen sport and good health in our employees are of as much practical importance to us individually as manufacturers as they are to the spirit of comradeship which seems to pervade the British Empire more than any other country in the world." Remembering the rector's words, he added: "Crime is much reduced and the temptation to slip into evil habits among the young is both checked by precept and avoided by lack of idle time."

Mobbs envisaged a number of clubs and societies for games, lectures and entertainment and said that, by helping to finance them, the companies on the estate could "set an example which may well be followed in other parts of England."

He announced the formation of the Slough & District Recreational and Instructional Fund and set as its initial target the raising of sufficient money to build a central hall capable of holding up to 500 people with a gymnasium and swimming pool. Members would pay weekly subscriptions for the facilities they chose to use; it would not be "a something for nothing" affair. There would also be a club building, a reading room and 20 or 30 acres of playing fields. Time, he emphasised, was running out because development meant suitable sites were disappearing.

Under the Mobbs plan, the funds would be invested by trustees and the expenditure controlled by an elected council. Industrialists would contribute seven shillings for each employee and individuals could become private members for an annual subscription of £5.

The chairman revealed that more than £2,500 had already been pledged and said he hoped that the fund would quickly be able to finance the type of facilities which might otherwise take 10 or 20 years to provide.

The response was immediate with companies like Horlicks, High Duty Alloys, Mars and Aspro putting up funds. Slough Estates, whose profits for the first time in 1936 breached £100,000, led by example with a donation of £20,000. Mobbs himself gave £2,600.

Donations poured in. Three of the largest British banks gave £50 each, with Lloyds and Barclays donating £105. Lord and Lady Astor donated £1,025, Lord Kemsley, the newspaper proprietor and a friend and neighbour of Mobbs, gave £100 while a fast-expanding retail business called Marks & Spencer gave £10.

Mobbs became chairman of the Fund's executive committee and the money was immediately put to work. By 1937, as the trading estate decked itself out with flags to celebrate the coronation of King George V1, the Fund had spent £52,500 developing buildings on a donated six-acre site close to the Farnham Road, where much of the town's development was underway. Designed by architects Wallis Gilbert, who had also been asked to draw up plans for the new Hoover factory in Perivale, west London, the centre boasted a hall to seat not 500 but 1,200 people.

The building was available for drama, dancing, badminton and "glider skating" - to become better known as roller skating - a separate youth club building partly funded by the Buckinghamshire Education Committee and a swimming pool. Plans for a £22,000 extension were at once put in hand.

The community centre hall - built to conform with other factory buildings on the estate so that it could be used as such if the venture failed - was opened by Lady Astor early in 1937. Less than two months later it received a visit from Queen Mary, who spent time looking round what must have been one of the first creches for the children of working mothers. She was presented with a dolls house as a memento.

Later the same year there was another royal visit. The new King, together with his Queen, were invited by Mobbs to see the centre in action, which now had 5,000 members. The visit would long be remembered as the first recorded instance of the King and Queen playing darts. Shown into the bar lounge at the centre, Her Majesty asked to have a go and, after a brief lesson from Charlie Harwood, the local darts champion, she proceeded to score 21. The King, using his left hand, managed only 19 and conceded defeat. Nine days later the "Sunday Chronicle" ran a story under the headline: "Women flock to follow the Queen's lead at darts."

For Mobbs, the visit seemed to set the seal on a very personal triumph. His plan had quickly taken shape and he was widely praised for his inspiration and encouragement. The chairman's resolve to enhance co-operation between business and the community, to the mutual well-being both, was far from being satisfied, however.

As his board colleagues agreed to his plan to set aside annually five per cent of profits "for purposes connected with the welfare of employees" Mobbs was thinking about his next experiment - the provision of health services for all employees on the estate.

Slough Social Centre, the realisation of a dream by Noel Mobbs to ensure that Slough Estates contributed to the non-commercial fabric of the local community. It was opened in 1937 by Lady Astor.

The chairman was acutely aware that health care facilities were every bit as important as leisure amenities and just as lacking. Windsor hospital was overcrowded and unable to secure sufficient funds to cope with a level of demand which mushroomed as the population grew. Two doctors made regular visits to the estate to offer health checks. Plans for anything more ambitious, however, were to be unavoidably delayed.

By the end of 1937 Slough Estates was prospering to the extent that hourly workers were, for the first time, granted one week's holiday with pay.

But the air of progress and optimism which surrounded the company's activities was now increasingly being overshadowed by events well beyond its control. In Germany, Adolf Hitler had been in power for four years and was being permitted to re-arm in the face of continuing reluctance by other European nations to intervene. In 1936, the Rhineland had been re-militarised and Hitler was preparing to embark on a succession of territorial claims which would lead to a repeat of the bloody chaos that had torn Europe apart such a short time before.

At home there were plenty of straws in the wind. The board was obliged to pay national defence contributions, which it argued should be treated for accounting purposes in just the same way as income tax.

Given the estate's likely strategic importance during any conflict and its relative proximity to London, the company also sought war risk insurance; its search proved fruitless.

As the prospect of war in Europe grew more likely, Slough Estates sought assurances from the War Office that it would provide an anti-aircraft battery to help defend it from German air raids. As it was likely that many of the manufacturers on the estate would be contributing towards the war effort by switching production to armaments and equipment required by His Majesty's forces, the War Office agreed.

Slough, the town which had just been granted a Royal Charter to make it Buckinghamshire's fourth borough, would finally be on the map - even if the map belonged to a German bomber. Plans to camouflage the factories were prepared.

In view of the mounting emergency the company decided to abandon any plans to expand its business through acquisition and it earmarked £1,000 for the protection of its own staff and documents in the event of air raids.

There was little optimism in the air by the start of 1939. The company went about its business, sanctioning a new advertising slogan: "Our success is no accident." It was also proving itself more inclined to use the services of estate agents to help it fill floorspace.

While estate land was identified for the construction of air raid shelters, the board tried to look beyond the immediate uncertainty to a brighter future by introducing an employee pension scheme. The staff were all issued with explanatory booklets and given examples of the benefits.

A 25-year old male employee earning £160 a year, for example, could expect to retire at 65 with a pension of £127 a year. A death in service benefit of up to £800 was also payable, though it was emphasised that this would not be forthcoming if the employee was a member of the armed forces engaged in warfare.

By April 1939 Mobbs was able to tell shareholders that the previous year had shown a further rise in profits and that the development of Slough and King's Norton, Birmingham, had been progressing on a greater scale than at any previous time.

His appearance before the Royal Commission on the Geographical Distribution of the Industrial Population, called to investigate and to suggest ways of restraining the growing shift of manufacturing industry towards the south, gave Mobbs a timely opportunity to sum up his company's progress.

The chairman reported that 23,000 people now worked on the estate at Slough, around 8,000 of them regarded as "immigrants" from distressed areas. The figure had earlier peaked at 15,000. He reported that, though the business had made mistakes, the estate had successfully pioneered a new approach to planning the industrial environment.

Only two other outstanding private trading estates were worthy of mention - those at Trafford Park and at Welwyn Garden City. He made it clear to the committee that, in his opinion, they did not measure up to the standards set at Slough.

The chairman also took the opportunity of using his appearance before the committee to set down his own views on the best approach to planning Britain's industrial landscape. He claimed that industrial planning would be best handled at a national level.

Queen Mary visits the Slough Social Centre in 1937. Noel Mobbs is accompanying her.

He warned that without a degree of centralised planning "there will be nothing to stop mushroom towns sprawling indefinitely over the adjacent countryside. They will mop up valuable agricultural land, beauty spots and coastal scenery in a mass of bricks and mortar."

Mobbs was no supporter of state controls and believed the nation's livelihood depended squarely on individual effort and private enterprise but, in this area at least, he saw the need for someone or some body to assume an overall responsibility. He told the committee: "I am dead against telling a manufacturer where he should go; I think that is his job; he knows where to go but to limit his choice by a system of national control seems to me entirely reasonable."

Mobbs called for a regime under which industrialists embarking on new factories should also provide areas of open space for use by workers. Even more controversially, they would have to contribute towards a fund established to provide a range of facilities for the benefit of the entire community. The contribution would be based on a fixed proportion of building costs.

Mobbs acknowledged that industrialists might not like the idea but that they would have to consider the national interests. The idea was not pursued, although a rapidly developing post-war development industry would rarely escape from the debate about its impact on the wider community and its responsibilities towards it.

Package 3 - 31

THE WORLD'S MOST SUCCESSFUL LIGHT CAR
THE NEW HILLMAN MINX
Greatest Value £169

Daily Express

WORLD'S LARGEST DAILY SALE

No. 11,728   Saturday, December 18, 1937   One Penny

22-IN-ONE GIFT
for the Children
Daily Express Model Book
contains 22 Free suits shown —
Queen Mary, Plane that flies 300 ft. etc. No winners at plus needed.
3/6

'Do Let Me Try,' Said The Queen

U.S. Cabinet Told Japan Will Make Full Amends

ROOSEVELT SEES CHIEF OF NAVY STAFF

From C. V. R. THOMPSON.
Daily Express Staff Reporter   NEW YORK, Friday

PRESIDENT ROOSEVELT prefaced a two-hour meeting of his Cabinet today with a summons to Admiral William Leahy, Chief of Naval Operations, for a full discussion on the sinking of the United States gunboat Panay.

Although Mr. Roosevelt told the Cabinet later that Japan was offering redress, Admiral Leahy's ...

War nears our Isle of Wight in the Far East—See map on Back Page

BARBARA HUTTON: NEW MYSTERY

Daily Express Staff Reporter
NEW YORK, Friday.
"CIRCUMSTANCES beyond her control" forced Countess Barbara Haugwitz-Reventlow to the sudden decision, which surprised even her friends, to renounce her American citizenship.

To her lawyers in New York the former Miss Hutton today dictated by ship-to-shore telephone from the liner Europa a message in which she expressed regret that her action had become necessary.

Some of her friends thought that taxation prompted the move. Experts calculated that her renunciation of American citizenship would save her several hundred thousand dollars yearly.

STOP PRESS

NEW BLOW FOR ROOSEVELT
U.S. House of Representatives by 240-to-9 vote resolved to take up the question of voting—$18 to 19—in favour of revising Bill to Judge Committee.

MAURICE TATE
Early today Tate reported slightly better.—See Page 23.

Telephone: Central 8000

Two Drowned On Joy Ride

Car Leaps Into River

Daily Express Correspondent
HULL (Yorks), Friday.

TWO young men starting on a joy ride were drowned tonight when their car skidded, broke through chains across Chapman-street Bridge, Hull, and somersaulted into the River Hull.

The men, nineteen-year-old William Padley and James Lawson, aged eighteen, were going to call for Lawson's brother.

They had driven only a hundred yards when their car plunged from the bridge, which was open to allow river traffic to pass downstream into the Humber.

Mr. S. Morris, the city engineer, wearing a borrowed macintosh over his evening dress, directed salvage work.

The car, with its roof ripped off, its red rear light still burning, was hoisted from the river bed by crane. Inside was Padley.

Search for Lawson will went on late tonight.

HOURS TO FIND MANSION FIRE

SHOOTING party guests arriving at Yattendon Hall, near Newbury, and Cambridgeshire mansion, last night, found the west wing burning and three fire brigades in charge.

The hall, owned by Viscount Chilcott, has 100 guides and stands in 500 acres of parkland. It was let recently to Captain Grenfell, whose wife is daughter of the late Rudyard Kipling.

Burning had been detected at lunch-time. Estate workmen failed to trace the cause and firemen were sent for. Floorboards were pulled up in many places, if smoke seemed to be everywhere.

It Was A Bean

Then, five or six hours later, a smouldering bean in the roof gave the clue. Firemen found that beams making the engine roof of the villa were burning. The whole of the insulated material ...

CAPTAIN SHOT DEAD IN WOOD

CAPTAIN C. F. MERMAIDEN, Royal Artillery, was found by a gamekeeper yesterday shot dead in a wood near Trowbridge, Wilts.

A 12-bore shotgun was by his side. He had been dead two or three hours.

Captain Mermaiden, who was thirty-six, was married, and lived in Bunton-road, Brighton. He had a daughter five years of age.

500 YEARS TO PAY

An order for payment of one penny a month—which, it is calculated, would take 533 years and one month to pay off—was made by Judge Watkins Cave in Bournemouth County Court yesterday in a judgment summons.

The amount owing, with costs, was £29. 6s. 1d.

HER FIRST DART

Daily Express Staff Reporter
THE Queen beat the King at darts in a match played in a bar lounge at Slough Social Centre last night. She won by two—but she stood a foot nearer the board than he did.

They were playing an informal visit to the Centre, which has 5,000 members. As they entered the bar, the Queen in emerald green, the King in grey tweed, several men were playing.

"Do let me try," the Queen said. "I have heard so much about this game."

"We'll have a match," said the King.

One of the players, Mr. F. Draper, handed three darts to the Queen. Her first throw was a 5, her second a 13. Then she scored again and bedded in the 1.

KING SCORES 19

"Very good," said the King, then took the darts. He used his left hand as he does at billiards. A 7, a 3 and a 9 was his score.

"So you've won at last," he said to the Queen.

"And I've never thrown a dart before!" she exclaimed.

"May have I," the King laughed "But it's a fine game."

"Very sporting," the Queen agreed. "We must play again. I must stop and watch for a moment more."

She popped at the door as the players they had beforehand started again. After she saw them throw a 99 and a 40 with two darts.

"Oh, isn't that marvellous!" she said. "What poor players we must be."

The visit of the King and Queen had been scheduled to last an hour that they stayed an hour longer.

DAILY EXPRESS RADIO STATION
London: Weather Forecast
Local fog patches in morning, clearing quickly in most places. Small amount of high cloud at first, with bright periods. Cloud increasing and falling later in day, with showers probable locally at night.

Carnera On The Telephone

"I Worry All The Time"

PRIMO CARNERA, world heavy-weight boxing champion four years ago, lay yesterday in a Budapest sanatorium, a giant broken by illness and worry.

He has kidney haemorrhage; he has been delirious. It will be weeks before he can leave his bed. He is bankrupt in two countries. But he accepted eagerly the telephone call I put in to him from London.

His voice was a husky rumble over the wires.

" Euro, I feel mighty bad," he said. "My English is somewhat Americanised. Whatever it is, it hurt me like hell. I can't eat—me, Carnera.

"I'm worrying too. I put the here and think all the time. Not much good, eh?

"I put no money, and here I got to stay."

(Primo in his train, had made and lost a fortune totalled at £200,000.)

"I have played in his bed for two weeks. I have to stay here for Christmas. What do you think of that?"

"The doctors come to see me every day. I see to them, 'Shall I box again?' They say, 'Maybe, Primo. We tell you when you're better.'

"So what am I going to do? I can worry all the time.

"I tell him he must not, or he would not get well. His doctors, in fact, say he has only the more tender chance of boxing again.

"It got to worry me," said Primo. "And I was going to box in Mexico again. By best bet.

"They knock me. They wouldn't again. But now—maybe I get well by-an-by."

SHOP EARLY

MOST of the great London shops and stores are keeping open late next week for the Christmas shopping. On Monday the average closing hour is at 7 p.m.; on Tuesday, Wednesday and Thursday one hour later.

But on Christmas Eve the closing hour is at 1 o'clock; in let staffs get away for the holiday.

These extended hours are for the benefit of those who have to shop late. All others are asked to

SHOP EARLY.

Eagle Oil Shares Fall By £1,250,000

Shares of the Mexican Eagle Oil Company, one of the most popular gambling counters in the world, fell in value yesterday by £1,250,000 on unconfirmed reports from Mexico City that the award of the Arbitration Board on the wages dispute, to be announced today, would add more than £2,500,000 to the annual expenses of the oil companies.

The dangers of booking Mexican Eagle shares, owing to the political risk, have been repeatedly pointed out in the Daily Express.

Details on Page Two.

The King Honours Austrian Minister

The King invested Baron Franckenstein, the Austrian Minister, with the G.C.V.O. at Buckingham Palace yesterday.

CHINA : 8 DAYS
London will be within sight and a half days' journey of Hongkong after tomorrow, when a new Imperial Airways service will be opened between Hongkong and Bangkok.

English Walk Off Liner

Daily Express Staff Reporter
NEW YORK, Friday.

HONEYMOON ship Monarch of Bermuda, the luxury Furness liner plying between New York and Bermuda, was at sea today with a cargo of good food and Christmas decorations, but without a single passenger.

Two hundred English stewards had walked off the ship and 200 passengers, including fifty-two honeymoon couples and the Duke and Duchess of Manchester, were asked to leave the ship.

MR. & MRS. J. W. BEAZLEY

The Daily Express published on Wednesday last a photograph which purported to be a photograph of Thomas Ronald Max Davies, who pleaded guilty at the Hampshire Assizes at Winchester to bigamy and who was on Thursday last found guilty of falsifying a Mr. "X" and sentenced to four years' penal servitude.

The photograph came to the Daily Express from such a source that there was no reason to question its authenticity. It was, however, not a photograph of Davies but of Mr. J. W. Beazley, of Maple-grove, Southall.

The Daily Express tenders to Mr. and Mrs. Beazley its deep regret for this unfortunate error and its apologies for the pain and suffering which has been caused to them.

'DON'T WED TOO YOUNG'

—Warns Air Chief

CADETS at Cranwell R.A.F. college laughed yesterday when Air Marshal Sir Cyril Newall, Chief of Air Staff, mentioned marriage during a passing-out inspection.

Sir Cyril remarked: "It is not a subject to be laughed at.

"If you marry too young you are doing your best. Your wife will go to seed. You will get to made for it, and you have probably not the taking responsibility which will take your blood and your time from your work.

"But Sir Cyril, who is aged fifty-one, married when he was thirty-six."

Mae West, As Eve, 'Insult To Faith'

NEW YORK, Friday.—Miss Mae West's interpretation of Eve in a broadcast skit, "Adam and Eve," been attacked by the Roman Catholic weekly Brooklyn Tablet as "an insult to every Christian."

The National Broadcasting Company, whose "deep regret" at having offended any one.—BUP.

3 Shot As Strikers Ambush Ford Men

KANSAS CITY, Friday.— Two policemen and a Ford worker were shot at Kansas City tonight when strikers ambushed a busload of about 300 men carrying non-strikers to the plant.

In a day of downtown night-time strikes, every arrived.—BUP.

Oh, Mr. Mercury, you did give me a start!

When Father Christmas, some years ago, changed over from reindeers to motor 'delivery, the faced a cold-starting problem that would make the ordinary driver shudder. We are, therefore, most gratified to be able to tell you that he is now running exclusively on National Benzole Mixture. He finds—as you too will find—that Benzole makes good petrol better for quick starting, even in Polar conditions.

NATIONAL
BENZOLE MIXTURE
The spirit of 'STARTABILITY'

Royal Darts. Slough Social Centre has regal visitors just before Christmas 1937.

All of a sudden, however, the question of north-versus-south became irrelevant; it had become a question of Hitler against most of the rest of Europe. On September 1, 1939 the dictator invaded Poland and, two days later, Britain declared war on Germany.

A year earlier, the poet John Betjeman had made his own effort to immortalise the town where thousands had now followed in the footsteps of Sir William Herschel to take a job. With a pessimistic, if prescient, turn of phrase he called out: "Come, friendly bombs, and fall on Slough. It isn't fit for humans now ...."

8

A BUSY WAR

FROM THE very outset of hostilities it was widely assumed that the Germans had earmarked the Slough industrial estate as a prime target.

It was a densely populated manufacturing centre, close to the capital, which the enemy correctly assumed would be almost exclusively turned over to helping the British war effort.

Any enemy bombers wishing to locate the estate - which was quickly to become one of the biggest centres of armaments production in the country - would have little difficulty. From 1939 onwards the estate and the town were to be deliberately shrouded in a foul-smelling smokescreen which may well have disguised the activities underneath but which made its general location fairly obvious.

The smokescreen emanated from giant, candle-like structures positioned about 20 yards apart all over the estate. A metal chimney rose from a drum base filled with oil-soaked rags and topped with a metal deflector intended to control the spread of smoke.

Arthur Martin, a chemist employed at Metal Colours, would often see enemy spotter aircraft overhead: "They sent down flares to illuminate the estate for the benefit of the bombers or to enable them to take photographs. The flares were so bright you could stand outside your own front door at midnight and read the newspaper. They were like so many chandeliers and, as soon as they started, the oil drums were lit up."

Lighting the smokescreen would become the responsibility of the Italian prisoners of war who eventually arrived on the estate. They were permitted to roam around unattended, identified only by the coloured patches stitched to their clothing. For the most part they appeared relieved simply to be out of the fighting.

If the smokescreen confused the Germans, it choked the workers and clogged the hair and clothes of the people of Slough. Barrage balloons hung overhead, occasionally breaking free and drifting away over the factory roof tops.

Company names were removed from buildings, to be replaced with simple identification numbers, and windows were blacked out. The first of 60 buildings and businesses began to be requisitioned by the government in order to contribute towards the war effort.

The urgent need for armaments and the entire range of equipment required by the armed forces meant that activity was never-ending. If anything, the pace of life on the estate stepped up as the conflict progressed and most businesses abandoned their peacetime activities.

The influx of extra "war workers" also placed impossible strains on accommodation. One expedient was known locally as the "hot bed" system, an arrangement by which a night-shift worker often got into bed, still warm from its day-shift occupant.

Tony Neville was a child living next to the estate in wartime and recalls how round-the-clock shift working meant that the streets, almost empty of cars, were thick with bicycles all hours of the day and night. "The whole place was going day and night, turning out guns and shells and aircraft parts. You could always hear, right across the estate, the steady thump of the presses at High Duty Alloys as it turned out armaments."

The company had at once become involved in the production of aircraft components, turning to good advantage its expertise in casting and forging light alloys. Daily, the factory turned out castings for Merlin engines, used to power the Spitfire, as well as undercarriages for Halifax bombers and components for the Lancaster aircraft.

Wallace Devereux, the owner, had a major contribution to make to the war effort. He had spent a great deal of time in the 1930s visiting Europe, and in particular the German aircraft factories, to watch and learn from the programme of industrial reconstruction underway. Devereux had reported back to the British government on the expansion of the German air force he had witnessed. As concern about Germany's intentions had grown, he had established a second components factory in the Midlands to help in the production of aircraft for the Royal Air Force.

His personal contribution during the war would be to organise, on behalf of the Ministry of Aircraft Production, the assembly of American engines and aircraft and the repair of the large numbers of immobilised fighter aircraft urgently needed back in action.

In June 1940, however, the role of High Duty Alloys itself would be temporarily halted by a massive explosion which killed six people and injured 40 others. The wartime activities of the company were shrouded in secrecy and the authorities were to prove no more forthcoming about what had actually happened.

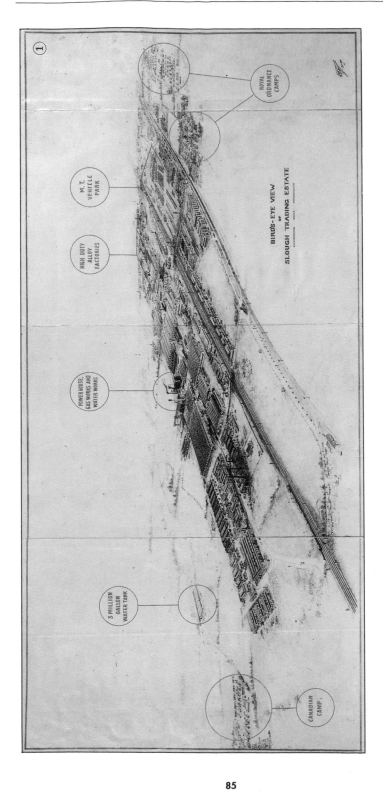

Top Secret. A wartime map of the Estate as it appeared during the Second World War identifying the most vulnerable targets for enemy bombers.

The explosion was eventually attributed to an incendiary bomb, though the hit had, like so many others during the war, been a matter of chance rather than good judgement. After the war it was disclosed that German intelligence believed the High Duty Alloys factory was, in fact, occupied by St. Helen's Cable and Rubber.

Value for Money at Slough. Marketing literature from the 1930s.

All over the estate the war effort was underway. A small company called Woodrims, normally manufacturing wooden bicycle wheels, turned to producing wooden parts for the De Havilland Mosquito aircraft. Citroen began making components for the Churchill tank; as tanks arrived, to be parked before being called into action, the estate began to look as it had decades earlier.

Gerald Mobbs, the second in the family to take the chair.

At nearby Langley, which Mobbs had considered the likely location for his proposed aerodrome, Hawker Aircraft were producing Hurricane fighter aircraft, which would bear the brunt of the fighting in the Battle of Britain. The factory was turning out five machines a day at the peak of its output. Other types of combat aircraft would also roll off the production lines, including the Typhoon, the Tempest and the Fury.

The Germans had other good reasons to be interested in Slough. They knew that much of the early work on the development of radar - later acknowledged by the enemy as one of the most decisive weapons of the war - was carried out at the radio research station at nearby Ditton Park.

Not all the factories were forced to suspend their normal operations. Mars, for example, was permitted to continue to produce its chocolate bars at reduced levels in order to supply the armed forces. The aim was to get a Mars Bar into every soldier's knapsack.

Chocolate production was only allowed to continue, however, after some intense special pleading. The Ministry of Food at first recommended that the factory should be completely given over to other purposes. It had argued that, with the chocolate ration down to two ounces per person a week, compared with the normal peacetime consumption of about nine ounces, there was no need to maintain pre-war levels of output.

Colin Pratt, who was managing director of Mars during the war years, recalls that the Ministry's logic was straightforward enough. "Being one of the last factories to start up, it was considered only right that it should be one of the first to stop production. We were visited by a stream of army officers of various ranks telling us we had to close down. I appealed to Noel Mobbs for help and, two days after we had discussed it with him, we were informed that Lord Beaverbrook, who was Minister for Aircraft Production, had agreed that we need not stop chocolate production." Forrest Mars would always be grateful to Mobbs for what he remained convinced was an effective intervention at the very highest level.

Even so, there were some changes at the plant. Derek Patterson, a Mars employee, remembers that part of the factory had to be given over to the canning of bacon and, in another area, there was a motor cycle assembly and repair operation going on. Both businesses had been bombed out of London.

Continuing Mars Bar production meant that consignments of chocolate still arrived in bulk form by rail, packed in sacks. Local children, inspired by the war-time spirit, blacked up their faces and launched commando-style raids on the sidings where the chocolate wagons sometimes stood overnight.

All the wartime activity placed enormous strains on the estate's power station and the intermittent supplies of poor quality coal did not help matters.

Henry Overshott, an eager 14-year old, joined Slough Estates as an office boy as war broke out and was to become the first employee to notch up 50 year's service with the company. He quickly took an apprenticeship in the power station workshops and remembers the herculean efforts made to keep the estate's power supply going under the ever-watchful eye of Sidney Harper-Bill, the intimidating chief engineer whose stature and bullying manner made him an effective, if unpopular, boss.

According to Overshott, who would eventually be manager of the power station: "Everything in the building was blacked out. There were no overhead lights inside; instead we had tiny lights over our gauges but, otherwise, we groped around with torches."

The power station was surrounded by a high wire fence and there were security guards on duty round-the-clock watch, not only for airborne aggressors but also for the possibility of attacks from the Irish Republican Army, which was again mounting a bombing campaign on the British mainland. Close by was a concrete water tower which became a useful vantage point for members of the Royal Observer Corps to watch for enemy aircraft. One of the less likely sightings must have been of Steve Hopkins, an eccentric power station superintendent, who insisted at all times on wearing a boiler suit and a bowler hat from which he cut the brim.

The power supply would repeatedly fail during the war, invariably breaking down under the demands of an overloaded system. It was also expected to help supply the national grid, a service which the Ministry of Power successfully argued should be supplied at cost.

Harper-Bill had waged a constant campaign for more power station plant but had repeatedly been frustrated by Dulley's tight financial regime. After a series of further mishaps he was finally replaced by Walter Cameron, a tough Scot who was to be one of a line of chief engineers charged with keeping the estate's power lifeline open.

As a decoy, a mock industrial estate comprising a series of wooden sheds which were partially lit up at night was constructed at nearby Datchet. Built on a bend in the Thames, in line with the real estate, it sometimes succeeded in confusing night-time raiders, though the residents of Datchet were not best pleased.

Dick Clifford, a building worker on the estate, was around one day when the Germans found the correct target. "I was helping to repair a leaky roof on Weston's biscuit factory when I heard the sound of an aircraft. I assumed it was one of ours but I looked up and had the shock of my life. It was a bomber with a dirty great black cross on the side and it was bearing down on me. All of a sudden he let go a hail of bullets that ripped along the roof, making a bigger mess than the one we had been sent in to sort out."

The strike turned out to be a rare success for the Germans. There were occasional hits but, by the end of the war, the rescue and demolition squad formed by Slough Estates, clad in boiler suits and steel helmets and ready for action day and night, had never been overstretched.

Despite the ever-present threat of destruction, the population made valiant attempts to carry on as normal, denying the enemy the satisfaction of turning people's daily lives upside down. The community centre found itself with an extra 30,000 temporary members.

Jim Rule, who worked for the Four Wheel Drive Company and took turns behind the lounge bar, recalls: "The army had depots all around Slough and the soldiers were permitted to use the centre anytime they wished. Sometimes they were seven deep at the bar."

The Aspro factory also became something of a social centre, regularly used as it was as the venue for entertaining the troops and children. With identification numbers pinned to their chests, the children would be entertained by the Aspro Orchestra and the Aspro Eight, a song and dance team of girl employees. At the end of a show the audience would sing "There'll Always Be an England" before making their way home in the blackout.

In the early stages of the war many youngsters were evacuated from London. Slough was considered a safer place even though the glow of the burning city could be seen in the night sky during the Blitz. Later, however, they were moved further away as the threat to their safety was considered to have grown.

Some Slough Estates' staff inevitably found themselves being called up for service. Among them was Gerald Mobbs, who joined the 1st Airborne Division and also spent a period on the personal staff of General Montgomery. He made the rank of Lieutenant Colonel before his war ended in 1944, during the battle for Arnhem, when he was severely wounded and captured by the Germans. His health would never fully recover.

The company did its best to operate as usual. Fortunately the government ensured there was no difficulty in keeping its buildings fully occupied.

It had entered the war in good shape. Profits in 1939 reached nearly £160,000 and the complete freehold estate was valued by the directors at just under £1.9 million. Further development, however, became impossible because of the absence of construction materials.

By 1940 profits had risen still further and the directors had to remind those shareholders able to attend the annual meeting in London's Great Portland Street that the company's performance might not actually be easily sustained once the war had finished and industry had to resume the search for more traditional business.

At the end of the year, Noel Mobbs appointed Victor Page as the company auditor. Page's partnership, Cocke Vellacott and Hill, would serve as auditors - from 1974 jointly with Deloittes - until 1976. Page himself would continue as a consultant up until his death in 1988.

Other professional advisers would come to enjoy similarly lengthy relationships with the business. Apart from Turner Kenneth Brown, Lovell White Durrant would serve as lawyers, Sedgwick Group as insurance brokers and Ewbank Preece as consulting engineers on the power station.

In 1941, though Noel Mobbs spoke of the "many serious problems" which the company had faced during the year, profitability was up again. The absence of any building programme meant that, for the first time in many years, Slough Estates had no overdraft. In a rough audit of the damage so far inflicted on the estate - mainly arising from incendiary bomb fires - the company estimated that the Germans had so far cost it £6,000.

Sidney Harper-Bill, chief engineer at the power station in the 1930s.

In spite of this, there was mounting concern about the estate's vulnerability. and the prospect of a real calamity. Along with the armaments production on the estate, the directors had anxiously watched as large numbers of military equipment and vehicles, particularly tanks, were brought on to the site to await despatch. Many of them had been shipped from Canada and large numbers of Canadian personnel had come with them to establish their own camp and repair shop on the edge of the estate. The more people and vehicles arrived, the more alarmed the company had become.

By the end of 1942 the government was also extremely worried. In an official document marked "Secret" which the enemy would have considered of incalculable value it was formally recorded that the complex had become one of the most vulnerable military and industrial targets in England.

The report stressed that there were more than 420 factories and workshops concentrated in half a square mile, mainly engaged in essential war production. The new influx of military equipment made the estate, now the daily workplace for more than 40,000 people, a prime target for air attack.

The document emphasised that an earlier agreement with the War Office had limited the number of military vehicles which could be stored on the estate but that no restriction any longer applied. It continued: "The purpose of all these precautions is being nullified by the arrival of large numbers of tanks and armoured vehicles with personnel and equipment, with the result that the military target has become substantially greater than at any time since the war began."

The report submitted that the new arrivals at an already vulnerable target were "dangerous to the utmost degree." To press home its point it stressed that there was one factory on the estate in which no fewer than 100,000 incendiary bombs were in various stages of production.

"If the present arrangements are allowed to continue, this estate will be the only one in England where a single stick of bombs can do immense damage both to the industrial and military installations at the same time." The tanks, armoured vehicles and associated personnel should be removed without delay, it added.

The War Department duly took note and began to disperse the vehicles, though some would remain. Only with the D-Day landings in 1944 did all the weaponry depart.

But however threatening the situation, the Slough directors attempted to plan for a future which they hoped the business would see. As early as 1941 Mobbs had instigated studies into the possibility of developing after the war new estates elsewhere in Buckinghamshire, Oxfordshire and Berkshire.

In the following year he attended a conference in Oxford on post-war development in the UK, where he reiterated his ideas for some form of central planning for industrial development and suggested the appointment of a "super minister" to oversee planning and development issues.

By 1943 William Morrison had been appointed to the new post of Minister of Town and Country Planning, political confirmation that public opinion now shared Mobbs' views about the need for far more stringent planning controls. The first Town and Country Planning Act followed shortly afterwards.

Though, by the middle of 1943, there was no sign of any end to the hostilities, the company submitted plans to Slough council outlining its proposals for the post-war development of the remainder of the estate.

Advertising began for tenants to take space once peace was declared: "When war is over you may require a factory at Slough or Birmingham." In a further optimistic initiative, the company began to consider plans to mount a permanent exhibition in London's West End to display the range of products manufactured on the estate.

Mobbs had also been busy on another personal venture. By 1944 he published an impressively detailed and well-presented booklet providing advice to developers and planning authorities on how to adapt war-time sites to post-war uses. Mobbs explained that unless plans were drawn up to put war-time industrial areas to good use once peace arrived, many would become "distressed areas." Others would simply revert to their previous "deplorable state."

Understandably the booklet, which was distributed privately to selected companies and councils, set out the benefits of encouraging a new generation of industrial estates on Slough lines.

A basic principle underlying their development, it claimed, was "the banding together of manufacturers for common purposes, to enable markets to be increased, inter-trading established, and co-operative development of the neighbourhood to be advanced in ways not visualised by the isolated companies of pre-war days."

The Slough Estates chairman continued: "It is, however, vital that manufacturers should be given a wide choice of neighbourhoods in which to establish their industries and that their success be not hampered by distance from markets and unsuitable surroundings. This is particularly the case with young men starting small industries in their home area. Some eventually become the great industrialists of the future and they need local capital granted from personal knowledge, local support for their earlier trading efforts and the economy of living at home, or they will never make the great adventure."

Mobbs went on to suggest the creation of industrial farming estates enabling farmers to hire the most modern, labour-saving agricultural machinery and to draw on communal stores, abattoirs and dairies. He called for the establishment of a national import and export organisation to help promote trade with the Empire and other world markets and suggested that, at home, manufacturers should be obliged to pay a levy, calculated on profits, towards the provision of local voluntary social services.

Mobbs also had views on the optimum size of the new towns which he expected to be spawned by the post-war expansion of industry. Remarking on government suggestions that towns of around 50,000 people might be developed, he claimed such a scale might not provide the amenities desired "either to the town-minded or the country-minded."

To Mobbs, the ideal solution was a number of cities with populations of around 200,000 inhabitants, which would have satellite centres of about 50,000 within 15 to 20 miles. Beyond them would be small rural-minded communities of about 3,000 people. In this way, he concluded, there would be adequate commercial, banking, educational, cultural, sporting and social facilities within reasonable reach of everyone.

There followed a series of examples of how large land areas devoted to war-time manufacturing purposes could be used to provide the basis for balanced and integrated post-war communities. The document's considered approach to the challenge of peacetime reconstruction was well received and a request for more copies came from the office of the new planning minister.

Noel Mobbs was increasingly anxious to put his philosophy to the test and the company began to investigate possible sites for the first post-war generation of industrial estates.

In the autumn of 1944 he despatched Dulley to South Wales to identify opportunities in an area where, to judge by the continuing outward flow of workers, employment was still badly needed. Although Dulley concluded that commercial prospects in Wales for a business like Slough Estates were poor, the company was persuaded by the Board of Trade to demonstrate its well-developed social conscience by co-operating over the creation of a badly-needed trading estate at Fforestfach in Swansea.

Slough Estates would not, however, own the development- it was financed by the Treasury - but would act as managers. In return, the company would receive a £5,000 annual fee plus five per cent of the rent roll.

A deal was struck and work on the new estate - which would eventually provide 520,000 sq. ft. of covered floorspace - began with a visit in November 1945 by the King and Queen. Five years later responsibility for its operation passed to the state-run Wales and Monmouthshire Industrial Estates.

The company also purchased a 22-acre ordnance depot at Greenford in Middlesex which comprised 21 factories and 644,000 sq. ft. of floorspace let to the War Department on leases running until 1959. It had been built by Alfred Allnatt.

The end of the war brought a wave of national relief. More than five years of fighting had claimed the lives of one third of a million British people. Among those lucky enough to return home to a new, if uncertain, era was Gerald Mobbs, who was at once elected to the Slough Estates board.

He was joined by another new director also home from the war. Lieutenant Colonel William "Billy" Kingsmill was Redmond McGrath's stepson and had commanded a battalion of the Grenadier Guards in France and Belgium during the war. He had returned, complete with the Distinguished Service Order and Military Cross , to stand for parliament in the July 1945 general election, which yielded a great and unexpected victory for the Labour party.

Even so he was comfortably elected for the safe Conservative seat of Yeovil. Kingsmill - like Gerald - would go on to become chairman of Slough Estates and, like his stepfather, chairman of the Taylor Walker brewery.

Though the return of peacetime was a cause for celebration, it left businesses to confront huge challenges. Just three days before the war ended in Europe on May 5, 1945 Noel Mobbs told the twenty-fourth annual shareholders' meeting of Slough Estates that the cessation of hostilities and the changeover from war production to meeting peacetime requirements would bring big difficulties. But with the company's trading estates embracing a well-balanced mix of manufacturing industries, he emphasised that he did not envisage any grave problems for his own company.

He reported that, in anticipation of an increased demand from tenants striving to meet new markets, investment in the power station was being stepped up. Inquiries from prospective tenants were being received but they could not yet be entertained because of the large number of building still requisitioned or leased by government departments and because of restrictions on new building. Development was being allowed only in areas of high unemployment.

The longer-terms prospects, however, appeared bright. A new development plan for Greater London, drawn up by Professor Patrick Abercrombie who had served on the Royal Commission on industrial development, provided for Slough's population to rise to around 110,000 and contemplated complete development of the estate. The objective would not, however, prove quite so easy to achieve.

Mobbs, who had now been appointed High Sheriff of Buckinghamshire, also disclosed that the company had decided to open up a subsidiary business to be sponsored initially by the Board of Trade and intended to complement the range of services already provided for its estate tenants.

The need to sell British goods overseas was paramount in the aftermath of the war. The slogan on everyone's lips was "export or die" and the company considered that, in addition to the national interest, its own ends could also be served in helping along the drive to win customers overseas for its tenants. It might also add another important dimension to a business whose immediate post-war future was unpredictable.

Slough Estates (London) was formed and set up in the former premises of the Bath Club in Berkeley Street. It provided a shop window for the products of tenants and offered expert advice on exporting and the intricacies of doing business in foreign currencies. The hire of a board room cost £4 a session and offices were 12 guineas a week.

Offices for tenants wanting representation in London were also available in the nine-storey building, which had been burnt out during the war. The London Club, with restaurant and private rooms, also opened in the building. The Club described by one member as very much "Noel's child," provided "ladies and gentlemen of good social position" with a useful meeting place in town. A bridge committee and a wine committee were at once elected.

The subsidiary was put in the hands of Peter Jones, the general manager, who set about recruiting help. An export manager, Jack Pearce, was appointed and a 25-year old Londoner by the name of Wallace Mackenzie, who had worked as a builders' merchant before the war, was taken on as his deputy.

Mackenzie, a bright grammar school boy, had found himself in uniform one month after his eighteenth birthday. Spending much of the war as a glider pilot with the 1st Airborne Division, he had the good fortune to be interviewed by Gerald, who spotted his divisional tie and revealed that he knew the young applicant's brigadier.

The merchandising operation would expand to handle products from companies based beyond Slough's own estates and would remain in its ownership until the end of the 1980s. Despite its modest financial contribution to the group its presence helped characterise the group's commitment to providing a complete service to its tenants.

Billy Kingsmill, a post-Second World War recruit to the board who would become non-executive chairman after Sir Noel. A stepson of Redmond McGrath, he was also an MP and chairman of the Taylor Walker brewery.

Much of its early business involved sales to Canada and among its early estate clients was Marcel Menko of Flexello, to whom Canada became an important market. Exporting services to Belgium and Australia were offered later, though no business was done in Australia.

The deputy export manager would thrive longer than the subsidiary he joined, eventually become managing director of Slough's main operating company and overseeing the closure of the subsidiary which had given him his first post-war job opportunity.

As the nation tried to pick up the pieces there were many other newcomers to the company in the months after the war ended. Roland Essery - a slightly-built West Country man with an infectious chuckle and a formidable reputation for calculating figures - arrived to be chief accountant, a role he would ultimately combine with that of company secretary.

Noel Mobbs also found himself a new chauffeur. Jack Luxton had worked for Slough Estates before in its works department but had been lured away by an offer to drive a grey Rolls Royce for an increasingly successful but demanding Garfield Weston. Now, he was re-employed to drive and look after Noel Mobbs' vehicle fleet, which included two Daimlers, an enormous Packard complete with telephone and cocktail cabinet, a Vauxhall 14-6 soft top coupe and a two-tone ivory and black Ford 10, a gift from the now ennobled Lord Perry.

Luxton, always dressed in his made-to-measure Saville Row uniform, would drive his boss backwards and forwards from Stoke Poges to his flat in Berkeley Street above the Club. One of his constant challenges was to prevent Sir Noel taking the wheel, something the chairman's wife dreaded.

Mobbs' driving adventures were legion. Once he drove from Angmering-on-Sea to Windsor with the handbrake on and could not understand the strange smell. The wings of his cars were invariably reshaped as a result of brushes with gateposts or walls.

Luxton was certainly not alone at Stoke Poges, now the scene of regular bridge evenings or weekend parties. Tom Cole, the footman, would greet guests and Bill Thompson would always be on hand to serve the cherry brandy on nippy mornings. There was a cook and gardener and all the trappings of a man who had used his energy and business skills to become one of a new generation of modern industrialists.

The Berkeley Street, Mayfair, offices - home of the company's exporting business and of Noel Mobbs' club for gentlemen.

Mobbs, however, was by no means content with what he had achieved. The end of the war brought new opportunities and gave him the chance to enact some of the initiatives which he had mulled over while the conflict raged.

Neither was he alone in seeing a challenging and potentially highly rewarding future. Already the values of commercial and other property had begun to rise; they had appeared to do so since the invasion of France, when a few businessmen began to believe that the ownership of land would prove an extremely good deal after an allied victory which had begun to look possible.

Some of them were estate agents, people like Harold Samuel who were turning from selling property for others to buying it for themselves; Charles Clore was another sparkling entrepreneur with a leaning towards property who, before the war, had built some factories and an ordnance depot in Berkshire. Two of the most enthusiastic buyers of commercial property were Sir Montague Burton and Sir Henry Price of the Fifty Shilling Tailors.

The immediate post-war inflationary spiral, which would last until 1949, meant that the value of property, purchased on money borrowed at fixed interest rates, began to soar. The message was not lost on people like Clore and Burton.

The Bath Road entrance to the Estate, pictured in the 1940s.

Land began to be bought and sold again within months at a profit. Sometimes vacant buildings were bought and leased; war-damaged offices started to be repaired. The straightjacket of building licences meant that new developments would be few and far between. The prospects were exciting and open-ended, even if the new Labour government was muttering out loud about measures to ensure the state shared in any property development boom.

In the year the war ended Slough Estates had notched up profits before tax of just over £247,000. Notwithstanding the best efforts of many governments to come, the company's performance was set to improve in each and every reporting period over the next 44 years.

9

OFF TO THE DOMINIONS

BOTH CENTRAL and local government were quick to make a mark on the early post-war activities of Slough Estates.

During 1946, the London County Council, charged with overseeing the capital's redevelopment, passed a resolution for the compulsory purchase of a large area of land to be used for overspill housing for up to 20,000 Londoners.

Included were 80 acres which lay within the Slough trading estate boundaries. To rub salt into the wounds the LCC also announced that it intended to use some of the land to develop a factory estate along the same lines as those successfully pursued by the owner of the land.

The only difference, according to the LCC, was that it could do it better. In particular, it wanted to build small units for new businesses, a strategy which Slough Estates itself was considering developing further.

Mobbs was quick to respond. "The duplication of services and industrial community facilities and the loss of efficiency which must result from two ownerships in one trading estate is, in the national interest, to be deplored.

"The council feels apparently that by acquiring an eighth of the company's property, building their own trading estate within the confines of our land, duplicating all the services, overheads and the industrial problems, they will be benefiting either Londoners or the nation. It should, in my opinion, be obvious that with no experience of running trading estates, the London County Council are likely to prove less efficient, to add materially to the overhead costs of running the estate as a single unit and to damage rather than benefit the economical productivity of the district."

An appeal, which had the backing of Slough council, was lodged. The subsequent inquiry found against the LCC and the land remained in the ownership of the company which had been drawing up its own proposals for the post-war development of its remaining land. The short-lived tussle with the planning authorities would, however, prove to be a mere skirmish when compared with the battle which lay ahead.

At national government level the Labour administration in 1947 pushed through its Town and Country Planning Act, which would introduce a measure of national planning reminiscent of the strategy which Mobbs had himself already called for in respect of industrial development.

For the first time the Act laid down a duty on local authorities to draw up development plans for approval by the government, to which they had to adhere. It was seen, in retrospect, as one of the most advanced and comprehensive systems of planning ever introduced.

But the Act was a double-edged sword. It also attempted to tax at 100 per cent the development value created when planning permission was granted. Alongside was a system of compensation for owners whose land values were hit by other planning decisions. The measure was complicated and full of loopholes and succeeded in stifling a great deal of post-war development activity until the early 1950s when Harold Macmillan, the new Conservative Minister of Housing and Local Government, abolished the tax.

Every estate employee had a numbered identity badge for security. This is thought to be the last in existence.

In 1947, however, Noel Mobbs saw the measure as an indication of the Socialist government's antipathy to free enterprise. The company began to make what would become regular contributions to Aims of Industry, a pressure group intended to protect and preserve an open and competitive business environment free from the "shackles" of government intervention.

Given its ownership of a power generating station and the government's decision to nationalise the electricity supply industry, Slough Estates had already faced the prospect of state intervention. Public ownership of the electricity industry did not appeal to Slough and it had sought, and been given, assurances that its own plant would not be included in any state takeover. The assurances were honoured but the company still felt the bureaucratic hand of the Ministry of Power on its shoulder once the industry was nationalised.

Although Slough Estates had ensured adequate supplies of power to its own tenants, the Ministry at once instructed it to implement regular power cuts to industries not on the government's post-war priority list. The decree arose from the invidious comparisons which were being made between the continuity of supply on the estate and the unreliable efforts of the recently-nationalised electricity boards.

The result was chaotic as factories were individually notified and affected tenants reacted angrily when they learned that neighbouring factories were still working. Experiences like this prompted the company to begin making donations to another pressure group, the Campaign Against Nationalisation.

At the same time Mobbs had another pressing priority on his mind. His plans to provide a modern and well-equipped hospital at Slough had been rudely interrupted by the war. A pre-war appeal for funds under the auspices of the Slough Social Fund had succeeded in raising £20,000 but the money had since remained frozen.

The chairman now realised that the responsibility of providing a local hospital - the nearest were at Windsor, Taplow and Maidenhead - would be taken up by the proposed National Health Service due to start life in the summer of 1948. His thoughts, therefore, turned to the creation of some form of industrial health centre to provide on-the-spot health care and accident services, to offer rehabilitation facilities for injured workers and to educate employers in the area of good health care. Already a trustee of the Nuffield Provincial Hospitals Trust, formed to help hospitals provide improved medical services, Mobbs asked his fellow trustees for help.

The Trust at once recognised the Slough trading estate as an ideal location for what it saw as a worthwhile experiment. It contained a large number of manufacturers, many of them so small that they could not contemplate providing their own health care facilities.

There were an estimated 300 companies based on the estate or within a three-mile radius, between them employing around 30,000 people. Only 15 had medical departments of any kind, the remainder merely conforming to their minimum statutory health obligations by providing a first-aid box.

The Nuffield Foundation, which was jointly administered with the Trust, was also particularly keen on funding research into industrial health problems and believed a centre at Slough would provide a valuable test-bed. The Foundation offered £15,000 to help get the project underway while the Trust provided a further £25,000 in grant. More offers of financial help came from several companies on the estate.

But other employers claimed that they had done well enough in the past and that they could not, in any case, afford the additional contributions towards the cost of running the centre - estimated in its first year at 27s per employee. Some companies considered that anything more than compliance with the Factory Act of the day smacked of "pampering" their employees.

However, with the backing of most local doctors (although some regarded the scheme as an unwelcome encroachment into their sphere of responsibility), of the health authority and of the Slough and Eton councils, the project finally got off the ground.

The former youth block of the community centre was adapted to form the central clinic and two sub-clinics were established in other parts of the estate. One of the buildings had been a paraffin and tyre store and had housed a giant press used to fix solid rubber tyres to First World War army vehicles. The walls still reeked of paraffin.

Farnham Park, the former home of Lord Kemsley, only two miles away, was acquired as the residential rehabilitation centre and the service was completed with a mobile medical unit.

Such units had proved very successful in the last war and this one consisted of a converted Morris five-ton tractor unit complete with trailer chassis. The £4,250 cost of the conversion, carried out by Pytchley Autocar, was met by Horlicks.

The provision of such facilities was not an entirely altruistic gesture. The ability to deal quickly and efficiently with illness and injury meant a more efficient workforce. The mobile medical unit alone was expected to save employers a thousand man hours every month.

Noel Mobbs, who had throughout been the driving force behind the project, was elected the first chairman of the service and Dr. A. Austin Eggar, who had been responsible for equipping and training all the medical units of the 1st Airborne Division after its formation, became medical director. Eggar and Mobbs had known each other in the 1st Airborne Division.

The service opened its doors on May 1, 1947 with 50 companies and 6,000 employees as members. Within two years there would be 115 member companies involving more than 11,500 workers. The Mobbs experiment, eventually to be known as the Slough Occupational Health Service, was to become an integral part of Slough's industrial life, as well as being a model for others to follow.

By 1948 Slough Estates had a full house. The last requisitioned properties had been returned to their tenants and the company believed that such was the demand for the limited supply of industrial space available it could let its factories at double the rents being achieved.

Mobbs had just been made a Knight Commander of the Royal Victorian Order, an Order of Chivalry in the personal gift of the King, with whom he had struck up a friendship. A near-neighbour who shared many of the monarch's social concerns, he had sometimes been invited to dinner at Windsor.

In his first shareholders' message since receiving his honour, the newly-knighted Sir Noel said the company would not be taking full advantage of the space shortage on the estate by demanding full rental increases as it wanted to help keep manufacturing costs as low as possible. Even so, as new leases came up for renewal, the company raised rentals by around one quarter. Some tenants sought permission to make improvements to their property, a trend which the landlord was happy to countenance provided the premises were always restored to their original condition when a lease expired or was eventually surrendered. The philosophy would stick.

Other occupiers, however, claimed that a prolonged period of low rents had helped make them financially strong enough to consider building their own premises off the estate. Despite its original intention to sell parcels of freehold land, the company had not done so. Companies like Black and Decker and Gillette would eventually leave to become owner-occupiers.

The landlord therefore decided to insert in all new leases a clause which required the occupier first to offer the lease back to the landlord. Sir Noel remarked: "It is not reasonable for new tenants, or tenants whose leases are being renewed, to be able immediately thereafter to take advantage of the position and sub-let or assign their leases at rentals this company has refused to charge."

Slough Estates was now in a position to begin some modest building work. With the power station's capacity newly boosted and with some new construction at both estates able to get underway before the July introduction of the government's development charge, the company took on its first staff architect.

It had been advertising for a surveyor to replace Bill Price, who had run his own private practice alongside his responsibilities on the estate and was now retiring. Instead it took on Cliff Richardson, a 35-year-old qualified architect and town planner who had been working for Sir Alexander Gibb and Partners, the civil engineers.

Richardson reckoned his arrival was long overdue: "I had the distinct impression that, up until then, the company's approach to factory development had been more than a bit haphazard. Sir Noel and Dulley would look at a piece of land and say: 'we'll have a go at that next.' They knew very little about the business of building factories and had just left the whole thing to Bill Price, the surveyor."

Richardson at once began to try and introduce some element of order to estate development, though progress was hampered by the continuing shortage and licencing of construction materials. He spent a lot of his time at auctions where he had to bid for the most basic of materials. Timber was particularly hard to find.

One of Richardson's first initiatives was the introduction of a new factory design which he christened the "Type H" for no other reason that types A to G had already gone before. It was a simple single-storey building which, most critically, provided just 5,000 sq. ft. of floorspace - the size beyond which an industrial development certificate, recently introduced to control commercial development activity, was required.

Under the new system the Board of Trade was to be given strategic responsibility to orchestrate the stimulation of "appropriate employment" in specific development areas. It had the power to veto applications for industrial development beyond designated limits - in some areas as low as 3,000 sq. ft. A certificate was not only required for new developments but also for a change of use. It would not be the last time that government would try to override the natural forces of supply and demand in the market place.

For the first time Slough began to develop buildings which showed signs of the "architect's touch." Those going up in Ajax Avenue, for example, incorporated facing bricks.

The drawing office, piled high with plan chests standing on battleship brown linoleum, gradually became an important element in the business. Among recruits to a department which expanded to include quantity surveyors and a team of draughtsmen under Edward Sibley was Arthur Kingman, who would eventually become deputy chief architect.

Although the business was again gathering some form of momentum, despite the restrictions and ensuing difficulties which still beset all commercial organisations, Sir Noel again decided to try and raise the sights of his company.

The board had already agreed to explore the possibilities of developing trading estates in the Dominions and, with conditions in the home market still extremely difficult, the directors were ready to sanction a closer look.

By early 1949 Sir Noel was reporting back to his board on a speedy visit he had made to Australia to study the prospects for establishing an arm of the business on the other side of the world. His colleagues had voted £1,000 expenses for the trip and were anxious to hear the outcome.

Sir Noel had gone to Melbourne because he believed its inhabitants were particularly favourably disposed towards the British. He intended to buy a small development site on which the business could replicate a minor version of the Slough estate.

He had been generously entertained by local dignitaries, visiting the races and playing bridge and was excited at the thought of doing business Down Under. The chairman returned not with a small plot of land upon which to carry out his Australian experiment but with news that he was planning to buy nearly 1,500 acres at Altona, eight miles west of Melbourne and alongside the trunk road which ran from the city to the port of Geelong. The main railway cut through the site.

The government of Victoria, he told the board, had also offered 300 acres of land, free of charge, for industrial development in the shire of Ballarat, 70 miles west of Melbourne. In the event the gift, though welcomed at the time, was eventually declined and the Altona deal was not to rank among Sir Noel's most impressive business initiatives, the poor location clearly overshadowed by his confident expectation that he would be able to purchase such a huge tract of potentially promising land for so little.

While the commercial property market in Australia was stagnant, with values stuck at pre-war prices and little or no development underway, any misgivings among Sir Noel's colleagues about the advisability of buying land so far away for development in a market about which the company knew little did not surface. They preferred, instead, to back a chairman whose judgement in the past had rarely let him, or them, down.

Sir Noel said the Altona land offered an excellent opportunity to extend the company's activities to the Empire although he acknowledged that work could not yet begin because of a shortage of building materials and construction workers. Development would begin as soon as material and labour was available.

However cheap, though, the Altona land was hardly a prize catch. The English were buying two square miles of scrub and swamp land separated from Melbourne by the Yarra River. The city had grown east and Slough Estates was going in the other direction; the company was definitely on the wrong side of the tracks.

To add to the challenge the site was beset with huge drainage problems. There were no services or internal roads on the site and there had been very little commercial development nearby.

Not everyone was pessimistic about the potential. The land had been mentioned to Sir Noel by Everard Baillieu, a local property man who envisaged huge commercial growth in and around Melbourne and believed Slough could, if it was patient, make a killing. When Slough Estates Australia Pty. was formally incorporated in 1959, Baillieu would become its first chairman, a position he would hold until Cecil Hyland, another of the original directors, took over in 1971.

Baillieu Allard, the business headed by Baillieu, was appointed to act as agents to the English business. One of Baillieu's own directors, Harry Seddon, was called on to help in what was going to be a marathon development saga.

It had fallen to Seddon to show Sir Noel around when he had first arrived looking for a development opportunity. He remembers: "Sir Noel wanted to be as close to Melbourne as possible but, by the second day, I got the message loud and clear. He wanted land cheap. We ended up in Kororoit Creek Road in Altona, with vacant land stretching as far as you could see. It was very unattractive, covered with thistles and stone and crawling with tiger snakes. But he saw it and at once made up his mind, telling me to find out how much we could buy and at what price."

The owners were the Sydney-based Rickard Estate and their representative, a Mrs Lawrence, lived in a shack on Altona's waterfront. She suggested a price of £100,000. Negotiations continued and the price was eventually settled at £22,000.

Although Sir Noel acknowledged the difficulties posed by the land he was convinced he had a bargain, believing that it had been acquired at a price which reflected the problems and which left plenty of room to enhance its value.

Charles Fairall went out soon after the land purchase to try and get the project moving. He made an impassioned two-hour speech to a full meeting of the Werribee Shire local council, asking for its help in providing roads across the site. He left, having wined and dined his audience, with a hard-earned letter of undertaking. It proved to be of no value because the council's area of jurisdiction was later reduced to omit the Altona site and Slough's Australian business would not get underway for years.

There was to be more immediate success further east, however. While Sir Noel had been investigating the Australian market, Charles Fairall, now a director, had been to Canada, where the board had already approved in principle the idea of factory development. In May 1950 it formed Slough Estates (Canada). Shortly afterwards Dulley and Fairall left for North America to sow up a deal.

Redmond McGrath had already conducted some basic preliminaries by discussing the company's ambitions with the Canadian High Commissioner in London, who had given him an enthusiastic reception as well as grounds for encouragement. The two emissaries did not take long to find a foothold. It took the shape of 40 acres of state-owned development land at Ajax, 24 miles east of Toronto on Highway 401, next to Lake Ontario and close to the Toronto-Montreal railway.

Ajax was, in effect, a post-war "new town" similar to those planned for Britain and had been named after the British warship which had pursued the Graf Spee, the German battlecruiser which had been sunk in the Battle of the River Plate. The town site had been agricultural land before the war and, although it had only 3,500 inhabitants, it was planned to expand rapidly as the Canadian economy grew. An influx of foreign workers, brought in by employers anxious to set up in Canada's first fully-planned industrial town, moved one local newspaper columnist to remark: "Most of the newcomers are from the British Isles. It gives the townspeople an Old Country air."

Ontario held a third of Canada's population and was responsible for more than half the country's national product; the choice seemed a good one and the English company also took up options on additional land. John Tory, a Canadian lawyer, was appointed the subsidiary's first president and the other directors were Gordon Arnold, his brother-in-law, and Gordon Fairley, a Canadian financier who managed to get a street on the Slough estate named after him.

Almost at once the subsidiary began to enjoy success with Julian Van Huyse of Van Huyse and Trusevych, a local architects' practice which would go on to design more than 150 of Slough's Canadian developments and would still be closely linked in the 1990s.

Once again, Slough Estates was buying itself a long hard slog, albeit at a reasonable price, and initial progress would fail to meet the company's early expectations. However, the decision to take the industrial development skills of Slough Estates across the Atlantic would eventually prove to be one of the best strategic decisions made by the company.

Back at home, where the company had concluded its involvement at Fforestfach in Swansea, limited new building work continued at the Slough estate. Progress was not being helped by the continuing inability of the local authority to provide a drainage system on a scale demanded by the complex and the nearby housing. The company, together with some of the largest tenants, had been forced to make a financial contribution towards the cost of extending the drainage system.

However the company continued to benefit from higher rentals being negotiated as pre-war leases expired. Pre-tax profits in 1951 reached £244,737, an increase of £10,000 over the previous 12 months.

Although the prospects for continuing profit growth were good Sir Noel and Charles Fairall were anxious to find some form of mechanism which could help protect the real value of the company's rental flow - and profits. Someone had previously attempted to tie rents to the price of gold but the courts had ruled against it.

Instead, they decided on a unique initiative to gradually introduce a system of indexing rentals to the increase in prices. It was formula which would quickly become commonplace in the post-war property industry.

As leases fell in at Slough the company began to explain to tenants that, if they remained on the estate, their rents would be subject to adjustment relevant to the subsequent increases in the wholesale price index. This offered an easy basis for calculation and which tenants knew could not be misinterpreted.

The new system gave the landlord a degree of certainty over income while the tenants generally had few objections, not least because inflation was low and there were few reasons to believe it might change. Indexation had arrived and would stand the test of time for the best part of three decades.

In 1951 there were to be changes within the boardroom.

After 28 years as deputy chairman Lord Perry decided to relinquish his responsibilities and stepped down. The man who had done as much as anyone to create Slough Estates and had gone on to be chairman of Ford of Britain now spent most of his time abroad, which suited his ailing health. His links with the company and with Sir Noel had, as a result, become increasingly remote.

The board paid full tribute to the company's co-founder and asked him to fulfil the honorary role of president. He gladly accepted and would hold the post until his death. Elsewhere Redmond McGrath replaced Perry as deputy chairman and Ted Dulley became a joint general manager with Gerald Mobbs.

There was also a new recruit to the board though Sir Owen Morshead may not have seemed the consummate businessman. An expert on claret wine, he was the King's Librarian and a friend and neighbour of Sir Noel, who welcomed the addition of another confidante in place of Lord Perry. It also appeared that the chairman sympathised with Sir Owen because the salary which accompanied his Royal appointment was hardly commensurate with the high honour attached to the office.

Morshead arrived as the company was girding its loins for a protracted planning fight, the outcome of which would have a fundamental bearing on its ambitions to fully develop its Slough complex.

While the war had been at its height Slough Council had approached the company to ask it to provide an outline of its peacetime proposals for completing the estate. The response had been a preliminary plan which the council rejected on the grounds of density. There had been further objections on the basis that there was an imbalance between freehold and leasehold factories in the borough.

Progress towards agreement was hardly given top priority because of the war and had been complicated by the London County Council's abortive attempt to compulsorily purchase some of the estate site for its own development proposals.

The issue had not been re-ignited until 1950, when a local plan for Slough was drawn up indicating the preferred pattern of development in the town for the next two decades. It suggested that some areas of the trading estate might be better utilised if they were allocated to non-industrial purposes.

Shortly afterwards Buckinghamshire County Council produced its first development plan for the area, which earmarked 80 acres - incorporating the land previously required by the LCC - as suitable for use as nursery and market gardens. A further 12 acres to the south west were also identified for non-industrial purposes.

Of the 216 acres of land owned by Slough Estates but not yet developed, more than one-third, all of it adjacent to the power station and the estate's three-million gallon water reservoir, was apparently to be taken away with the full connivance of the Board of Trade.

Sir Noel was furious. The company immediately lodged an appeal and an inquiry was held in 1952. The Slough Estates chairman stormed: "The creation of 80 acres of market gardens in the heart of a great trading estate, upon whose industrial development millions of pounds have been spent, seems past all comprehension."

At the inquiry the company argued that to use land which had the benefit of estate services for any other purpose would be inexcusable. More critically, the business had in its possession a planning permission dated 1945 which, it claimed, gave the company authorisation to develop the remainder of the estate.

But the existence of the document was, inexplicably, not fully exploited. The company lost the battle and proceeded to fight for £500,000 compensation from the Central Land Board under the terms of the Town and Country Planning Act. As a gesture the Slough Estates board temporarily halted the donations which it had begun to make to the Conservative party.

The company would, in 1957, be awarded £178,000 compensation and the issue of whether or not it possessed all the authority it required to complete the estate would be resurrected years later with challenges to the planning refusal in both the High Court and the House of Lords.

In an especially extended 1953 annual report to shareholders Sir Noel said he believed no money would compensate the company or the town for the loss of such valuable industrial facilities. In a highly critical account of the episode, which underlined the chairman's frustration with what he regarded as damaging and bureaucratic interference, he backed Slough's publicly-stated intention to limit the town's population growth to around 115,000. But he vehemently disagreed with the plan it had devised to achieve it "by cutting off a limb from a highly developed industrial body when that body was quite capable of keeping within the population limits without any surgical operation."

Sir Noel pointed out that, in the early days of the estate, the average factory employed approximately 100 men per acre, a figure which had now been substantially cut with the growth of mechanised production methods. He emphasised that homes for 20,000 Londoners were being built on the estate's northern boundary and that the town's population would soon reach 100,000. He suggested that up to 75,000 of them would be dependent for their living on the good management and ordered development of the industrial estate.

He continued: "In their re-zoning, the authorities have industrially sterilised 90 per cent of the remaining land which can be available to manufacturers requiring railway sidings; they have sterilised 80 per cent of the remaining land upon which, by reason of its proximity to the power house, we can produce steam for industry and they have sterilised against factory building a water area upon which we have spent £50,000 in sinking four wells to 1,500 ft. to yield soft and pure water which is industrially so useful to many manufacturers."

Under the ominous heading "Finality of the Decision," the chairman added: "The authorities can, as they have done, prevent us from building on this land but should they change their minds it will be difficult for your company to build thereon as and when they deem it necessary. In a time of trade depression and incipient unemployment they may probably be anxious for us to build more factories, but neither we nor anyone else can build and find tenants for factories in such times. One can only develop successfully in times of success and not to suit planning schemes."

He warned, in sombre tones: "Your board consider that this land, with its great industrial resources and the great expenditure thereon, has been lost to industry."

Neither could the chairman resist an unflattering comparison with the company's treatment at the hands of the authorities in Commonwealth countries where, he said, planners had only been too glad to help the process of industrial development.

In fact the enthusiasm of the Australian authorities had not begun to be tested because of the company's reluctance to start any development while the local economy languished. But good progress had been made in Canada.

The Canadian operation was now in the hands of Wallace Mackenzie, who had done well during his spell in the merchandising subsidiary. The chairman, having been advised that the North American business should preferably be run by a Canadian or a Scot, had promptly appointed someone born in Kensington.

Mackenzie at least had a Scottish name and had been asked by Sir Noel to go over to build up the agency business and to begin factory construction.

Until then Mackenzie had rarely met the chairman and was understandably in awe of the elderly, patrician figure who now walked slowly with the aid of an ebony-handled walking stick. To someone like Mackenzie, the chairman's advancing years made him no less formidable.

In Toronto the land, lawyers and architects were all in place but there was no staff on the payroll to take charge of the development operation. "I knew a bit about construction and costing but as for leasing and managing properties I had absolutely no idea," he recalls.

Even so Mackenzie and his new wife had set sail on the Empress of Canada on January 2, 1952 to take up an opportunity he felt he could not afford to miss. He had arrived in a blizzard to find the company's office - one room in the British Canadian Trade Association building in downtown Toronto. He took a bus to Ajax where the first two buildings, constructed more or less to English specifications, were underway.

Mackenzie had a long, hot summer ahead of him, trying to lease at $1 a sq. ft. factory floorspace in a less than ideal location. To make matters even more difficult, the local property market was not used to the concept of renting while potential customers made clear their belief that the asking price was too high.

It would take Mackenzie, who was also working on building up the agency business, nearly a year to let the two buildings, one of which he managed to sell to a company owned by Sir George Dowty, who happened to know Sir Noel.

A major problem was to get funds out to Canada at a time when exchange controls made such transactions extremely difficult. Loans from the parent company were, however, arranged and income from the merchandising operation also gradually became available.

At home the company's solid progress was inevitably arousing interest at a time when the British property market was finding its wings. Though development activity was still difficult because of the continuing need for licences, a new breed of takeover specialist was emerging.

They concentrated on buying up companies which held their property assets in the balance sheet at pre-war values and had little idea of just how much they had appreciated. In many cases property portfolios included non-revenue-producing bomb sites.

Wallace Mackenzie, recruited by Gerald Mobbs and sent over to Canada to run the North American business. He was subsequently brought home to run the UK industrial property subsidiary.

Among the masters of the so-called sale-and-leaseback deal were Isaac Wolfson, the financier, and Charles Clore. In 1953, when Clore successfully bid for Sears, the retail shoe chain, its directors told shareholders that at least £6 million could be raised on the acquired properties, a figure which came as something of a shock since they appeared in the books at just over £2 million. When Clore won control he immediately sold shops worth £4.5 million, taking long leases on the properties. There was another £4 million worth of property left, leaving Clore well-placed for his next deal.

By March 1954 Clore was casting an acquisitive eye over Slough Estates, no doubt with exactly the same strategy in mind. He contacted Sir Noel and suggested that the two men should meet to discuss a subject of mutual interest.

They duly met at the Portland Club and, after a short conversation, the two men parted, never to discuss the subject again. Clore dropped the whole idea, giving rise to endless and unresolved speculation about how Sir Noel so decisively saw him off at a time when he was being most acquisitive.

The entire board backed their chairman in opposing any form of deal with Clore but began to man the barricades - just in case.

Mobbs at once recruited to the boardroom Nutcombe Hume, who was chairman of the Charterhouse Investment Group and vice-chairman of the Metropolitan Estate and Property Corporation. He had a reputation as a very tough corporate finance strategist and deal-maker. If a defence were needed Hume, who would in 1956 receive a knighthood, was just the man to have on board.

The directors also took the precaution of placing a value on all the group's properties - at April 1954, Slough Estates property portfolio was given a worth of just over £4 million.

The outcome of the valuation exercise was, as the hapless directors of Sears had felt during their own date with destiny, something of a revelation. The business was developing into something quite capable of tempting the taste buds of prowling predators.

Though Clore walked away, the company was again soon to find itself the object of renewed interest from several sources. It was becoming clear to any outside observer that Slough Estates now held out great promise. Revenues and profits were continuing to rise, UK development was being accelerated and the company had now embraced its first overseas markets.

The best news was yet to come. On November 2, 1954 the government fired the starting gun for what was to develop into a full-scale property boom creating dozens of new millionaires on the way. Nigel Birch, Minister of Works in the first post-war Conservative government, announced to the House of Commons that building licences were to be abandoned. The cheers from the Tory benches were nothing to those heard coming from the property industry.

The end of the licensing system - combined with the decision a year earlier by Harold Macmillan, the Minister of Housing and Local Government, to scrap the development charge - promised to lift the lid off the demand for property which had been mounting since the end of the ward. Freed from the frustrations of a bureaucratic straightjacket which had outlived its purpose, every developer was anxious to win a slice of the business, even if he still faced acute shortages of materials and of skilled workers.

Almost from the moment Birch sat down Slough embarked on a fresh building programme in response to demand for extensions and additional factories from existing tenants. New customers also wanted space on the estate.

In the autumn of 1955, as Gerald Mobbs became general manager in advance of Ted Dulley's retirement and final preparations were made for a £500,000 rights issue to fund further development work, the company received another takeover approach. This time, it was from an anonymous group of businessmen gathered together to launch a bid under the name of Seton Trust.

The offer, made through a merchant banking intermediary, was to buy a minimum 40 per cent of the ordinary share capital of the company with a view to eventually assuming control. Some of Slough Estates' equity had already been acquired by the mystery grouping but, in the face of implacable opposition from the board, the challenge failed.

The company would not have to wait long, however, for its next, unwelcome approach.

10

TO MAKE A MILLION

IN EARLY 1956, shortly after the last passenger train had left the estate at Slough and the station had been closed down, the board of directors were informed that an outside party had purchased 300,000 shares in the company. Overnight, someone else owned nearly 18 cent of the business.

To make matters worse, the buyer was yet another anonymous vehicle operating under the name Dawick Trust and, by the time the directors were aware of its activities, it had circulated Slough Estates shareholders with news of its purchase. It emphasised that it had no intention of seeking outright control of the company and that it regarded the share deal as a sound, long-term investment.

As an anxious board attempted to discover who was behind the transaction, Sir Noel received a letter from none other than Alfred Allnatt, the man who had approached the chairman in 1928 to ask whether he would co-operate on a development at Acton. Allnatt, like Sir Noel, had subsequently prospered and built up his private property development business. It had, in common with many other businesses, been liquidated at the end of the war.

At a hastily arranged meeting he told the Slough Estates chairman that he was acting as the agent in the share purchase. He was not obliged to disclose the identities of those involved but wanted a seat on the board.

Sir Noel called together his directors to discuss strategy, after which he wrote to Allnatt: "The board hold the view that undisclosed shareholders holding their shares through nominees could not expect any representation upon the board of the company." He said that the circulation of a letter to shareholders, without any prior consultation, had "naturally created a poor impression and indicated something more than making an ordinary investment."

There was, however, an olive branch: "If this impression can at a later date be removed and the names and intentions of the new shareholders given, I will again bring the matter before the board."

Allnatt was not prepared to let the matter drop. He wrote again to Sir Noel, suggesting that the shadowy investors he represented would be prepared to tell the company who they were as long as their identities were not made public. If the idea was acceptable, he suggested, then the chairman could tell his boardroom colleagues whether or not he approved of the new shareholders.

The cat and mouse game would continue until July. Just as the death was announced of Lord Perry at his home on New Providence in the Bahamas, it emerged that Allnatt was acting for Arthur Guinness, the brewery group, which had financed the share purchase. The disclosure ended a period of worrying uncertainty and there was some relief that the stakeholder itself had excellent credentials, even if it knew little about property development.

Allnatt then suggested that a business associate from Guildhall Properties, which now owned a portfolio he had originally helped build up, should join the Slough Estates board. The nominee was Ron Diggens, a former Colonel in the Sappers who had gone to work for Allnatt as a 17-year-old and had become his right-hand-man before the war.

Apart from running Guildhall, Diggens had also joined forces with Leslie Smith, a man with unlimited stamina and an impressive eye for detail, to develop property under the Allnatt (London) banner, using the name as a courtesy to their former boss.

After the chairman and Gerald had cast an eye over him Diggens was invited to attend his first board meeting and elected a director. Sir Noel told shareholders, in a message which belied the air of mutual suspicion and wariness which surrounded the appointment, that Diggen's estate experience would be of great benefit to the company.

The new director, however, was seen as nothing less than a Trojan horse; he was not welcome nor made to feel welcome, at least at first. He had been imposed by a shareholder insistent upon boardroom representation and both sides appeared quite aggressive towards each other during their first encounters. After he left the boardroom a separate confidential agenda was often discussed.

Diggens, a 44-year-old bachelor, was a determined, tough and shrewd businessman but always the perfect gentleman. A former amateur boxer, ballroom dancer and light aircraft pilot, he also had the kind of property experience which a company like Slough Estates could not easily afford to ignore.

However, his obvious value to the company and his undeniable charm soon enabled both sides to warm to each other. His knowledge of town planning in particular was formidable and he would insist to his colleagues that planning books represented his preferred bed-time reading.

It was a messy start to what would be a long, if unconventional relationship, in which Slough Estates, Allnatt and Guildhall would be linked by Diggens but cast for many years as competitors in a tough market anxious to keep off each other's patch.

At the end of 1957, the year in which Harold Macmillan reached 10 Downing Street and the new generation of property companies for the first time justified their own dealing section on the London Stock Exchange, Slough Estates had a boardroom reshuffle.

Sir Noel, after 35 years as chairman and managing director, decided that the time had come to step down. He assumed Lord Perry's mantle of company president and Billy Kingsmill took his place. Kingsmill was soon to hit the headlines by receiving a record £60,000 in compensation for giving up the chairmanship of Taylor Walker when it was taken over by Ind Coope. The political row provoked by the payment, made despite the fact that Kingsmill was made joint deputy chairman of the enlarged brewery business, led to a change in the law to ensure that similar pay-offs were taxed.

With Kingsmill becoming non-executive chairman, the real authority now passed to Gerald, who had been preparing for the job for 26 years and was now appointed managing director.

Gerald was to prove a more cautious character than his outgoing father and it was clear to those around him that, although he was the epitome of a true English gentleman, he was essentially reticent and hard to get to know. He would inevitably be working in the long shadow of his predecessor.

Gerald maintained his father's broad view of the role which industry should play in the life of the nation but he was not to fully share his father's imaginative approach to business or his readiness to take a gamble. The new managing director won a £500 pay rise to take his annual salary to £4,000; Charles Fairall became general manager.

One of Gerald's first tasks was to consider an issue which had become a matter of increasing concern to the board. Given the marked switch to road transport by an increasing number of tenants, the estate railway had become a loss-making operation.

Despite a levy on tenants towards the cost of rail transportation on the estate, the system was seen as increasingly under-utilised. There were also mounting problems in keeping road and rail traffic moving alongside each other; lorries often parked across tracks and some locomotive drivers made it their business to make life difficult for road users. The railway's fate was not to be helped by a strike of railwaymen during early 1958, which forced many of the line's customers on to the road, never to return.

Slough Estates sought legal advise to establish whether or not the company was obliged to provide a railway link to tenants. The railway company was not interested in taking over the estate network, so it was decided to test tenants' reaction by telling them the railway system was to be dismantled.

The exercise ended in something of a compromise. The company decided to shut down about two miles of the track but to renew more than six miles of estate railway at a cost of £70,000. The railway would run for another 15 years before the power station was left as its only customer and the last two steam locos would be pensioned off.

Ron Diggens of Allnatt, who became a board member after Arthur Guinness, for whom Allnatt was acting, acquired 18 per cent of the company. He was first treated with suspicion but the relationship subsequently burgeoned. Eventually he would play a key role in Slough's acquisition of Allnatt itself.

Gerald had inherited a sound and successful company. Pre-tax profits in his first year as managing director reached £618,000, with the rent roll rising healthily as more leases came up for renewal.

In Birmingham the estate was almost fully developed while the War Office had indicated that its lease at Greenford was not going to be renewed, thereby freeing its 21 buildings at modern rentals. The estate would be sold in 1970.

The long hand of government, however, still conspired to make life uncertain. The government was strictly enforcing the Industrial Development Certificate regime as part of a co-ordinated effort to "persuade" industry to expand in areas of higher-than-average unemployment.

The company expressed its disappointment that the government had seen fit to put a brake on new development but, with IDCs not required for buildings of under 5,000 sq. ft., extensions and small factory building continued.

Progress was also being made in Canada, where Wallace Mackenzie would occasionally play host to his English masters, who were anxious to see how the young man was doing in a young country.

In Australia, however, very little moved. Nearly a decade after the purchase of Altona, the local business was still petitioning in vain for water and sewerage services to be extended to the site.

There was, at least, some comfort to be had from indications that the Melbourne location was showing signs of promise. A consortium which included Vacuum Oil of America, Distillers of London, Dow Chemical Company and the Union Carbide Corporation of New York had joined forces to construct a petroleum plant. They had chosen Altona as the most suitable site. The consortium had been persuaded to locate there, rather than Sydney, by Henry Bolte, the Premier of Victoria, who worked tirelessly to bring new industry to his state.

Without any hesitation Slough Estates sold for A$950,000 more than 500 acres of the tract of land it had originally purchased for a fraction of that figure. Apart from the useful cash injection into company funds, there was some comfort to be gained from the evidence that the area was, at last, beginning to attract industry and to show some of the promise which Sir Noel had envisaged. The Australian subsidiary was finally incorporated in August in readiness for a long-awaited start on development.

Sir Noel would not see it. On November 25, 1959 he died, aged 79, his ashes interred in the Stoke Poges Gardens of Remembrance. It was 39 years since he and Sir Percival Perry had approached the War Office with their plan to buy the "white elephant" at Slough. Lord Perry and Ted Dulley were already dead and, within a few months, Redmond McGrath would follow.

But it was Sir Noel's death which represented a watershed in the development of the company. Though he had already withdrawn from daily involvement in the affairs of his business, his influence had remained. A generation of Slough Estates management had nearly run its course and the baton was being handed on.

The co-founder and company president of Slough Estates left behind him a business with a balance sheet value of £5.65 million but which the share price put at more than £12 million. There were 600 factories occupied by 240 manufacturing firms at Slough alone, with another 100 at Birmingham and Greenford. Abroad, there were high hopes of more success.

Among the many tributes to Sir Noel, a friend, writing appropriately enough in "Bridge Magazine," summed up a life and a career: "His life was built on a tripod: business, games and charity - and the greatest of these was charity.

"In business, his Slough Estates has ramifications as far afield not only as Birmingham but Melbourne and Toronto. His activities have been primarily responsible for the development of Slough itself from a country town of 15,000 to an industrial centre of more than five times the size. But Slough is no mere mushroom growth; for Mobbs, Lord of the Manor of Stoke Poges, exerted a careful and benevolent control over the swift expansion.

"Even in his most arduous days, Mobbs devoted an enormous amount of his time and energy - and money - to charitable work; as he gradually relinquished his professional activities, more and more work for altruistic motives absorbed the dynamic drive of the man. No other figure in our little world - few, indeed, in the great world - has done one-hundredth as much for others, or has devoted himself so ruthlessly to purely honorary tasks."

As one generation of the Mobbs family gave way to another, so a third generation joined the company.

Gerald wanted to bring his only son Nigel into the business. After an education at Marlborough and Christ Church, Oxford, mirroring that of his father, Nigel had pondered on a career in the army or, alternatively, farming. However, he had started his career by joining Hillier Parker, May & Rowden, the long-established chartered surveyors and agents which had West End offices in Grosvenor Street.

He arrived at Slough in October 1960 as a management trainee, where he was joined by Charles Clifford, a nephew of Billy Kingsmill, who also wanted to see his family play a role in the future development of the company.

The young Mobbs, who would shortly marry Jane Berry, the daughter of the second Viscount Kemsley, was at once struck by the air of Victorian formality which pervaded the small head office. His father, he at once noticed, would never dream of referring to the senior managers by anything other than their surname.

Slough Estates
Engine No 3 crossing
Buckingham Avenue.

Gerald would tell his son that his ambition was to make one million pounds in profits and then to buy himself a Rolls Royce. Neither objective was far away.

Nigel shared his father's determination to succeed and, from the outset, it was clear to most of his colleagues that he possessed the intellect and drive of his grandfather, even if he could not yet fully understand the business.

This was obvious to Wallace Mackenzie who was not particularly impressed when he first met Nigel while on a visit to Canada with his father. "He was a tall, slim, gawky youth and that was about it," he recalls.

But he soon recognised the managing director's son as a force to be reckoned with. "Nigel had a very quick brain and always did his homework. He had a tremendous sense of fun and was much more outward going than his father. He could also sum up a situation very quickly and make a decision when it really mattered."

The two newcomers were put to work to test their mettle.

The young Mobbs joined the estates department, where he worked with the self-effacing Tommy Wood, who was running the operation because Peter Jones was ill. Wood had been recruited to the company as an office boy and had stayed loyal to it, finally becoming estate manager.

Despite his eagerness to get on with the job, he was nevertheless politely reminded not to come in too early as the secretaries were embarrassed to see senior staff arrive before the mail had been opened.

The art of good business appeared fairly basic to him. "The budgeting was rudimentary and there was no such thing as performance analysis. Brokers were amateurs when it came to judging progress and journalists were not intrusive.

"The principal objective was simply to beat the previous year's performance, which we were very good at doing. It was all very cosy; there was no sense of urgency."

In reality the young Mobbs, who took over the estate manager's job when Wood died, was wrong about the stock brokers. Several City houses had, in fact, devised an excellent source of information in the face of the company's polite reluctance to talk about itself. They would telephone late in the afternoon after the office was closed and get put through to the power station. An indiscreet contact would invariably impart valuable gossip and report the level of demand from tenants for power - and hence the company's current state of health.

Mobbs was given responsibility for the power station - where work was underway to increase its capacity still further, from 38,000 kilowatts to 50,000 kilowatts - though some duties there were delegated to Charles Clifford, who was also put in charge of the still-dormant Australian business. By 1963, after their lightning apprenticeships, both would be appointed directors.

Before they reached the boardroom, however, the company reached an important milestone, reporting pre-tax profits of more than £1 million during 1961.

In an interview with a local newspaper Gerald was effusive about his company's state of health: "You could say that the Slough Estates group is now worth between £25 million and £30 million." Over the next few years, he predicted, the company would spend another £4 million at Slough alone.

The country, too, was facing an important step in its post-war development with its application to join the European Economic

Community. Mobbs gave the impression that his company would be well prepared. Pointing to a high pile of files. he told the reporter: "Over the past few months we have been studying the prospects in every Common Market country. The whole matter needs very careful thought but, as yet, nothing has been definitely decided." But he stressed that, whether or not Britain joined the EEC, Slough Estates would be looking to the continent to expand.

For if Britain signed up, UK companies would want a European foothold to provide manufacturing, distribution and servicing facilities; if the membership application failed, then companies would still have to manufacture in Europe to take advantage of the tariffs and other economic advantages which were available to EEC-based operations.

Even as Mobbs was giving his interview Charles Fairall was scouring the continent looking for Slough's first European foothold.

Though a site near Orly airport at Paris seemed encouraging, France was eliminated because of the stringent conditions which the French were imposing on foreign property developers. A little further afield West Germany was also rejected because it was considered to be suffering from levels of inflation which made the business environment too risky. Holland, too, was discounted because of restrictions on development and because of the country's expensive social security structure.

But Belgium appeared to Fairall to meet most of the company's requirements. It was highly developed, offered a rich market and was only one hour by air from London.

Fairall, who was being helped in his search by Charles Clifford and Arthur Kingman, one of the company's architects, reported back to the board with his recommendation. He believed Belgium was the right market and that St. Niklaas, a town of 50,000 people 14 miles from Antwerp and 28 miles from Brussels was the right location.

St. Niklaas boasted the largest market square in Europe and warmly welcomed the British and their plans to develop at a cost of £2 million just over 62 acres of land for industrial use.

The site had been expropriated from small farmers for industrial development to help broaden the local economy at a time when the area's textile industry was in decline. The authorities, from the Minister of Economic Affairs downwards, all proved helpful. To add icing to the cake there was a package of financial concessions for anyone moving into what was officially designated a development area.

The letting of factory space was a new concept in Belgium and, once again, initial progress was slow at a location which was not entirely ideal in terms of communications. There was little interest from British companies, with most tenants emanating from the United States or West Germany.

Slough Estates Belgium was formed to handle the business which, despite Britain's initial failure to join the EEC, would become a permanent part of the group's European business. M. Roger Lepoudre, who would remain with the group for 26 years, was appointed general manager. He would eventually be awarded the OBE for his services to the British community in Paris.

Back in England the property boom was at its height, with large numbers of developers who had not even existed before the war taking their place on the London stock market.

By 1962, the year in which Gerald Mobbs would follow in his father's footsteps to become High Sheriff of Buckinghamshire, the total value of shares in the 169 publicly-quoted property companies stood at exactly £800 million, eight times the value recorded only four years earlier.

Almost all of them had been built up from nothing since the end of the war. They came to the market partly to satisfy their backers, the insurance companies, which had begun to provide fixed interest finance in return for slices of the companies' share capital. Before long, the insurance companies and pension funds would increasingly dip their toes into direct development activities.

The institutional partnership was a fashion which Slough Estates would prove reluctant to follow, although there would be joint projects. The business was not to become closely identified with any particular investment partners, choosing to leave open its funding options and not to have its sphere of operations restricted by the preferences or prejudices of second parties. In any case the company usually preferred to call on its shareholders for development funds when they were required.

Some of those companies acquiring share listings were also seeking relief from private income tax and surtax liabilities which could be as high as 18s 3d in the pound.

They were, almost without exception, interested in office and retail development. Industrial property was not regarded as sufficiently glamourous or lucrative and it rarely caught the imagination or the headlines in the same way.

As the publicity-shy Harry Hyams began work on the infamous Centre Point office tower in London's West End and Jack Cotton and Charles Clore and a whole new breed of property specialists began to change the face of the capital and of Britain's provincial cities, Slough Estates quietly got on with its job.

By the end of 1962 the group had notched up pre-tax profits of nearly £1.2 million and was reporting higher rental values at all its UK estates. Billy Kingsmill told shareholders that Britain's failure to join the European Common Market was a disappointment to businesses like Slough Estates which had already started to operate on the continent. The company did not believe, however, that Britain's continuing isolation would prevent Slough Estates from pressing on with its long-term plans for expanding in Europe.

There was further profits growth in 1964 to nearly £1.4 million.

Demand for industrial floor space in Britain ensured a busy building programme for the company, which also experienced record demand from tenants for electricity, steam and water supplies.

In Canada the company's Ajax estate was now half developed and home to more than 30 companies. Work on developing St. Niklaas in Belgium was well underway. Nothing changed, however, in Australia where a start on work still seemed a long way off.

At home the effective ban on office building in London imposed with the introduction of office development permits by George Brown in November 1964 was of no consequence to factory-builders like Slough Estates and, to the Labour government's ever-lasting embarrassment, only helped office rents in the capital to merrily escalate further. In 1965 the government published proposals which the company would not be able to dismiss so lightly.

Although the company did not figure among the giants who were now making all the running in the British property development industry, it could not escape all the political consequences of the sector's behaviour. At the end of the year, in which the number of employees on the Slough complex reached nearly 28,000, the government resurrected the idea of a levy on commercial developments scrapped by Harold Macmillan more than a decade earlier.

The Land Commission Bill, an extremely complex piece of legislation, envisaged the public acquisition, management and disposal of land to help lubricate its supply. It also introduced a betterment levy, set at 40 per cent of any gain in development value arising out of local authority planning decisions.

In a reaction which was to characterise Nigel Mobbs' attitude towards the role of government in industry and, in particular, the property industry, he would say: "I am as much against speculation for speculation's sake as anybody else but the same ends could have been achieved by strengthening existing legislation. Too many senior executives have to waste time in just running to keep up with new, complicated legislation."

His chairman agreed, informing shareholders: "This is a legislative measure of an unprecedented complexity, the restrictive effects of which will be felt not only by property companies but all sections of the community."

Slough Estates already had another of its own local development battles going on. As the company formulated and pursued plans to build on its remaining acreage at Slough, the local council had become increasingly concerned about what it regarded as a lack of car parking space on the estate, which would become still more acute after further development.

After protracted negotiations in which the company offered to make available car parking space, to be operated by the council, in return for permission to construct more factories, a public inquiry was called.

During the hearing the company again raised the apparent granting in 1945 of planning permission to complete its estate. The council again insisted that it had never granted such approval.

Even so, the Inspector gave his consent for 70 per cent of the company's applications, allowing the phased development of further warehouse and factory space. The company was not, however, prepared to let the matter rest there. Apart from the principle involved it argued that the existence of planning permission for the remainder of the estate meant it could build up to two million square feet of additional floorspace without having to apply for industrial development certificates.

Slough Estates warned that if the authority wanted to revoke an established planning permission it could find itself facing a £4.5 million bill for compensation.

The company decided to take the matter to the High Court and on to the House of Lords in a legal process which would not be completed until 1969. It was concluded that any permission granted nearly 25 years earlier was ambiguous. In the event, the outcome was of academic interest.

Well before the final, inconclusive judgement some of the undeveloped land which stood at the centre of the legal wrangle had been sold to the council for housing. The company, in turn, was granted permission to develop other estate land. It reached a deal just in time.

The passage of the Land Commission Bill had been delayed because of the 1966 general election and would only reach the Statute Book in 1967. The planning approval from Slough council, which added considerable value to the land in question, was concluded the day before the new development gains tax took effect.

Such protracted wrangles seemed light years away in Canada, where in 1966 the company had managed to build a 65,000 sq. ft. factory with offices in under four months, a "significant improvement" on the work rate experienced in England, Billy Kingsmill reminded his shareholders.

The Canadian business was steadily growing under Harry O'Neill, an oil man by profession, who had been joined on the local board - where majority Canadian representation was a legal necessity - by John Howard Taylor, a local businessmen who held a string of directorships with major Canadian companies.

The subsidiary had by now acquired 109 acres at Malton, a mile from Toronto's international airport, to which it would quickly add further development land. The Ajax site had also been enlarged and, together, they housed 800,000 sq. ft. of factory space.

Though the directors and shareholders must have doubted that it would ever happen, the company had finally started work at Altona in Melbourne. They had not been alone in their scepticism; in 1962, the subsidiary had appointed John Greenshields on £3,250 a year to take command and to ensure work started. He resigned two years later in total frustration at the complete lack of any progress in preparing the site for development.

Greenshields was eventually replaced by Redmond Nolan, an unlikely successor given his qualifications as a chemist. He, in turn, would leave in 1975.

In an effort to speed up progress Charles Clifford had at one stage tried to enlist the help of Henry Bolte, the State premier, by inviting him to the Athenaeum Club in Melbourne. When the question of financial assistance towards the provision of site services was raised, Bolte replied curtly: "If you are asking for government help, the answer is no. I suggest you have done very well out of the deal and can well afford the development costs involved. Now, may I enjoy my lunch."

Not long after Greenshields' departure, things did, indeed, begin to move. Fifteen years after Sir Noel had bought the land his company signed an agreement with the Melbourne & Metropolitan Board of Works under which water and sewerage services would be laid on.

The Board, in return, assumed ownership of 220 acres of low-lying swamp land for use as a water catchment area. On November 10, 1966 the estate was finally declared open by a newly-knighted Sir Henry Bolte, whose earlier reluctance to become involved was obviously not held against him. He had, after all, encouraged the process of development by his earlier success in luring an international oil consortium to the area.

David Christensen, secretary of the Australian business since its inception and later to succeed Cecil Hyland as company chairman, was at the opening. He remembers that there were perhaps half a dozen factories on this vast acreage of land. "They looked like pimples on a pumpkin."

Some new ground was also being broken at home, despite the deep wounds inflicted on the economy by continuing financial crisis. In 1967 the company had moved further north by acquiring 17 acres of freehold land in Wakefield, Yorkshire. The Monckton Road industrial estate might not have appeared an obvious choice but the selection was limited.

A further tightening of industrial development certificates, reducing the 5,000 sq. ft. limit to 3,000 sq. ft. and limiting each approval to a single building, made life hard in the highly competitive south-east market.

The IDC system had already been exerting upwards pressure on industrial rents, to the extent that the company's system of indexation was failing to keep up with what was happening in the market. As a result Slough Estates adopted a regular rent review pattern - the initial, seven-year period was later changed to five - which was superimposed over the index calculation. When the review came, rents were raised and then the indexation link was reactivated.

Market conditions were certainly more relaxed in Yorkshire and the purchase of some former rhubarb fields from vendors strapped for cash gave the company something new into which it could sink its teeth. Like the mutually beneficial deal agreed at Slough with the local council, the Wakefield purchase was concluded immediately before the deadline for the imposition of the new development tax.

The site changed hands for £65,000 just two days before the all-important day, the town clerk working wonders in ensuring planning permission for a valuable source of local employment. The British development process, it seemed, could get its skates on if it had to.

Harold Wilson's government had more to worry about than development taxes, having been forced into a humiliating devaluation of Sterling in an attempt to rescue the nation's ailing economy.

But, as it had always done, Slough Estates was still managing to weather the storm with pre-tax profits in 1967 heading towards £2 million. Indeed, Wilson's "pound in your pocket" announcement meant slightly better contributions from the overseas subsidiaries.

The same year saw new appointments to the parent company's board following the death shortly after his retirement of Charles Fairall and of Sir Nutcombe Hume. Owen Morshead, too, decided to step down.

In their place there were to be two newcomers. John Vaughan was deputy chairman of Charterhouse Group and followed in the footsteps of Nutcombe Hume. He was joined in the new board line-up by Douglas Lofting, who had recently retired as a partner in Henry Butcher & Co., the surveyors and auctioneers who had a high reputation in the industrial property sector.

In 1968, as the group reached another milestone by passing the £2 million pre-tax profit target, Roland Essery retired, to be replaced by Joe Harding, who had once worked for Horlicks but joined Slough Estates from Harris Intertype, the US-owned printing machinery manufacturers where he was company secretary.

Harding already knew Nigel Mobbs. He had previously had to negotiate additional car parking space for Harris Intertype on the estate and the two men had reached a deal over a meal. Mobbs would say later it was one of the few occasions when a tenant succeeded in bribing him with a lunch.

Harding would be a director within three years. As he arrived, he could tell change was in the air. "A younger team was taking over at the helm and it was making itself felt and heard. The chemistry of the organisation was changing," he recalls.

Almost at once Harding found himself involved with his new employer's acquisition of an investment trust called Yorkshire and Pacific Securities, one of the last companies to be quoted on the Huddersfield stock exchange.

The attraction of the company, headed by George Norton, who

would prove to be a tough negotiator, was that its share portfolio was held in Canada. Exchange controls had made it impossible for the growing Canadian business to arrange a badly-needed injection of equity from the UK business and the dollar premium made any such transaction prohibitively expensive.

The plan was to acquire a company in Canada whose assets could be sold off in order to release investment cash with which to feed the business. The deal which was concluded in 1969 was complex but, over a period, it allowed the shares to be liquidated and nearly C$5 million to be injected into the Canadian subsidiary's operations.

In the same year - as Sir Roderick Barclay, the recently-retired British Ambassador in Belgium joined the board to give it the benefit of his experience on European issues - another business was scooped up. This time the action was closer to home.

Bill Baker, who was taken on to search out new industrial sites around the country and would eventually join the board, had come across Hertford Industrial Estates, a small but formidably well-connected operation which owned three well-located estates at Hertford and Bishop's Stortford in Hertfordshire and Braintree in Essex. The owner, Cyril Brazier, had been killed in a road accident in France and the business, embracing 264,000 sq. ft. of floorspace over 23 acres and with an annual rent roll of £115,400, had been left in the hands of solicitor Gordon Hyde to dispose of. It was sold to Slough Estates in a cash and shares deal worth £854,000.

No-one would have suggested that the Hertford assets acquired in 1969 were particularly exciting but the deal provided further evidence that the company was prepared to seek out and conclude deals which would help an increasingly expansionist strategy.

During the 1950s and for much of the 1960s the company had seemed largely content to amble along, its business still firmly rooted in the original estate and with its half-hearted overseas operations failing to live up to their early promise. But now, it seemed, the business was beginning to make up for lost time.

11

CHAMPAGNE AND TEARS

NINETEEN SEVENTY was a year of champagne and celebration. Slough Estates had reached its fiftieth anniversary and the election of Edward Heath's Conservative government raised hopes in the property development industry that an era of intervention in its affairs was at an end.

The statistics at the end of the first half-century would have made incredible reading both to Lord Inverforth, the man who had unwittingly helped create the business, and to Lord Perry, who had helped it through its early years.

As the directors planned a champagne party for 250 guests at the Savoy, an inventory of the company's assets showed 717 acres of industrial land in Britain containing just over eight million sq. ft. of floorspace. At Slough, where the now dual-fired power station was now big enough to supply a small town, there were six million sq. ft. of factories and warehouses employing nearly 30,000 workers. The company was landlord to nearly 500 tenants around the country.

There were, in addition, 235 acres in Canada supporting nearly one million sq. ft. of factory and warehouse space. While 706 acres in Australia housed a meagre 92,000 sq. ft. of floorspace, there was almost twice that amount on the 63 acres in Belgium.

In Jubilee year, as all 200 employees received a celebratory two week's extra pay, the company would receive £2.8 million in UK rental income with another £500,000 from abroad. Sales of electricity, steam, water and gas added another £2 million to turnover. The merchandising operation, which now extended to selling laxatives to Kuwait and golden syrup in Sudan, contributed another £1 million. Group pre-tax profits rose to £2.6 million.

The estate at Slough was valued externally at £29.7 million, there was another £3.5 million worth of properties in Canada, £1.6 million in Australia and nearly £1 million in Belgium. The "family firm" had taken on another dimension.

The company now chose to establish another new subsidiary. The continuing domestic credit squeeze meant that finance was hard to secure and Slough Estates (Luxembourg) was set up as an overseas vehicle which could be used to raise funds. With the aid of Charterhouse Japhet, its merchant banking advisers, the company in 1971 began using the Euromarkets to raise finance essential to its development programme.

The company's strategy was now being discussed in a more deliberative way than had previously been the case. A management committee comprising directors and senior personnel met once a month for a boardroom lunch to exchange views.

Ted Brooks, the commercial manager who would rise through the ranks to become company secretary, was invited to join the select band. "It was a very formal occasion but it helped draw thoughts and ideas together, giving us a sense of direction. The meetings were always followed by lunch in the senior dining room. It was permissible to pour yourself one drink - and one drink only - before you sat down."

The concept of a top management forum would later be further refined.

The celebrations were crowned in November with a visit from the Duke of Edinburgh, who toured factories under construction and visited the power station. He had arrived at the estate under his own steam from nearby Windsor Castle, driving his favourite Alvis OXR 1. Jack Luxton, by then chauffeur to Gerald Mobbs, was deputed to park the vehicle before driving the Prince around the estate in the managing director's Rolls Royce. "He told me to watch it, as he'd already blown a couple of engines in it," he remembers.

At the very end of the year it was the power station workers who threatened to spoil the celebrations. At a national level the electricity workers were in dispute in support of a 26 per cent pay claim and, despite their generally good relationships with the management, the men at Slough threatened to walk out in sympathy. In a celebratory spirit, their claim was effectively met in full.

In 1971 Billy Kingsmill died and was replaced by Gerald Mobbs, who took the chairman's seat 13 years after it had been vacated by his father. Nigel, after 11 years with the company, became managing director and Wallace Mackenzie, still running operations in Canada, joined the board.

The reshuffle was a signal for the beginning of a new phase in the company's development, aided by the easing of the tight credit restrictions which had been curbing its potential for so long.

The return to "cheap money" was intended to strengthen British industry prior to entering the EEC. The property industry was quick to grasp the opportunity, taking advantage of falling interest rates to borrow heavily for new schemes in the conviction that rising values would provide a cushion until their schemes were completed and began to pay off.

Though Slough was not about to adopt the "borrow or bust" creed - shortly to become "borrow and go bust" - it was indeed stepping up its debt, using the Eurodollar markets to finance its own expanding development programme.

The company had just purchased 22 acres of development land at Yate, near Bristol, to take advantage of the impending completion of the M4 and M5 motorways, and would add to the UK portfolio further by acquiring a seven-acre development site at High Wycombe and 14 acres at Aylesbury.

The Slough estate itself, however, still contributed about 80 per cent of group profits.

Over in Australia, where progress was excruciatingly slow - the collapse of a section of the West Gate bridge across the River Yarra, intended to open up the area to the west of Melbourne, killed 34 workers and seriously delayed its completion - another 40 acres were bought at Waverley to the east of Melbourne in an area of established demand. Canada and Belgium were growing.

At home there was a distinct change in the economic atmosphere, not least because Britain, under Edward Heath's patient diplomacy, was finally heading for membership of the EEC.

According to Nigel Mobbs: "The whole outlook became more exciting. Property just took off and we started to go out and buy things. Just as the Old Guard had gone, the market place was transformed and we began to inject new life into the company. We were actively looking for new opportunities and becoming far more aggressive in seeking opportunities than we had ever done before."

An early opportunity to pursue its ambitions came in 1972 through Suttons Seeds, an old-established seed business which had been bought by Douglas Collins, a wealthy businessman who had founded the Goya cosmetics business.

Suttons wanted to realise the extensive assets within the business but they did not want to see it disappear. The situation provided an ideal opportunity for Slough Estates, which was not interested in entering the seeds business but keen to assume ownership of the 43 acres of prime - and expensive - development land which the business owned on the edge of Reading and used as a seed trial ground.

Slough worked out a package under which it would buy the business and then sell on the seed operation to an interested Swedish company. Two sets of negotiations were conducted in parallel.

At the eleventh hour, with contracts about to be signed, Collins died suddenly and the deal collapsed. But it was agreed to talk to Suttons at a later date and the purchase, for £3.2 million, was resurrected in 1975 when estate duty problems had been sorted out. The seed business was sold on to the Swedes in 1978.

There was to be another new initiative in Europe during 1972. With Belgium making steady but unspectacular progress, the company was hungry for more action on the continent where British office and shop developers were by now racing each other to conclude development and investment deals.

Prince Philip makes a visit to mark the group's fiftieth anniversary in 1970. He is pictured with Gerald Mobbs.

British developers had tried once before to invade Europe, at the end of the 1960s, but most sorties had ended in abject failure. The laws varied widely, long-term capital was hard to find and the idea that estate agents could in some countries act for buyer and seller - and be paid by both - was more than the British could take. Exchange controls had put the lid on the whole exercise.

Now, however, the scene was different. Europe offered higher yields and happy hunting grounds where the locals still had a lot to learn about the art of commercial property development. The British were everywhere, from Brussels to Paris to Frankfurt to Amsterdam. The early flights from Heathrow were crammed with Europe-bound property men, ready to sign up and return home the very same day.

Slough's style was somewhat less high-risk - the Lex column in the Financial Times said it "lacked sex appeal" - but it shared some of the enthusiasm for joining in the gold rush.

According to Wallace Mackenzie: "Everyone was jumping on a bandwagon without regard to the fact that everyone else was getting on it. The criticism of us for being too conservative and ultra-cautious clearly had some effect on our thinking but we agonised over every decision we made in Europe, unlike many of the others."

One high-flier who ran into Slough Estates was Charles Mackenzie Hill, a highly capable property entrepreneur, complete with helicopter, who was already established in France. He approached Slough Estates.

A Cambridge boxing blue with a reputation for being "a bit of bruiser" in business, Mackenzie Hill had flair and charisma and seemed to personify the swashbuckling approach to property development. Slough Estates was impressed and agreed to join him in Anglo-French Industrial Developments, a 50-50 partnership for developing industrial estates in the Paris area. Two sites were quickly started at Colombes and Bures-Orsay and a £9 million development programme began.

There would be more board changes and a complete reorganisation of the management structure in 1972. The intention was to better utilise the skills of those within the company whose voices had not previously been fully heard.

Charles Clifford - who had changed his name to Charles Clifford-Kingsmill as a pre-condition to inheriting the extensive estate of Billy Kingsmill, his childless uncle - stepped down as an executive director. He remained on the board until 1977.

But the pivotal element of the company reorganisation was the return from Canada of Wallace Mackenzie.

Nigel Mobbs, now firmly in control of day-to-day affairs and increasingly showing the qualities which had made his grandfather a force to be reckoned with, was acutely aware that his management team was "a bit too thin for comfort."

As he cast round for fresh managerial talent Ron Diggens quietly suggested that the company might have just the sort of expertise within its own organisation, though it was hardly on the doorstep. He suggested Wallace Mackenzie.

Nigel Mobbs had certainly appreciated Mackenzie's sense of judgement and mental agility and flew out to Toronto to offer him a directorship of the parent company and responsibility for the group's UK industrial estate developments.

The proposal came at a time when, after years of dogged hard work, Mackenzie's efforts were beginning to pay dividends. There was a record rent roll, a progressive and substantial increase in earnings and the Canadian subsidiary was tackling its biggest-ever construction programme. The business was also on the verge of reaching a partnership agreement with the American company Draper & Kramer, to enable it to cross over the border and begin operations in the United States.

Draper and Kramer, founded in 1893, was a well-respected Chicago-based real estate management and mortgage banking business with a successful development arm. Douglas Kramer, its president, had been introduced to Slough Estates in England by the First National Bank of Chicago. He had paid a visit to the Estate and he and Nigel Mobbs had got on well. Kramer subsequently offered reciprocal hospitality in Chicago which led to the creation in 1973 of SDK Industrial Parks. Douglas Kramer would become a non-executive director of Slough Estates in 1981.

For the astonished head of Canadian operations it was a hard choice. "I was 50 and had decided Canada was our home. I saw me ending my business career there and was certainly not pushing to come back to England. It took a great deal of thinking about."

The thinking done, he and his wife returned in September 1972. John Taylor was now chairman of the Canadian business, a post he would hold until 1972, when Jack Rhind would take over the helm.

Behind him, Wallace Mackenzie left the day-to-day running of the business to James Appleyard, who had emigrated to Canada after a spell as chief estates officer for the East Kilbride Development Corporation.

Appleyard had experienced an extraordinary introduction to the company. On his arrival at Slough for an interview with Mackenzie and Nigel Mobbs, he was blissfully unaware that Mobbs faced something of a predicament. The chief executive had just split his trousers, which were being repaired in another office by Mackenzie's secretary. The two men had agreed that Mobbs would, consequently, stay seated at his desk throughout the interview. Appleyard got the job and, when he next saw Mobbs on one of the chief executive's visits to Canada, was surprised to see that his boss was not disabled.

Shortly after his return to the UK Mackenzie would be awarded the OBE for services to British commercial interests in Canada. He had, apart from his Slough Estates duties, been closely involved in the promotion of British trade in Canada and had served terms as chairman of the British Commonwealth branch of the Toronto Board of Trade and as president of the British Canadian Trade Association.

He arrived home to find a company preparing to boost its ordinary share capital from £18 million to £28 million and achieving annual pre-tax profits worldwide of well over £3 million. Independent valuations of the group portfolio produced a combined figure of £76.3 million. But for a government-imposed five per cent ceiling on dividend payments, which formed part of an emergency, anti-inflation package, some very frustrated Slough shareholders would have been expecting a much improved year-end payout.

His unexpected return to London caused some surprise among those who might have expected preferment. It also gave Mackenzie plenty to ponder on. "It struck me at once that the whole process of creating property assets in Britain was extremely inefficient and cost ineffective and that it loaded the dice against us. The planning process itself was so tortuous that if you could get permission you did not worry too much about what you could build. You had won the prize when you won permission and the end result would be let, even if you were not particularly proud of it. The actual construction process, too, was slow and costly."

It was a theme which Nigel Mobbs would also later publicly pursue.

Mackenzie's arrival also represented the starting gun for the management reorganisation in train. Nigel Mobbs realised that more independence was being given to senior staff overseas than to their counterparts in the UK and that the time had come to devolve more authority away from the small group of executives at the centre.

The move enhanced the status of the senior management, recognising their role in helping to determine company strategy. With day-to-day responsibility for the group's operations handed down to a series of subsidiaries, managers would be given their head to make more important strategic decisions.

Under the changes the company would be reconstituted as a group organised around a holding company responsible for policy-making and planning. Slough Industrial Estates would become the principal UK industrial property subsidiary, headed by Mackenzie. Within his control would be the nine estates now operated in the UK.

Beyond this there would be a string of other companies with special interests, one of which would put a Slough toe into another part of the property pool.

A new company, Gauntlet Developments, was set up to establishing Slough Estates in office development both in the UK and in Europe.

So far the company's history and success had been based almost exclusively on its expertise in the industrial sector, building only the occasional office block to complement factory and warehouse units. Robert Phipps, the UK estates manager, was made general manager of the new subsidiary, which at once proceeded with two office developments - its first in Europe - in the Quartier Leopold in Brussels.

Slough Estates (Overseas) would provide the umbrella for the foreign businesses, Slough Estates (London) would press on with its export sales operations and Slough Estates Finance would act as financier to all the subsidiaries. Joe Harding took on the job of group finance director alongside his responsibilities as company secretary.

Slough Estates (Utility Services) would provide utility services to tenants, although the company was now anxious to make the power station, which had always been a quite distinct operating entity, a more free-standing unit.

The result was a decision to promote a private Bill at Westminster in order to permit the company effectively to run a separate electricity supply business contrary to the provisions of the 1948 Electricity Act which secured state ownership of the electricity supply industry. Though it did not say so at the time, the company was also increasingly nervous about the growing militancy in the electricity supply industry and was becoming less enthusiastic about a continuing involvement. There was always a chance that a separate utility business could be sold off.

The Bill was abandoned, however, in the face of open hostility from the Central Electricity Generating Board and from the Southern

Electricity Board. Slough Estates would continue its unique role as a private provider of power to its tenants.

The year also saw the beginning of another initiative which was to end in more concrete results. Though the company's offices at Slough were held in some affection by those who had grown with the business, they were now hopelessly cramped and hardly appropriate as the focal point for an organisation which promoted itself as a pioneer in industrial property development.

Head office staff were, in fact, distributed around five buildings on the estate and were forced to spend their time scurrying between them. Nigel Mobbs decided that the ramshackle arrangements had to go and that the company required a "signature" building on the estate. He told his board colleagues it was likely to cost around £750,000, though it would inevitably prove much more expensive.

Mobbs wrote the architectural brief and, after consulting a series of architects, chose Geoffrey Salmon Speed Associates to design what was to become, when it opened five years later alongside the Bath Road, the subject of considerable controversy. The building's appearance provoked some criticism from those who were uncomfortable with its modernistic design but was stoutly defended by Nigel Mobbs. He would refer to the new headquarters as "my baby."

But even as the project reached the drawing board, the economic world outside was becoming increasingly tough. By November of 1972, as part of a further package of anti-inflationary measures, the Heath government announced a rent freeze.

The property industry was understandably angry though the measure was initially regarded more as an irritant than a catastrophe; the expectation was that it would not have to last long.

For many landlords the timing could not have been worse. In numerous cases their tenants held 21-year leases on fixed rents, many of which were now, finally, coming up for renegotiation. The prospect of huge increases, some of them up to 1,000 per cent, had been taken away at the stroke of a ministerial pen.

Things were nothing like as bad for Slough Estates which was at least partially protected by its indexation formula and its cash flow would remain healthy. The company could not expect to escape completely, however. It would, for example, have to wait until 1981 before it finally found a tenant for a 175,000 sq. ft. office building in Rue du Luxembourg Brussels which had been started in 1973.

Many other developers responded in the only way they could if they wished to boost artificially restricted rental cash flows - by building even more property in the hope that conditions would quickly improve.

The rush into Europe gathered pace still further. By the summer of 1973, by which time David Simons had been appointed a director and general manager of Slough Estates (Overseas), the London Evening

Standard had drawn up a list of British property interests in Paris, estimating that the value of their schemes underway in the French capital alone was more than £600 million.

The newspaper identified nearly 150 individual projects associated with the British. The names made familiar reading: Slater Walker, Heron Group, Town and City, Lyon Group, Compass Securities, Stern Group, Peachey Property and, among dozens of others, the Mackenzie Hill - Slough Estates joint company. Slough was making progress in France though Simons was to find that its efforts at promotion were not helped when one marketing initiative, which it helped fund, referred to the company as "Slow Estates."

The picture of frenetic activity, of spectacular deals promising undreamed of profits, provided welcome contrast to the continuing and deepening problems at home. But the euphoria was unsustainable and the seeds of calamity were sown.

Nevertheless 1973 saw Slough Estates - the rent freeze denying it about £130,000 in rental income during the year - maintain its profitable progress. The rent roll touched nearly £4 million, as did pre-tax profits. For every square foot of floor space under construction in the UK, it was now providing two abroad.

The board, on which Wallace Mackenzie now served as deputy managing director made another break with the past. It finally bowed to the inevitable and authorised the dismantling of the last one and three quarter miles of estate railway. The tracks which had first brought life into the estate had finally reached a dead-end. The last two 39-ton steam engines - Number 3 and Number 5 - made their final journeys to railway preservation societies.

As the company, for the first time, moved into Scotland - buying a site in oil-rich Aberdeen - it was also ready to make it first move into the United States.

SDK Parks, the joint venture with Draper & Kramer, in which Slough took an 80 per cent interest, unveiled plans to build up to 800,000 sq. ft. of industrial floorspace on two sites near Chicago's O'Hare airport with an expected investment value of more than $10 million. Nearby was the 2,500-acre Centex Industrial Park, which managed to make Slough's home base look modest.

With every British developer and his dog running around Europe, the deal made Slough Estates the first British property company to tackle the industrial sector in the United States.

The choice of Chicago was hardly surprising given Doug Kramer's experience in the city and its record as one of the fastest-growing commercial and population centres in the US. He told a London press conference: "Chicago is a thrusting, expanding city - not the run-down place portrayed in movies about Al Capone."

Nigel Mobbs, who was by now beginning to emerge as one of the industry's more prominent and knowledgeable spokesmen, was quick to use the United States as an inspiration for his vision of industrial property development. With many of the factories at Slough now 50 years old, his desire to rebuild and to provide more generous landscaping would only be further encouraged by what he saw on the other side of the Atlantic.

It was in America that the first industrial estates, or parks, were developed and from which the best definition of the perfect industrial complex had emanated.

In one of a growing number of articles he was asked to contribute to property journals, he spelled out the basic criteria of good location, proper communications and further room for physical development - all of which his grandfather had championed - before turning to the industrialist's environmental obligations.

Pollution control, he stressed, was to be the problem of the age. Pollution was "the accumulation of a century's ignorance of the impact of industry" and was impossible to remedy quickly. The developer's principal contribution, he added, was the provision of modern buildings, offering better working conditions and easier ways of controlling the polluting effects of industrial processes.

National and local government, Mobbs claimed, had a role to play in ensuring that suitable land was zoned for industry and that its development could be phased to enable construction costs to be minimised by large-scale development.

He repeatedly took the opportunity to call on the government to relax Industrial Development Certificate controls so that existing buildings could at least be demolished and replaced with more efficient buildings.

Mobbs suggested that the future success of industrial development would be dependent upon a partnership between the planners, the environment lobby and industry in ensuring that new industrial growth was developed in a way acceptable to the whole community.

It was a theme to which he would regularly return and an issue over which he would not hesitate to criticise if he believed it was being ignored.

The end of 1973 crudely brushed aside such worthy sentiments. An already weak economy, assailed by rising unemployment and mounting inflation, was about to be felled by a series of further blows.

A miners' strike brought further problems for the beleaguered Heath government, which was forced to introduce a three-day working week for industry in order to try and conserve energy.

The Slough estate, however, was to win an extraordinary exemption. With its own power supply the company made urgent representations to the Department of Trade and Industry asking for the estate not to be included in the government's emergency orders for fuel and energy economies.

The company had taken the precaution of writing to all its tenants on the estate telling them of their special pleading but warning that it was unlikely to be successful. The DTI confounded everyone and agreed to classify the power station as an "emergency standby generator."

While the lights went out all over Britain, the estate kept working, though the company asked all tenants to make voluntary economies so that it could reduce output at the power station, now fuelled almost entirely by North Sea Gas. To add to the national misery the Organisation of Petroleum Exporting Countries quadrupled oil prices, adding to the wave of global inflation and forcing the British government to abandon its "cheap money" policy.

As fresh shudders went through the economy, the property sector in particular took its next body blow. Anthony Barber, the Chancellor of the Exchequer, introduced in December an emergency budget which singled out the property development industry and which contained a pledge to limit what he called the "obscene gains" it had been achieving.

Barber announced the imposition of a new 50 per cent development gains tax in place of the existing 30 per cent capital gains charge. It was to be the start of a new era of political intervention in the business of property development.

There was at least one sigh of relief at Slough, which was in the process of finalising the sale to the council of 55 acres of land for affordable housing, part of the agreement which finally paved the way for further development of remaining estate land. The £3.5 million sale contract having being confirmed before the date nominated by the Chancellor, the company escaped liability.

There was to be a lot more pain inflicted in 1974. The commercial property bubble was about to burst in spectacular fashion, destroying companies and reputations literally overnight.

Gerald Mobbs was moved to say that at no time in the past had it been so difficult to foresee the prospects for business in the UK, or anywhere else. All industrial nations were in recession, there was high and rising inflation and business confidence was at rock-bottom.

The crash stemmed directly from the chaos which encircled the secondary banking sector, the source of finance for much of the development and investment activity which had taken place in the early 1970s.

When Keyser Ullman, heavily committed to the property industry, had to be rescued by a Bank of England "lifeboat" operation - Wallace Mackenzie would later join the bank's board to help sort out the mess - the game was up. One of the bank's customers was William Stern, whose property empire collapsed with debts of £143 million. He would later be declared personally bankrupt with world record debts of £118 million.

Bank lending had been backed up not by the assets of their property developer customers but on the promise of huge gains on the completion and sale of projects. Development planning had been predicated on the basis that cash flow would come through from ever-higher rents.

While rents were frozen interest rates were not. With the arithmetic supporting development and the servicing of debt no longer adding up, the house of cards collapsed. In Europe, where developers had scrambled to escape the problems at home, the picture was no better. Some developers had, in any case, failed to adapt to markets which looked deceptively familiar to those at home but which were often full of expensive pitfalls.

Companies began to haemorrhage; confidence, the lifeblood of the property industry, flowed away. The liquidators were set to become the biggest landlords of them all.

In common with all the other developers, Slough's shares slumped, falling briefly below par. But though the company inevitably fell victim to market sentiment, its sound asset base and inherently conservative approach to the business of property investment made it a relatively safe haven. Throughout the property slump the vacancy rate at Slough never rose above three per cent.

This inherent strength brought a number of pleas for help.

In March 1974 another client of Keyser Ullman contacted Nigel Mobbs, who was on a visit to Paris. Ronald Lyon had started in business making garden sheds for £16 each and graduated to building industrial estates. By 1974 he had built more than 2,000 factories in the UK and Ireland.

His organisation spread around the world, from Germany and Spain to Singapore and Australia. But his private empire became fatally overstretched and, when the market collapsed, he was left facing personal guarantees of more than £50 million against his company's debts - by then totalling about £85 million.

He told Mobbs he was in "temporary financial difficulty" and asked for help. He wanted to borrow £10 million which, he said, would keep his business afloat long enough to pull through. In return, Slough could have 80 per cent of the equity.

Mobbs was hardly enthusiastic. "We could have had 80 per cent of nothing. A panic injection of funds can never be sensible and, in any case, we did not have any experience of dealing with him."

Six weeks later, after further strenuous efforts to avoid collapse, the Lyon group folded, inflicting fresh misery on the sector.

"It was an awful period," Mobbs remembers. "The atmosphere was terrible, the market was full of rumours and the whole thing appeared to be going down the chute. Others would seek help from the Slough Estates managing director whose stature, at 36 years of age, was steadily rising within the business community.

But Slough Estates was not going to be tempted into mounting rescues. "The Financial Times share index fell to 147 and even the National

Westminster Bank was said be in trouble. Some big names were on the brink and we just got our heads down and concentrated on self-protection. The scene was so desperately gloomy, it did not seem like the right time to be brave," Mobbs recalls.

With the advantage of hindsight, however, he believes a bit of courage would have enabled the business to take advantage of the desperate plight of the market by securing never-to-be-repeated property deals. "The banks were coming to us, offering us money because they saw a strength in us they did not see in many of the others. In early 1973, brokers had been saying we were sleepy and undergeared. Now they were saying we were clever and perceptive."

The company's apparent timidity would become a regular theme of future criticism of the group's approach to business.

Mobbs would later acknowledge: "There was an element of judgement in our own, secure position but it was probably more luck than anything else. There was no profit to be had in deals so why should we have borrowed merely in order to maintain a big development programme?"

Mobbs also later offered his views on why the events of the early 1970s were so catastrophic. He told a London conference that prudence had been abandoned at the prospect of making a quick buck. "The concept that trees grow to Heaven in a period of inflation became all-apparent and people were more concerned with asset values and their growth rather than with cash flow and the ability to service debt from real earnings."

He recalled being "amazed by the manner in which financial institutions were willing to advance large tranches of money on minimum security terms for projects which at the best depended upon a high rate of inflations of rents."

Mobbs claimed that the shortcomings of the banks and institutions had been magnified by the lack of professionalism displayed by consultants while managements of developments had found it possible to gear up to such an extent that they were inevitably vulnerable to any downturn. There were serious lessons for everyone to learned, he suggested, if another disaster was to be avoided.

With his prestige riding high he became a non-executive director of Charterhouse Group, which would eventually acquire Keyser Ullman, adding to his directorship of Barclays Bank Trust and to the 14 others he now held within the Slough Estates group. He was also elected chairman of the National Council of the Association of Chambers of Commerce.

There was more bad, and a some good, news for the property market at the end of 1974. The earlier return of a Wilson government by an electorate which had given Edward Heath the wrong answer to his question about who really governed Britain had hardly been a cause for spontaneous rejoicing among property men.

Chancellor Denis Healey, like Barber only a few months previously, had singled out the property sector for special treatment. There was to be a new tax on development land and - even more damaging for some companies like Slough - a tax on first lettings.

Gerald Mobbs had some harsh words to say about the new government at that year's annual meeting. They had, he alleged, set back industrial investment in Britain by 10 years in attacking the property sector.

He told shareholders that the measures would halt industrial building, force up rents and ensure the continued use of obsolete and inefficient buildings. At the same time the package would place an additional burden on property companies' liquidity when they were already under severe pressure.

Commercial and industrial property, he reminded the government, was owned by the nation as a whole through pension funds, insurance companies and shareholders. Everyone would suffer.

Nigel Mobbs, wearing his Chambers of Commerce hat, also publicly castigated the government for failing to prevent crippling rate increases being imposed by local authorities. To complete the cheerless picture, the government pledged to embark on the nationalisation of development land.

Against this gloomy outlook Anthony Crosland, the Environment Secretary, suddenly surprised everyone by giving notice that the freeze on commercial rents was to be scrapped from February 1975, more than a year ahead of the date which had been penciled in for its demise.

With the announcement coming only a week before Christmas, the newspapers dubbed him "Santa Crosland" and, for the property market, festive celebrations were more cheery. Shares rose sharply in value and the news was warmly welcomed, with some companies predicting a big boost in profitability.

Nigel Mobbs calculated that the rent freeze had cost his company about £1 million in 1974 and that its removal would bring some stability to a market badly in need of new confidence.

By the end of the darkest year in living memory for the British property industry Slough Estates turned in yet another rise in pre-tax profits - to £4.2 million. The company was reporting strong demand for accommodation at home, where it opened its £4 million Huddersfield estate. In June alone, it let more industrial space than in the first six months of the previous year, while Gauntlet Developments planned several new office schemes.

The picture abroad was also surprisingly buoyant. There had been more site acquisitions with Mackenzie Hill in France, where it now had a £7.5 million development programme underway, and, despite earlier reservations about the market, it had also joined its new partner in the creation of Anglo-German Developments to build office, factory and warehouse space in West Germany. It kicked off in Cologne.

Even though the domestic outlook was bleak the Slough Estates board earmarked £75 million for expansion in Europe up until the end of 1977. Nigel Mobbs was in no doubt about the longer-term prospects across the Channel, telling staff that the European market would be a major target for expansion now that continental industrialists had finally caught the Slough habit of renting, rather than buying, their premises.

12

CARRYING THE BANNER

VICTIMS OF the property crash were still licking their wounds when, in April 1975, Slough Estates helped give the market a badly needed shot in the arm by revealing plans to raise cash from shareholders to finance an expanding development programme.

While it had been adopting a cautious approach to new projects, it still had around £10 million worth of work on its books at a time when several major developers such as Town and City, English Property Corporation and Hammerson said they were not developing anything in the UK until conditions improved.

With Chancellor Healey now talking about the introduction of a Capital Transfer Tax - levied up to a possible 75 per cent and backdated to March 1974 - more than a few surviving property entrepreneurs wondered out loud about the use of going on at all. Nigel Mobbs, on behalf of the Chambers of Commerce, reminded Healey that, even in the Soviet Union, the top rate of comparable tax was 10 per cent.

But, despite the rhetoric, Slough Estates still had ambitious plans and needed extra funds at a time when property was hardly the most fashionable investment vehicle around.

The directors realised that the company needed to increase its longer-term capital to repay bank borrowings. Two parallel initiatives were started.

Firstly it began to negotiate a £5 million loan from Finance Corporation for Industry, the organisation owned by the clearing banks and which had been set up to help provide investment funds for the commercial sector. The loan attracted a 15 per cent interest rate and had a maturity date of 10 years.

At the same time Slough Estates investigated the possibility of having a convertible loan issue underwritten. But with the chances of a conventional underwriting arrangement seeming impossible, the company approached the Kuwait Investment Office to see if it would act as sole underwriter.

The KIO, which carried huge investments in Britain, was already a fairly substantial shareholder in the business. It was particularly interested in increasing its exposure to the development market, an ambition it fulfilled with the acquisition of St. Martin's Property Corporation, a leading player on the British property scene.

The Kuwaitis agreed to underwrite the whole £5.5 million rights issue, effectively undertaking to provide all the required funds. But as the deal with the Kuwaitis was being finalised the stock market rallied, not least because of the end of the rent freeze.

As a result Slough Estates was able to approach the market for conventional underwriting. The KIO became merely a sub-underwriter and a subscriber on the basis of its own shareholding.

The Slough fund-raising operation was successful and the event helped restore some of the industry's fragile confidence.

On April 28, 1975 Slough Estates finally moved into the new headquarters building which had been conceived when the property market was in better shape. After 55 years at 27, Bedford Avenue, the 90 head office staff moved around the corner into a striking pre-cast concrete and bronzed glass building.

With each floor providing more space than the one beneath it, the 55,000 sq. ft. building was immediately dubbed an "inverted pyramid." According to a highly impressed Architectural Review, the structure "could be described as the Modern Movement's answer to the Doric temple or, perhaps, the Palladian villa; the square form on plan, the device of the oversailing storeys and the columnar peristyle give an impression which is rightly called 'monumental.' Such a building, you instinctively feel, could never die."

Nigel Mobbs, it appeared, had got his "signature building." The following year the company would close down its offices in the Berkeley Street building where Sir Noel had played bridge and "ladies and gentlemen of good social position" had met to wine and dine.

Four weeks after moving in Slough Estates faced one of its livelier annual meetings at the Savoy Hotel in London. A group of local Liberals, headed by Philip Goldenberg, the party's prospective parliamentary candidate for Slough, had given notice that they intended to use the annual meeting to attack the company's record on two fronts; that it did not contribute enough to the local community - and that it contributed too much to the Conservative Party.

Given its pioneering initiatives in creating both an industrial health service and a social centre, the accusation that the company was not sufficiently community-minded was not well received by the board.

The centre itself had, only six weeks earlier, been handed over to Slough Council as a gift.

The week before the meeting the band of critics - including the two Liberals on Slough council - warned of a no-holds-barred invasion. Why, they demanded to know, should the council permit the continued expansion of the trading estate "without the company making some effort to support that expansion with reciprocal efforts to help provide the extra housing and new roads needed to meet it?"

The company, they insisted, should develop a social conscience which had been sadly lacking in the past. The injustice of the remarks stung.

The annual meeting itself proved to be something of an anticlimax. Goldenberg asked Gerald Mobbs why the company had, in the previous year, given £4,000 to the Conservative party and allied organisations. The answer, he was told unapologetically, to loud cheers from the 50 people present, was because the company believed a Conservative government would most benefit its shareholders.

On the question of contributing to the local community, the chairman reminded his audience that, as a result of the company's endeavours at Slough, the local authority was receiving around £4 million a year in rating income. He added: "I think, therefore, that the council do not do too badly out of us."

Goldenberg would return to his attacks on the company's political donations three years later when he questioned the company's contribution to the local Conservative Party at a time when it controlled Slough council. Mobbs vehemently denied any suggestion that Slough Estates was seeking to influence local politics and warned his critic of the risk of defamation. The issue was not resurrected.

At the end of the 1975 shareholders' meeting, in a reference to a well-publicised jibe from Edward Heath about "the unacceptable face of capitalism," a shareholder praised the company for showing "the proper face of capitalism" by producing another set of record trading figures, with pre-tax profits reaching £5.3 million.

Tucked away in the annual statistics, the really keen shareholder would have spotted another milestone - the company's annual payroll had now topped £1 million for the first time.

It was to be the last annual meeting with Gerald Mobbs in the chair. On medical advice he cut his workload and announced that he would retire in 1976. Nigel Mobbs was made deputy chairman and Wallace Mackenzie stepped up to managing director.

The arrival of Derek Millis, the former treasurer to the Electricity Council, brought another new face to the board. Millis was quickly appointed finance director.

Gerald Mobbs had been with the company for 45 years, 19 of them as chief executive and six as chairman. Though he was not regarded as one of the property industry's more flamboyant or daring practitioners, he had overseen the steady and uninterrupted growth of his business through good and very bad times.

He had presided over the company's regeneration during a period when government contracts had severely restricted the development of most industrial property. The estate and the power station had expanded under his guidance and he had left behind a system of sound management and a group inextricably integrated into its local community.

Mobbs was leaving in place a new generation of executives to carry the banner and was handing over to his son in a way which would enable Slough Estates still to be regarded as something of a "family firm." The worldwide property portfolio was by now valued at nearly £140 million.

He was also leaving behind him a property market which was, again, finding its feet. No major developers had gone out of business in 1975, interest rates had tumbled, property shares had outperformed the FT index and the investment market was growing stronger.

But the government was again set to send shudders through the market with the publication of its Community Land Bill, which would empower local authorities to buy up all development land at existing use value and, if they wished, to undertake any development themselves. The legislation also envisaged that authorities would eventually have a duty, rather than merely the power, to purchase all development sites.

Alongside the plan was the proposed Development Land Tax, the latest in a line of government-inspired mechanisms for ensuring the community shared in the benefits of increased land values.

Predictions of disaster were quick to follow, with some property men warning that their industry was about to be squeezed to death. John Silkin, the Minister for Land, gave comforting reassurances that there would always be a positive role for the private developer.

As the Community Land Act reached the statute book in November Wallace Mackenzie added to the chorus of criticism. The measures, he claimed, could well lead to a dramatic increase in industrial rents as development land dried up. The inevitable bureaucracy within local authorities, he added, would lead to long delays in making land available.

The real problem for developers was that the individual landowner who stood to benefit from a windfall profit as a result of a change in planning permission would not sell and would simply sit back to await events. The development industry would be deprived of its raw material.

Once again, while the sector smarted, Slough Estates was looking in fit shape for whatever lay ahead. As the business engaged in its year-end review, there was plenty to report. Lettings were confirmed in Chicago, the Cologne estate was progressing, tenants were being signed up for a new project in Montreal and the office development in Brussels was on schedule for completion.

In Sheffield, the company's £9 million Fountain Precinct office and showroom scheme, on offer at a record £5 a sq. ft., was being topped out - even if the ceremony had to be conducted on the first floor because the lifts were not commissioned in time. It would, however, be nearly two years after completion before any space in the 127,000 sq. ft. building - locally dubbed the "ghost block" - was let at £4.50 a sq. ft. The deal followed a well-publicised controversy surrounding the unveiling outside the building of a 12-ft. high stainless steel statue of a horse and nude female rider. The lady was said to bear an uncanny resemblance to Princess Anne.

Group pre-tax profits in 1975 continued their remorseless upwards climb, bringing some cause for celebration among the company's 16,000 ordinary shareholders.

Ownership of the company had spread significantly in the previous few years, so that by the end of 1975 insurance companies and pension funds held between them 15 per cent of the equity. Nearly 20 per cent was held by nominee companies but 42 per cent remained in the hands of individuals.

One month before taking over as chairman Nigel Mobbs gave shareholders, the property industry and the government plenty of food for thought when he published a detailed survey comparing the time and costs involved in developing a typical 50,000 sq. ft. factory in all its markets.

The conclusions, which received considerable publicity, made fascinating - and depressing - reading. They also further helped endorse Nigel Mobbs' reputation as a man whose contribution to the development sector, at 39 years of age, went well beyond the construction of modern industrial and office buildings.

British businessmen, he said, had been regularly criticised for not investing sufficiently and for delaying their investment decisions. In fact Denis Healey, the Chancellor, had chided the business world for its poor performance and had specifically asked business to demonstrate how industrial investment was frustrated in practice.

The detailed 26-page document was the case for the defence. There was, Mobbs acknowledged, some truth in the accusation but the critics had conveniently overlooked the deeply ingrained structural difficulties that impeded investment in the UK. In the six other countries studied, he stressed, the ground rules relating to investment in a new factory were more easily comprehended and quicker to implement.

The statistics said it all. In Britain it took an average 26 weeks to obtain planning permission, in France 16 weeks, Germany 12, Canada and Belgium six, the United States just over four and in Australia just three weeks.

In almost every other aspect of development - from the preparation of architectural drawings to the pricing of projects and actual construction - the British performance was bad. While investment plans in most other countries proceeded with some degree of certainty, those in Britain were invariably subject "to the vagaries of unqualified comment of planning committees" and decisions which could delay or veto important investment.

The document warned that unless businesses found competitive investment conditions available in the UK, new factories would inevitably be diverted to those countries where the building process was easier and cheaper.

In that event "UK employers will be denied the modern working conditions they deserve; industry will be denied the modern and cost effective accommodation they must have and communities will be saddled with continuing industrial dereliction."

The report ended with three basic recommendations. Not surprisingly, Mobbs singled out the abolition of Industrial Development Certificates - a system which he had increasingly attacked in public as being the most inhibiting factor in preventing industrial growth - as an urgent priority.

To Mobbs, industrial policy in the UK had for too long relied too heavily on negative controls and cash incentives as a substitute for a positive industrial strategy. The needs of industry, he emphasised, should not be related to the need to relocate employment opportunities to areas of high unemployment but to the requirement to invest in the most cost effective manner for the good of the economy.

Some areas, the chairman believed, would no longer be able to attract the industry that local interests demanded. Rather than forcing industries into declining regions, new forms of employment should be generated.

Mobbs called for a more controlled form of development plan procedure under which land would be designated by a local authority after consultation with all relevant government departments. The existing and potential needs of industry to locate and expand in the area and the availability of labour and services would all be taken into account.

The report suggested that the Department of the Environment should publish clear and unambiquous building regulations specifically for industrial buildings, claiming that the existing regulations hampered effective industrial building design.

The document also called upon architects to adopt a more pragmatic approach to the design of factories. It said building material suppliers should reduce the wide choice of special products and encourage the use of building components and systems which were readily available from stock. Taken together, it said, the measures could achieve major cost savings and improve industrial investment performance.

The debate took off and was still running at the end of the year when Slough Estates helped organise a conference, presided over by Sir Frank Layfield, QC, to examine the issue.

The subject was still very much alive when, three years later, Nigel Mobbs repeated his investigation. The conclusions were alarmingly familiar; once again, Britain's performance was comparatively poor despite the intervening easing in the criteria governing industrial development certificates. In some areas, the position even seemed to have deteriorated with, for example, the average period for receiving planning permission lengthening from the 26 weeks recorded in 1976 to 35 weeks.

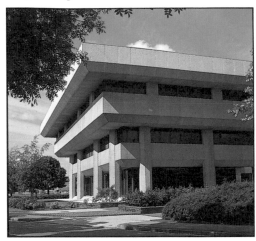

Slough Estates' headquarters building on the Bath Road.

In August 1976, just a few months after retiring and handing over the chair to his son, Gerald Mobbs died suddenly. The tributes were warm and numerous and clearly reflected his wider contribution to the local community which he had helped sustain. The funeral service could only have been at St. Giles' Church, Stoke Poges.

A few weeks before his memorial service in London, six of the nine main board directors left for Canada and the US to mark the 25th anniversary of the foundation by Gerald's father of the Canadian business. In those 25 years the subsidiary had developed more than 2.5 million sq. ft. of industrial space in Toronto and Montreal. There were 227 tenants as well as a land bank providing scope for a doubling of existing floorspace.

Australia, where the first overseas land had been purchased, had failed to show anything like the same progress, though the arrival of Alex Cameron, an outgoing, red-bearded general manager promised to liven things up. Before long the Australian company would make its first move out of Victoria and purchase a prime 14-acre development land in the heart of Sydney.

There was a parting of the ways in France, however. Mackenzie-Hill's appetite had proved too big to be satisfied by the scale of projects which the two partners were undertaking and they severed all links in

December 1976, leaving Slough Estates with three completed investment estates and one undeveloped site in France.

In July 1977, shortly after John Backes, a partner in Kenneth Brown, Baker Baker, one of the company's solicitors, joined the Slough Estates board, Nigel Mobbs was appointed non-executive chairman of Charterhouse Group, replacing John Vaughan.

Redevelopment along the Bath Road. A new building takes shape alongside the Celltech building.

It was to be his first major external business post and signalled a phase in which, with Wallace Mackenzie back in England and managing the business, Mobbs could spend less time at Slough and begin to pursue more fully other business interests.

He was not, however, to quietly slip away. Only a month later he delivered another set of telling home truths for those concerned with property development.

Nigel Mobbs, the third member of his family to run Slough Estates. He joined in 1960, became a director in 1963, managing director in 1971, deputy chairman and then chairman in 1976.

New accommodation at Innovation Park, Hamburg. The group opened a management office to oversee its expanding German activities in 1989.

During the summer the government had published its eagerly-awaited White Paper on a new approach to the challenge of the inner cities, based on the regeneration of industry and the provision of affordable housing. Mobbs did not mince words. The document, he suggested, formed "a useful statement of intent." There was little else in the way of praise.

The government, he claimed, had made the fatal error of assuming that the solutions to the post-war decline of Britain's inner cities lay wholly with the injection of public sector money and on the assumption that local authorities were the natural agencies to tackle the problems.

Many private developers, he said, would be ready to play their part, provided they were allowed to operate under "more sympathetic conditions - another plea for the abolition of Industrial Development Certificates.

The Mobbs report - "The Inner City - a location for Industry?" - provided a detailed account of the evolution of industry in cities and a critique of the problems facing modern centres of population. It also contained sections on the role of planners and the arguments for refurbishment as well as redevelopment.

Among the conclusions was a call for closer partnership between public and private sectors and the identification of the need for new methods of funding inner-city commercial construction via the creation of US-type tax-free development bonds or capital cost allowances. Mobbs also called for the creation of Industrial Improvement Areas within which boards of management would be able to provide a range of financial inducements to promote development.

For too long, Mobbs declared, Britain's cities had been the subject of changing policies and consequent indecision which had contributed to their decline. Positive leadership and partnership was required to breathe life back into Britain's urban heartlands.

The group promptly put its money where its mouth was and soon began work with the local council on an inner city nursery unit scheme in Salford.

The British Property Federation, in which Mobbs had became senior vice-president in 1977, set up its own working party to formulate its response to the government White Paper. Wallace Mackenzie served on the eight-man committee, whose conclusions were remarkably similar to those of his chairman.

The inner city issue would remain the subject of deep political contention. There would be some pockets of progress but generally little evidence on the ground to suggest that the challenge had been comprehensively and effectively met.

Slough Estates, meanwhile, entered 1978 with more than one problem of its own to resolve. The first was the increasing impact of incessant inflation upon the company's system of indexing rents. Given the addition of the five-year review pattern, the formula had worked well but now the index was increasing considerably faster than the lettings market could justify. Tenants began to complain and, like British Tissues, leave.

A decision was taken to cap any indexed increase to a maximum of 10 per cent over the previous year. It was the beginning of the end for a system which had endured for nearly 30 years and which had enabled Slough to maintain the type of consistent performance denied many of its competitors.

The concept of periodic market reviews was taking over and the idea of indexation becoming less relevant. By 1983, the company would face a mounting rebellion among tenants, some of whom formed the Slough Industrial Tenants' Association, over what they described as the "inexorable and constant rise in costs" associated with their tenancies.

Under the banner "United We Stand, Divided We Fall," the Association's members would accuse their landlord of not providing the best possible service and of charging excessively for space and services.

Slough stoutly defended itself, pointing out that the local market supported higher rents. Bill Baker, by then general manager at Slough, would retort: "This image of wicked landlords charging what they like is outdated. If we were not charging a fair rent, the estate would be empty, which would do us no good at all."

Eventually a truce was signed, with every tenant being given the chance to come off the index and agree a market rent with three-yearly reviews. More than 200, nevertheless, preferred to stick with the old system. If no more are granted, the last indexed rent - to National Westminster Bank - will expire in June 2011.

The company, meanwhile, faced a far more complex problem during 1977, a year in which it managed to build one million sq. ft. of new floorspace at home and abroad.

The estate at Slough now comprised 7.5 million sq. ft. of factory and warehouse accommodation, with Mars alone occupying around 900,000 sq. ft., more than twice as much as any other company. More than 800 companies and 27,000 people worked within its boundaries. It had become a manufacturing power-house, embracing the full kaleidoscope of modern industrial activity.

The power station at its heart, which also supplied electricity to 2,000 residential and commercial users outside the estate, was ageing, increasingly inefficient and costing the company, which was struggling to cope with wildly escalating fuel costs, a great deal of money to run. Although it had invested in new generating equipment during the 1960s, the company had simply chosen to replace existing plant and had failed to opt for more advanced equipment with a potentially longer operating life.

The company had never really looked to the power station to provide big profits, though it was expected to be self-financing and anything extra was regarded as something of a bonus. Now, however, it was facing losses on a scale which would badly dent the performance of the core property business. With a major investment decision looming, the old arguments about abandoning the utilities operation altogether once more came to the surface.

The arguments were familiar enough. Slough had become a power generator by an accident of history; a property developer had no real business in providing energy; the running of a power station required a different breed of people and different skills and the two businesses had never really properly dovetailed. The company could save millions by calling it a day.

But how on earth would the company organise the transition to the national grid given the inadequate capacity of the connection and the fact that, during a long and complicated process, all the aces would be in the hands of the power station workers?

To Fergie Wiggin - recruited in 1975 as chief engineer to replace Arthur Park, who had been promoted to general manager - the dilemma had been clear since the day of his arrival and his first tour of the outdated plant. Wiggin, a lifelong power engineer with a commanding knowledge of his subject and a penchant for pushing at the frontiers of new technology, knew that the crunch was coming.

"Investment mistakes had been made in the 1960s. We had changed from coal to heavy fuel oil or gas and when the price of both went through the roof we had nowhere to turn. We faced serious technical and economic problems; it was clear we needed new technology to give us more flexibility in fuel usage and we needed a decision fast."

But the board was not easily convinced, with some members wanting to pull the plug, revert to the grid and withdraw altogether from the utility operations. Others were prepared to consider an ambitious commitment to new generating plant.

According to Wiggin: "They had not recognised that it was almost as difficult to get out of the utilities game as it was to get in, particularly if you do not have an adequate replacement in terms of electricity supply. I told the board it would take five years to withdraw." Faced with that sort of choice the directors had little option but to press on and bring the power station up to date whilst enhancing the capacity of the national grid connection.

"The board realised we could not delay any longer and finally bit the bullet. I decided we had to make a 20-year jump in technology to compensate for earlier wrong decisions."

The company settled for a 23 megawatt heavy duty gas turbine which could also burn heavy fuel oil, a system able to use fuel more economically that any other. Untried anywhere in the UK, similar plant had been employed in the United States for refuse disposal. Mobbs announced that contracts worth £9 million had been placed with John Brown Engineering Gas Turbines and Babcock & Wilcox.

According to Wiggin there were many who believed the decision was highly risky. "People at the Institution of Mechanical Engineers said what we were doing was impossible and the leading gas turbine designer at Rolls-Royce said it could not be done. I never had any doubts, although it was frontier stuff."

The new plant - complete with 275-ft. steel-lined concrete chimney - would be commissioned in 1982 after considerable teething troubles which encouraged the critics to believe that Wiggin had got it wrong. Henry Overshott, who worked alongside him, recalls that it was "a nightmare for the first two years. But we got everything sorted out and the plant did everything Fergie said it would. He stuck his neck out and was proved entirely correct."

Wiggin at once found himself with another fight on his hands. The company was already accusing the British Gas Corporation of abusing its monopoly position by securing excessive profits at its customers' expense. On the commissioning of the new plant, the Corporation imposed a new premium on gas supplies to the company, a decision which Slough challenged, inconclusively, with the European Commission.

The wider debate on the strategic wisdom of remaining in power generation would re-emerge within a decade and again would be resolved with a decision to implement an even bigger investment programme. The eventual privatisation of electricity would add another twist to Slough Estate's continuing involvement in the power business.

13

A QUANTUM LEAP

THE ELECTION on May 3, 1979 of a Conservative government under Margaret Thatcher, Britain's first woman prime minister, was the cause for almost universal celebration within the property sector, one of the pillars of free enterprise.

When Nigel Mobbs reacted to the Tory victory he was speaking not only for his own company. He had been elected President of the British Property Federation and was now also on the board of Barclays Bank.

The electorate's decision, he suggested, represented a watershed in British politics, marking the shift in emphasis from an ideology of intervention to one of opportunity creation. For too long, he said, the "pervasive influence of over-regulation and excess intervention" had increased costs and stifled business initiative.

The new government wasted no time in displaying its market-oriented credentials. If the property market stood for initiative, enterprise and entrepreneurial spirit, then the market should be set free to show its full potential.

At once the rate of Development Land Tax was cut from 80 per cent to 60 per cent, while the payment threshold was also raised. The tax would be scrapped by 1984.

The government also announced the abolition of the Community Land Act which had failed to make much impact but which the development industry feared could soon have started to bite, adding to administrative bottlenecks, increasing bureaucracy and bringing further costly development delays.

A pledge to streamline town planning procedures was also welcomed, as was the ending of exchange controls which, for a company like Slough Estates, would enable its growing programme of overseas development to be funded by the direct transfer of sterling. Funds were immediately injected into Australia.

The government, Mobbs declared, had made "a sound start in their programme of restoring incentives and rewards for risk." He added: "The challenge is there. It is now the turn of business to respond."

In developing an early initiative to encourage the regeneration of industry, Sir Geoffrey Howe, the new Chancellor of the Exchequer, had called on Mobbs for help. While the Tories had been in opposition he had been asked, along with other advisers, to join a policy working party to help develop a new planning initiative. It was to be dubbed an "enterprise zone" - areas within which companies would receive financial incentives to carry out their business.

Companies locating within the zones would receive capital cost allowances and rate-free periods to help stimulate expansion. They were, according to Mobbs, "an experiment in deregulation, the elimination of bureaucratic intervention and the restoration of faith in enterprise."

The zones were soon established after the election victory despite controversy over their effectiveness and claims that they merely encouraged existing businesses to relocate and offered unfair advantage over other companies. They would last for a decade and the debate over the efficacy would outlive them.

Weeks before Margaret Thatcher had entered Downing Street, a newly-confident Slough Estates announced a £24.9 million rights issue to help fund the power station improvements and a £40 million international investment programme planned for the next three years.

The chairman had already spoken of the need for a greater emphasis on new development and now the necessary resources were being lined up. Given the hike in interest rates and decline in stock market values which quickly followed a bout of post-election euphoria, the move was well-timed.

The rights issue had been described in the financial Press as one of "cautious opportunism" but the company itself sounded confident enough.

During the year there would be 300,000 sq. ft. of new floorspace constructed in the UK, with two new sites acquired. One, the purchase from Cadbury Schweppes of a 15-acre site at Hendon, north London, represented the company's first move into the Greater London area.

Overseas the Canadian business would achieve record profits and, over the border, expansion was gathering pace. Around 80 per cent of the floor space was so far let in 33 West Monroe, the 860,000 sq. ft. Chicago office building in which the group had a 25 per cent equity interest. More land was also acquired to expand existing estate developments, including a site at Elk Grove, close to the existing and fully-developed Regent Center Estate.

In Australia 60,000 sq. ft. was added to the four estates now operated and, in Belgium, the group's first major shopping centre was opened in the southern cathedral town of Tournai.

Group pre-tax profits in 1979 leaped by 22 per cent to reach just over £10 million, with rental income touching £20 million. Around the world the group's property portfolio was in the books at £366 million. The business, as it entered the 1980s,could look back on a decade in which earnings and assets had grown progressively. Ten years earlier earnings per share had been just 1p and net assets 21p; now they were 5.57p and 184p respectively.

From 1980 onwards the value of the group's worldwide estate would become the subject of an annual valuation. Until then, and in common with many other property businesses, Slough had only bothered to undertake such an exercise when it believed the outcome would be flattering.

The move came about after a protracted battle with the accountancy profession which had proposed the introduction of a new standard requiring annual depreciation of all freehold and long leasehold properties.

The idea hardly endeared itself to the property owners and the industry went into battle. As president of the British Property Federation Mobbs found himself at the forefront of the fight. At one stage the 20 largest companies informed the Stock Exchange that they would prefer to accept qualified accounts rather than accept the depreciation principle. The Stock Exchange, they said, would simply have to suspend them all.

After a period of prolonged bargaining a deal was struck under which companies would not have to depreciate assets providing they undertook an annual valuation of the property holdings.

Slough Estates first opted for an annual review to be carried out internally and a three-year valuation exercise conducted by independent valuers. The group quickly abandoned the internal valuation procedure and adopted annual external valuations.

With the depreciation saga out of the way the president of the BPF turned his public thoughts to other issues. His reputation as a man who was increasingly prepared, in the words of Wallace Mackenzie, "to stick pins in conventional beliefs," was further enhanced when he decided to challenge as a myth "the spectre of the property developer as a wealthy tycoon, solely concerned with maximising short-terms profits."

In an uncompromising counter-attack on the industry's critics, Mobbs alleged that property development was "largely as a result of ignorance and emotion," misunderstood and widely regarded as being anti-social. He added: "The notion that an investment return has to be made from the use, development and improvement of resources is confused with the spectre of speculation."

Property development, he stressed, was an economic activity

which improved national resources. The developers provided entrepreneurial initiative for new development and investment, in which substantial elements of society - through pension funds and insurance companies - had a direct interest. The implication was clear enough - lay off the property developer.

There were more "pins" in evidence later the same year when Mobbs fired a broadside at "nosey" analysts and "bossy" valuers.

At a conference organised by the Incorporated Society of Valuers, the BPF president acknowledged the need for adequate and reasonable valuation information to be disclosed to the management of the company itself, to investors, creditors and bankers. It was not reasonable, however, to expect management to provide a commentary on valuations or to give details of the spread of yields used in valuing a diversified portfolio.

Some questioners, he asserted, went much too far. Analysts did have their virtues and some of them were polite. But in some cases their search for knowledge was bordering at best on intrusion and at worst impertinence.

While they had a duty to question management, when that function extended to the probity of external valuers advising management then the process was going too far, he added.

Mobbs also suggested that valuers, too, should get their roles straight. They were there to give advice to management, which should then make up its own mind. They should not expect the same treatment as an auditor who was appointed at a company meeting. Those who aspired to a similar pedestal could lose the support of their clients, he warned.

They were themes to which Mobbs would regularly return, the wider role of the estate agency also coming in for an occasional tongue-lashing. Though the Slough Estates chairman would deny he disliked estate agents - he had, after all, been one himself and would eventually be made an honorary member of the Royal Institution of Chartered Surveyors - he would criticise the manner in which they undertook their agency role.

His case rested on the conclusion that agents were attempting to be something they were not. "They have allowed professional ethics to get in the way of marketing competence. The profession is largely driven by wanting to be seen in the same light as, for example, chartered accountants.

"But if they are brokers, which is what they basically are, it comes down to moving space. They are bad on marketing, bad on cold calling and have been pretty amateur about the whole business." Mobbs would concede the agents were getting better but the group, while using their services worldwide, would continue to prefer to organise its own lettings at Slough itself.

The end of 1980 brought pre-tax profits for the year of £11.4 million despite high interest rates worldwide and strong Sterling. The group had further increased its domestic land bank with purchases at Crawley, Walsall and Welwyn Garden City.

The year had also seen departures from the group's normal activities, reflecting its readiness to react to opportunities which arose beyond its mainstream business.

In the United States, for example, it participated with Draper & Kramer in a Chicago housing development. In Australia, it undertook a housing development in the heart of Sydney and took a fee for underwriting a shopping development in the same city. It would later adopt the same role during the development of an office building in Perth.

There were also two new appointments to the main board, which in themselves reflected the group's broadening horizons and the need to bring in some new blood among the non-executive directors.

Paul Orchard-Lisle, a managing partner in Healey & Baker, the London chartered surveyors and agents, was a Marlborough contemporary of Mobbs and widely recognised for his extensive knowledge and experience of the commercial property sector.

800 Fairway Drive - Slough's Ultra-modern business space under Florida's blue skies.

A member of the Council of the Royal Institution of Chartered Surveyors and a future President, Orchard-Lisle's skills were already employed in his capacity as a consultant to the Milton Keynes Development Corporation and the Welsh Development Agency. He was also advising the Environment Secretary on the disposal of new town assets and would become his own firm's senior partner.

The other newcomer was Roger Brooke, a former Foreign Office diplomat who had quickly progressed through the world of corporate finance. He had been deputy managing director of the Industrial Reorganisation Corporation, a main board director of Pearson Group and had most recently been managing director of EMI until the company's merger with Thorn Electrical Industries.

Brooke had the City background which Mobbs believed could greatly benefit the business. Later the same year Brooke would set up

Candover Investments, a business specialising in management buy-out investments and in which Slough Estates would itself eventually participate.

Mobbs himself took on additional outside responsibilities, becoming chairman of the Property Services Agency Advisory Board

This 70,000 sq. ft. office building in Rue Belliard, Brussels, was let to the European parliament and pre-sold to a Belgian pension fund.

charged with advising the Environment Secretary on all aspects of the PSA's activities. He also accepted new directorships within Charterhouse Group.

Continuing recession in 1981 did not prevent the group, now preparing to register as a PLC, from notching up yet another big rise in profits to £13.4 million. Net assets per share stood at 243p against just 79p only five years before.

Stylish offices for Credit Factoring International at Feltham, west London.

The worldwide portfolio was given a year-end value of £475 million. Of the group's total international portfolio, nearly 75 per cent of it by value was now located in the UK, generating £22 million of the total

£30 million annual rent roll. North America represented the group's second largest market in terms of value, with Europe next and Australia just behind. Mobbs was confident enough to predict that the rental income in the UK should increase by at least 55 per cent over the next five years.

The group maintained progress during the following 12 months, despite the continuing difficulties being experienced by all the economies within which it operated.

Nearly half a million sq. ft. of new floorspace went up in Britain under the Slough Estates banner, although the total vacancy rate rose to nearly 10 per cent.

In the United States, where high interest rates and an over-supply of property made the going tough, Slough Parks opened its own office in Chicago to work alongside the partnership with Draper & Kramer but also to seek out its own investment opportunities. Bill Pickrell, a Draper & Kramer man, was appointed president.

Elsewhere, business for the group was generally hard-going but a spot of excitement arose during 1982, the year in which Nigel Mobbs followed his father and grandfather to become High Sheriff of Buckinghamshire.

It came when F W Woolworth, the ailing retail chain, found itself on the receiving end of a £310 million bid, which included the purchase of the 52 per cent controlling interest held in the ailing stores group by its American parent. A consortium named Paternoster Stores, put together by Charterhouse Japhet and Rowe & Pitman, stepped forward with a bold plan to turn the business around. Given the state of the business and the lack of retailing experience among those involved in the deal, many observers regarded the move as suicidal.

Paternoster's largest shareholders included Norwich Union, the Merchant Navy Officers' Pension Fund, Robert Fleming, Prudential Assurance and Charterhouse Group.

John Beckett, a former chief executive of British Sugar, was named as chairman and, among the non-executive directors were Alan Hurst-Brown, former senior partner of Rowe & Pitman, and Nigel Mobbs from Charterhouse. His knowledge of property would clearly prove handy in a business operating 950 High Street stores as well as a national network of Do-It-Yourself centres.

Despite the awesome task confronting the new owners, the business would be revived and renamed Kingfisher Group. Mobbs and Hurst-Brown remained non-executive directors.

Following pre-tax profits of just over £16 million in 1982, the group took another stride forwards in the following 12 months when profits exceeded £20 million for the first time. Demand for space in Slough's properties around the world, now valued at £515 million, was rising.

The pattern of steady but unspectacular progress was, however, about to change and Mobbs would find himself at the centre of a deal which would prove to be the most important to date in the history of Slough Estates.

For years Ron Diggens and Gerald Mobbs had casually discussed the possibility that, one day, the Allnatt business and Slough Estates might arrange the perfect marriage; it appeared to be an entirely logical prospect.

Despite the earlier unfortunate history, Diggens and Nigel Mobbs had enjoyed an increasingly warm relationship.

Diggens and Leslie Smith, the blunt Yorkshireman regarded by his colleagues as an unrivalled workaholic, had separately continued to build up their impressive property investment business. By 1962, the year in which it was publicly floated as Allnatt London Properties, their business embraced 39 different companies.

Going public had made millionaires of both of them but, despite their wealth, they lived modestly and never sought publicity.

Under their tenacious and tireless management, the enterprise had subsequently flourished, developing unsophisticated, simple-to-maintain industrial property on a "bespoke" basis to meet the needs of individual tenants. Like Slough Estates, they rarely had to go out and look for industrial tenants.

Visit of Secretary of State for Energy, Nigel Lawson, in 1982, to open the new gas turbine/waste heat boiler at the Slough Estates power station. Nigel Mobbs is on his left and Fergie Wiggin, general manager utilities services, on his right.

The two men had developed for themselves a reputation as a formidable duo who knew their business like the back of their hands. By the early 1980s Smith was chairman in place of Diggens, whose health was failing but who remained by far the largest shareholder.

Diggens now increasingly believed the time had come to seek a partner to carry forward a business which was no longer sparking as it had done in the 1960s and 1970s. He told colleagues: "I have had enough. Where do we go from here?"

Ramsay Hack was Allnatt's finance director. "Ron wanted to make sure that the company was safely merged with another property company. His decision had nothing to do with the state of the market and nor was he influenced by any outside pressures. It came down to a personal decision to secure the future of the company and the position of its shareholders."

Allnatt sought the advice of Baring Brothers, its merchant bank, which counselled the company not to rush into any deal with a favourite partner but to establish how many suitors might be interested and to pursue each carefully.

There was little doubt, however, which suitor Diggens preferred. According to Norman Hartford, another Allnatt director at the time: "Diggens was absolutely convinced that a merger with Slough was in Allnatt's best interest. Leslie Smith was more inclined to see what other options existed. There was no split within the Allnatt board, however."

Though other companies did show an interest, it was with Slough Estates that serious discussions began shortly before Christmas 1983.

The talks, aimed at finding a mutually acceptable basis for an exchange of shares, were amicable and business-like, though at one stage a deal did appear to be at risk. For a brief period what was supposed to be a friendly merger began to take on the appearance of a hostile bid. Mobbs recalls that Allnatt's advisers behaved as though they were being employed to fight off an unwanted approach.

"We eventually got so frustrated that we made a public announcement to the effect that the whole thing was off, basically to let Ron see that his team was jeopardising the deal."

Given that such a declaration could have tempted another suitor to come forward with a bigger offer, the tactic was not without its risks But Slough Estates was determined not to pay too much to win the prize.

After a spell of final horse-trading - in which an initial offer was rejected and then followed by another - a deal was struck for a three-way merger between Slough Estates, Allnatt London Properties and Guildhall Property, in which Allnatt now held 39 per cent of the equity.

Shareholders were offered a share-swap or cash alternative in a package which reflected Slough's antipathy to the idea of a significant dilution in assets per share. Diggens became the largest single shareholder in Slough Estates, which was still not dominated by any large institutional shareholders. He was joined on the board by Smith.

The £140 million merger, accompanied by a £32 million loan stock issue, brought with it £157 million of assets, achieving overnight what Slough Estate's preferred philosophy of organic growth would have taken decades to achieve.

There was more than seven million sq. ft. of investment property, much of it in the Park Royal area of west London, together with 70 acres of development land and a £14 million rent roll. The merged group began life with a combined portfolio valued at £689 million and a net asset value of £460 million. Seventy per cent of it was located in the south of England. Overseas property accounted for 22 per cent of the total portfolio value.

The deal was arranged to leave virtually no dilution in earnings per share and also provided welcome tax advantages.

Ramsay Hack, along with other senior executives at Allnatt, was to find himself out of a job because Slough Estates already had its own finance director in the shape of Derek Millis. But he believed the merger to be "the happiest and most logical outcome." Allnatt, he stressed, had almost reached the end of its operational life.

Mobbs told shareholders, who in January 1984 gave approval to the deal and an associated increase in share capital from £65 million to £84.8 million, that the merger provided considerable scope for new development and redevelopment, as well as a strong financial base on which to construct future expansion plans. He added, with some cause for satisfaction: "The combined group will be the largest industrial property development and investment company in Europe and, possibly, the world."

The merger gave Slough Estates plenty of work to do as it began to integrate properties and management. Some buildings were old but very well located, offering income-producing land banks capable of future redevelopment. Though the Allnatt assets were undeniably attractive, they were invariably scattered and not grouped together in Slough Estates-style.

Joe Harding remembers: "It was all so very fragmented. They did not have many large estates, half a dozen properties here and half a dozen there. But it was an extremely worthwhile acquisition and signalled the start of a marked thrust forward on the development side of the business."

Within a year disposals from the Allnatt portfolio had raised nearly £3 million. The job of weeding out, selling and redeveloping would last for most of the remainder of the decade.

Slough Estates left 1983 behind it, having broken through the £20 million pre-tax profit barrier for the first time and having appointed to the board a man whose role would be to help ensure that the group's new potential was realised.

Mobbs announced that Robert Phipps had left, to be replaced by Roger Carey, the development director responsible for development and marketing. He was also joined on the board by Sir Donald Maitland, the former Permanent Under Secretary at the Department of Energy.

Maitland was a former Foreign Office man who had become chief press secretary to prime minister Edward Heath after serving as British Ambassador to Libya. He went on to become Ambassador and the UK's permanent representative to the European Community.

Carey, a Black Country grammar school boy, had been with MEPC since 1970, for a while running its operations in Ireland and looking after some of its European activities. He had become unhappy on his return to London and jumped at reports that a board vacancy existed at Slough Estates.

Dubbed "a self-styled empire builder" by his former boss, Carey was the consummate property developer, ever-anxious to find new opportunities, stitch together projects and get on with the next challenge. But Carey's expertise did not extend to the industrial property sector and he knew little more about Slough Estates.

His new employer certainly gave him something to get on with. "There had never been a strong focus on development at Slough; there was no such thing as portfolio balance. It was 98 per cent industrial with a few other bits and pieces added on," he remembers.

Carey believed that the development process under Bill Baker, director of estates operations, and Bernard Rimmer, had been pursued largely on an ad-hoc basis. However, earlier planning for new developments had been constrained by restrictions which impinged on new industrial building work and the demand for space.

Carey began to do things differently. "In the old days the development function began the day anyone looked at a piece of available land and ended the day the tenant signed the lease. After my arrival my department began to decide what went where. The design and construct operation would then get a brief and the completed property would be handed over as a created investment to the investment division."

Subsequently the design and construct activities would be fully integrated into Carey's development and trading division. Rimmer became general manager.

It was not just a matter of re-allocating responsibilities. Slough Estates had to water down its overwhelming dependence on industrial property and take retail and office markets more seriously than it had done in the past.

Its selection, therefore, to develop jointly with British Rail Property Board the 220,000 sq. ft. Howard Centre, a shopping and office complex at Welwyn Garden City, was not only particularly encouraging but indicative of a newly-emerging approach to its business.

The retail sector was a notoriously hard nut to crack, especially in terms of large-scale town centre developments, where local authorities were looking for developers with proven experience. According to Mobbs: "You could not tell a council that you had not done any big retail schemes but that you would like to cut your teeth on their town centre."

Slough had, however, made the breakthrough, even if the project would prove to be complex and fraught with difficulties, forcing the group on more than one occasion before the centre opened in the autumn of 1990 to wonder whether it had been wise to pursue the retail sector with such determination.

The momentum was maintained in 1984, underpinned by a £40 million debenture issue offering the benefit of long-term fixed interest finance. The enlarged business constructed nearly 900,000 sq. ft. of new floorspace around the world.

In Britain new construction was planned or underway at Birmingham, High Wycombe, Reading, Swindon and Slough. The group, in partnership with Prudential Assurance, was also selected to develop a 200,000 sq. ft. freeport adjoining Birmingham airport. In another joint venture it teamed up with the Midland Bank Pension Trust to begin a pre-funded 100,000 sq. ft. project at Feltham, west London.

With the benefit of Allnatt's contribution, the investment portfolio in 1984 was valued at £737 million and group pre-tax profits rose to nearly £35 million. The group's net worth, for the first time, exceeded half a billion pounds.

The utility operation remained a blackspot, however, turning in more losses and convincing the management that urgent action was required to improve its viability. Redundancies appeared inevitable, the entire future of the power station looked to be in serious doubt and the workforce threatened a fight.

But with the 1983 Energy Act permitting private electricity generators like Slough Estates to sell surplus power into the national grid, the group would again decide not to withdraw. Instead, it would embark on a plan to further enhance its connection to the national electricity supply network.

The group also began dipping its toes into the property trading market, an area which, traditionally, it had been happy to leave to companies more readily inclined to trust their futures to the short-term vagaries of the market place.

Slough Estates had not jettisoned its traditional caution but had come to recognise that, by not participating in trading activity, it was being bypassed by those with opportunities to offer. By entering the market the group would at least expose itself to a wider choice of projects which could be tackled as investment or trading opportunities or simply rejected. The philosophy could also prove attractive in its overseas markets, where less dynamic rental growth patterns might be augmented by trading activities.

The bones of a portfolio of trading projects were put together and, within a short time, the group's domestic trading operations would be gathered together under the Guildhall Properties umbrella and would make an increasingly significant, if volatile, contribution to profits.

Further afield both North America and Australia turned in better results in 1984, aided by favourable exchange rates. The Australian business completed the first 132,000 sq. ft. phase of its Silverwater Estate in Sydney and began work on the next.

In Canada, as a 122,000 sq. ft. office building was completed and began to fill up with tenants, the group was preparing to part company with its Ajax estate. It had by now become apparent that the main thrust of development in Toronto was on the other side of town with the eastern suburbs suffering from lack of infrastructure and high local tax rates.

It was decided to sell Ajax rather than persevere with its development and improvement. It was disposed of to a consortium and the funds re-invested in more profitable loocations ariound the city.

Elsewhere in North America projects were underway in the United States as far afield as San Diego, Chicago and Florida, while others were progressing in Brussels and Paris.

Slough Estates really was beginning to look like a dynamic, international business.

14

AN UNEXPECTED SETBACK

WITH ROGER Carey firmly in place, Nigel Mobbs now began to search for someone to help complete the new-look management line-up which would take the group towards the 1990s and beyond.

Wallace Mackenzie, after 36 years with the company, would be retiring from his post as group managing director and confidante to the chairman in the middle of 1986. Other long-serving executives would soon be following him, making way for a younger tier of top management.

Mobbs, who was again beginning to spend more of his time on group affairs and less pursuing his other business interests, wanted a broad administrator and head of operations. Graeme Elliot fitted the bill.

Elliot, a Cambridge-educated chartered accountant who was born in the United States and had worked around the world, had spent the previous 17 years with RTZ and had returned from Los Angeles to London.

At 43 he knew little about property but had excellent international banking contacts and the sort of broad business experience which Slough Estates now required at the top. Mobbs was intent upon changing the culture of the business, to further augment its property interests. Elliot, who was to become executive vice-chairman, seemed ideal.

His first impressions were telling: "It all looked very conservative and rather slow moving. It was a big contrast to RTZ with its young and thrusting meritocracy."

Part of Elliot's job, as set down by Mobbs, was to help develop a new second leg to the business. The chairman wanted positive and significant diversions from its bread-and-butter business, now split into four divisions in the UK.

An indication of the group's readiness to embark on the new strategy had already become apparent during 1985. It had, albeit in a very small way, begun to invest in what Mobbs would describe as "entrepreneurial businesses."

The first such venture involved a commitment to invest £9.7 million in Charterhouse Group International of New York, a spin-off from the Charterhouse Group which specialised in managing leveraged buy-out deals. Following a change of ownership it became known as Charterhouse USA, or CHUSA.

To those who raised eyebrows at a property development group participating in such arrangements, Mobbs emphasised that the move was quite logical and complementary as leveraged deals were not at all dissimilar to those struck in the property world.

The balance sheet, he insisted, could sustain some alternative investments and the leveraged buy-out business could provide useful returns at a time when property was performing below par.

Before long the group would be participating in similar deals in the UK through Roger Brooke's Candover operations. It initially committed itself to invest £2.5 million in Electra Candover Direct Investment and later took a 10 per cent equity stake worth £25 million in a subsequent Candover fund.

The group also acquired a 20 per cent stake in CHUSA as well as investing in another CHUSA vehicle called Charterhouse Equity Partners and in the CHUSA Recovery Fund, set up to revive financially troubled businesses. Further non-property investments would soon follow.

Slough Estates made another uncharacteristic investment at home, taking a four per cent stake in Stock Conversion, the property investment group founded by Joe Levy, one of property's post-war giants. The plan was to raise its stake further but was thwarted when another property company purchased one quarter of Stock Conversion before selling it on to the Peninsular and Oriental Steam Navigation Company. P & O then made a successful bid for the business. Slough Estates sold its own holding for a profit of just over £1 million.

The group did, however, complete one successful corporate acquisition in 1985 when it paid £36 million for Helmlace, a private investment and development business under American ownership.

The company, brought to Slough Estates by Drivers Jonas, the London surveyors and agents, held development sites in the City of London, at Basingstoke and close to Reading. The purchase of Helmlace, which also owned properties in Glasgow, Leeds, Newcastle and York, provided some useful opportunities to augment the group's development portfolio.

The most significant opportunity lay in the so-called Winnersh Triangle at Reading, a parcel of development land close to the M4 motorway. Part of the site had already been developed by Wimpey Property Holdings to provide 800,000 sq. ft. of warehouse-style units occupied by names such as ICL, Hewlett Packard and AEG Telefunken and Mars.

In early 1985, however, Helmlace had moved in to acquire 65 acres of the 100-acre estate from Wimpey and, almost at once, approached Slough Estates, offering itself for sale.

The new owners of the Winnersh site decided the remaining undeveloped land lent itself to a high-tech industrial park and threw out a challenge to architects by staging a design competition for the first stage of the development.

It was the start of a project which would prove very demanding in terms of group resources. The concept would also be altered to reflect changing requirements among tenants, although an ensuing oversupply in the local office market meant that, by 1990, as work began on a new speculative phase of mixed office and warehousing space, part of the office accommodation constructed earlier was still unoccupied.

By the end of 1985, as Ron Diggens retired, Slough Estates worldwide had nearly two million sq. ft. of new floorspace under construction and had, over the previous 12 months, leased about the same amount of accommodation. Pre-tax profits were just under £40 million.

Surrey Quays in London Docklands, one of three shopping centres jointly acquired with Tesco in early 1989.

The group would again don its acquisitive hat during 1986, a year in which 1.5 million sq. ft. of new floorspace was added to an investment portfolio now valued at £851 million. Nearly £50 million was spent during the year on acquiring future development opportunities.

The business was increasingly keen to step up its exposure to the retail development market at a time when a buoyant economy had led to a consumer boom and busy High Streets. The Welwyn Garden City development was its only significant retail project and that was still only just getting underway.

A telephone call from Rowe & Pitman, the group's joint stockbrokers with Sheppards, would change all that. Mobbs was told that an interest in Bredero Properties - a Dutch-owned developer primarily involved in retail projects and increasingly well regarded for its high-quality town centre schemes - was up for sale.

The group jumped at what appeared to be an excellent opportunity to buy overnight a track record and management experience in retail development which rarely became available on the market.

Model of the 654,000 sq. ft. Centre West office and shopping complex being developed by Bredero at Hammersmith, west London.

Bredero, headed by Alan Chisholm, a tough and highly competent development man, was heading for record profits of nearly £3 million in 1986 and had an active development programme underway.

The business had started in Britain in 1974 building homes in Scotland but quickly expanded into the retail market. There were large shopping centre schemes such as the Ashley Centre in Epsom and the first

Premises for Sony, developed at St. Ouen, Paris.

stage of a retail centre in St. Albans already under its belt. There were more lined up in Aberdeen, High Wycombe and Nottingham, while the potential for the development of the Centre West site in Hammersmith, west London, as a major office and retail centre was substantial. Bredero's reputation was, justifiably, riding high.

There was no prevarication on the part of Slough Estates, which promptly purchased a 49.5 per cent stake - subsequently increased to

52.2 per cent - for £15.7 million.

The acquisition meant that Slough Estates now had the foothold in the retail development market that it had wanted although it would continue to pursue separately some of its own shopping schemes.

After the Bredero deal Mobbs summed up the group's strategy to be orchestrated by a board of directors with more new faces on it. Derek Millis was about to retire as finance director, to be replaced by Derek Wilson, who had joined from Cadbury Schweppes, having worked previously for Cavenham and Wilkinson Sword. Peter Johnston also arrived to assume responsibility for the UK property investment portfolio after spells with Lloyds of London, Sun Alliance Insurance and MEPC.

Their chairman emphasised that the primary strategic aim for the business was not only to enhance and expand its industrial property investment and development activity but also to widen the portfolio with the addition of new office, retail and retail warehouse park projects.

The group, he said, would continue to concentrate on improving the quality of its revenue-producing portfolio by positive estate management, the sale of low-performing assets and the modernisation of buildings already owned. Mobbs stressed that Slough Estates would also maintain its interest in the sort of entrepreneurial businesses in which it had already invested.

In 1986 pre-tax profits rose to just under £50 million, reflecting increased development activities in all the company's operating markets. A total of 1.5 million sq. ft. of new industrial, retail and office space was added to the worldwide investment portfolio. In addition, nearly £50 million was spent on acquiring new projects for future portfolio development. By the end of the year another 1.5 million sq. ft. was under construction.

During the year it took the strategy another step forward by entering joint ventures intended to take advantage of the depressed state of the US oil and gas markets. The investments, through SDK Industrial Parks, the Draper & Kramer joint venture, entailed the acquisition of businesses in Texas and Oklahoma at substantial discounts before recapitalising them in order to put them back on their feet.

Under the joint ventures SDK would become significant shareholders in two independent energy companies and hold an interest in 160 oil and gas producing wells.

But however potentially interesting or profitable the non-property investments appeared, their relative importance in the scale of things became abundantly clear when placed alongside the mainstream activities of Slough Estates.

In the middle of 1986, the company and its chairman would receive another accolade. Nigel Mobbs followed in his grandfather's footsteps and was awarded a knighthood. It was seen as fitting recognition for his broad contribution to the world of commerce and his role in advising government on a range of issues.

By the end of 1987, the group's international portfolio had been valued at just over £1 billion. It comprised 27 million sq. ft. of industrial, office and retail space occupied by 2,000 businesses. Of the total, 7.4 million sq. ft. were on the original estate. There were more than 800 acres of land worldwide awaiting development and the group had a forward development programme in the UK alone of £430 million.

Abroad, the group had built 1.3 million sq. ft. of accommodation during the year, acquired land in the USA, Canada, Australia, Belgium and Germany, sold properties around the world worth £47 million and planned another £120 million worth of development.

As the property market in Britain enjoyed buoyant demand, improving rental rates and strong investment activity, the group acquired, through a jointly-owned company with Tesco, three fully-leased shopping centres to help provide a strong income flow. The schemes, with a combined floor area of more than 750,000 sq. ft., had an initial market value of around £80 million. The business also formed a partnership with Bredero to buy from Grosvenor Developments the Lewisham Centre in south London, a 350,000 sq. ft. prime retail shopping centre in need of selective refurbishment.

Trading activities, intended to heighten the group's profile in the market place and make a contribution to earnings, were also stepped up under Clive Handford, who joined the group as managing director of Guildhall Properties.

The group's rapid progress would again be reflected in ever-bigger numbers. Pre-tax profits in 1988, including a sizeable contribution from trading activities, rose to £75.1 million. Earnings per share rose by nearly 22 per cent, net assets per share by nearly 38 per cent.

There were other milestones. The group finally divested itself of the Altona estate in Melbourne which some believed Sir Noel Mobbs would have been well advised to leave to the tiger snakes.

At the same time, however, its commitment to Australia - where some relaxation of long-standing controls governing foreign interest in property now made life easier - was maintained with the purchase of 38 acres of land in the suburbs of Melbourne. The group also acquired a 70 per cent stake in Pacific Property Investments, a developer of high-quality industrial space in Sydney.

In Canada the group bought more land in Toronto and Montreal, purchased three office schemes in Chicago and Florida and there was continuing expansion in Europe.

By the end of 1989 Slough Estates had made further enormous advances. Its position as one of Britain's largest and most successful property development and investment groups was secure.

It had, however, finally decided to extricate itself from the merchandising operation which had been started by Sir Noel as a device to help the company's tenants prosper. Slough Products, which had experienced a chequered financial history but which, by the end of the 1980s, was again making useful profits was sold off to Standex Corporation, an engineering products supplier.

For Slough Estates, which no longer believed that a business primarily selling casters formed an appropriate adjunct to its mainstream operations, Canada was now, exclusively, a property market.

There was another non-property activity, however, which would continue. After yet another review of the strategic case for maintaining ownership of the power station, the group embarked on a further £40 million plant modernisation programme. The new plant was designed to meet exacting environmental standards and to improve operating efficiency. Once again the power station would be able to burn coal, heavy fuel oil, gas, kerosene or even refuse pellets, whichever was the cheapest.

With the privatisation of the electricity supply industry enacted in late 1990, Slough Estates was to find itself deeply involved in complex negotiations with the Department of Energy to safeguard its position as the principal supplier of power to its own tenants.

The group began the last decade of the 20th Century owning properties in seven countries. Its unbroken profits record was maintained with pre-tax figures up another 16 per cent to £87.3 million, while earnings, dividends and net asset values all rose handsomely.

The previous 12 months had seen the construction of more than two million sq. ft. of new property, two-thirds of its overseas. The group was committed to spend £400 million over the next three years on new projects and it calculated that the cost involved in developing its entire international land bank would exceed £1 billion.

In the UK the group's investment portfolio, spread among 45 locations, now produced an annual rent roll of nearly £87 million.

The improving quality of the UK portfolio, now under the watchful eye of Hugh Thomson, had enabled average rentals to grow by one-third in the previous 12 months.

The development division, where Bernard Rimmer and John Keogan were supporting Roger Carey, completed 666,000 sq. ft. of new property and had a further 656,000 sq. ft. under construction.

In Germany the group opened a management office in Dusseldorf and Dr. Udo Titz was appointed general manager of a business busy selling off some properties and developing others to take their place. A management office was also opened in Paris in early 1991 headed by Philip Loysel.

In the United States a number of development properties were acquired and new development partnerships created. During 1990 Marshall Lees, the group's general manager responsible for corporate planning, would take over as President of the US subsidiary, which now had property interests from coast-to-coast.

At home the company had also invested nearly £8 million to take an initial 20 per cent stake in London and Paris Property Group, a private company specialising in office development in around London. The new shareholder's finances would help fund a £100 million development programme.

But while the London and Paris equity stake and the Tishman partnership appeared promising, another US joint venture was to prove disastrous. In conjunction with CHUSA the group established Charter Hendrix Realty, another vehicle for converting poorer properties into higher-value investments attractive to institutional owners.

The partnership acquired the 400,000 sq. ft. Sanwa Bank building in downtown Los Angeles at a time when prices were peaking and shortly before the market took a dramatic turn for the worse.

The group, as a result, disclosed provisions for Charter Hendrix of £8.5 million in its 1990 half-yearly accounts. Other write-offs for possible trading losses helped drive down profits from £44.4 million to £35.3 milion, a performance which left the City extremely disappointed.

The faltering halfway performance was not to be the end of the story. The group's worst expectations would be borne out in full-year figures which would bring to an end successive decades of rising profits.

However temporarily, Slough's achievements were also to be interrupted by the impact of a deteriorating domestic economy. Continuing high interest rates, diminishing rental growth and weakening property values took their toll.

For once Slough Estates could not buck the trend. The group's single faltering step was, ironically, certain to arouse interest within the City and the financial Press, both of which were only too accustomed to the group's predictable progression from strength to strength.

The newspaper headlines for the half-year figures had an unfamiliar ring. "Slump reaches Slough" said The Times. Somewhat predictably Today opted for "New Slough of Despond." According to the London Evening Standard "Even rock-solid property investment companies are being hit by the slump."

Slough Estates itself brushed off the disappointment as a temporary set-back, though it provided a useful reminder to the business that it could never take its success for granted.

The group would press on with the objectives which lay behind its business: to maintain real growth in net earnings per share, dividends per share and net assets per share - growth which had to exceed the underlying rate of inflation to provide real value to those who invested in the group.

In order to achieve them, it would maintain a small but professional management team, remain active and opportunistic, redevelop existing property assets into better quality space, develop selectively in different types of property and continue to hedge political and economic risks by operating overseas.

The formula had stood the test of time and Slough Estates had no reason to believe that it could not and would not provide it with the basis for a new era of successful growth.

15

UNDER THE SPOTLIGHT

NEARLY 70 years after its formation Slough Estates had received more than one uncomfortable reminder that its past achievements and consistent progress provided no guarantee that the future would necessarily go according to plan.

During the summer of 1989 the Stock Market was suddenly alive with rumours that the business was being eyed up by a potential predator. Its shares began to outperform the market in expectation.

A favourite suggestion was that a bid, if any, would emanate from overseas, probably from one of the vast corporate conglomerates with resources available on a scale which could fairly easily digest one of Britain's largest property companies; all eyes were on the United States and possibly Japan.

The City enjoyed the guessing game and eagerly anticipated some action. Who could be interested? What sort of company could take over Slough Estates without wrecking its own portfolio balance? What could a new owner make of the business without the management which had built it up? Or perhaps it would simply be broken up and sold off in bits to the highest bidders?

Would Nigel Mobbs fight to the death to preserve a business which, since its inception, had been entrusted to the care of his family? Or would he, as a man dedicated to the best interests of his shareholders, simply be forced to succumb to an offer to which opposition could not be justified?

As the speculation buzzed about the Square Mile and triggered off increasingly fanciful gossip around the industry, the group itself was left to wait and ponder on its fate.

In the event the rumours died away. No approaches and no bids materialised and the spotlight was switched off. But whatever the future holds for Slough Estates - as takeover target or, indeed, the instigator of its own ambitious expansionary bids - the group will continue to be driven by its primary strategy - the pursuit of continued real growth in assets and earnings via the development, acquisition, ownership and management of commercial property.

Since its earliest days Slough had adhered to the philosophy that, by leasing or renting premises, companies can avoid the necessity of tying up capital which could be more usefully employed in developing other aspects of their business.

It is a view not universally shared by industrialists but one which appeals to sufficient numbers to ensure Slough Estates has nearly always had a ready demand for its product. It is also an idea which Slough itself has helped establish and popularise in some of its overseas markets.

Despite its image as an innately conservative property company which rarely excites the taste buds of those whose job it is to monitor and comment upon its progress, Slough has invariably managed to combine a pioneering approach to its business with a steady and deliberative style which has enabled it to escape the fate of many other contemporary property businesses.

Whether it was to develop a single, serviced manufacturing community, its readiness to branch out and seek new markets overseas or to innovate with mechanisms like index-linked rents, Slough Estates has always tried to stay abreast of an ever-changing market and of the requirements of its tenants.

It is doubtful, however, whether it can ever completely escape its rather lacklustre image given the very nature of its core business. Industrial property, however efficient, modern and environmentally sensitive, is not widely credited with the same level of corporate "sex appeal" attached to some other sectors of the business, or indeed property, world.

At the beginning of 1990 a group of stockbrokers met privately for dinner in Westminster to discuss Slough Estates, part of an exercise sanctioned by the company to prepare the ground for a fresh campaign to improve its image and to boost investor relationships. The meal gave Slough Estates plenty of food for thought.

Once again, the group found itself on the rack - condemned for being unexciting, unimaginative and predictable while simultaneously pilloried for trying to wean itself away from what it did best in order to diversify into new areas of business.

The views, predictably enough, were hardly welcomed back in Slough, though they unquestionably underlined the scale of the challenge facing the group in promoting and explaining itself better to its audience.

If the group could take some comfort from the fact it was not alone in being criticised - various other publicly-quoted property companies were variously described as "dangerous," "paranoid" and "monolithic" - it believed it had excellent grounds for rejecting many of the criticisms aimed at it.

The group accepts the conservative label, though it deems the description a compliment not a criticism. As Wallace Mackenzie puts it: "Is that not a characteristic of all companies that prosper and survive? When you have been in business as long as us, you become conservative because there is a great deal to conserve."

Nigel Mobbs acknowledges that his business has never been fully understood in the City but is, unsurprisingly, also ready to query the credentials of some of his City critics.

"We have always been seen as slightly boring and lacking in excitement but it is partially a reflection of the underlying business. We do not have the 'pazzazz' associated with some property businesses and are not so often involved in headline-making deals. A new building at Slough is rarely regarded as news and the fact that we have rebuilt a lot of the estate is not particularly visible.

Industrial space for Flexible Hose Supplies on Edinburgh Avenue, Slough Trading Estate.

"Many of today's investment analysts are more susceptible to today's glamour than tomorrow's underlying long-term performance. They are too influenced by the asset side of the business and do not pay enough attention to the longer-term cash flow position."

For Slough Estates, the strength of its all-important cash flow comes from the diversity of its tenant base and of the location of its property. Its asset base increasingly enables it to use international markets to secure creative and innovative funding schemes, arranged on terms which further enhance development performance. Peter Hardy, a director of S.G. Warburg Securities, who has followed the property sector and, through Warburg's Rowe & Pitman offshoot, advised Slough Estates for many years, argues that the group is not as conservative as it once was. Even so, it remains "immensely secure."

He adds: "The City is terrible in appreciating this sort of company. They go down to Slough on a lousy day and look around the estate and are not always impressed. But it is a goldmine and the group has a stunningly good record."

The "goldmine" at Slough, given a market value of about £600 million, remains at the heart of the group's regional and international activities.

By the end of 1990 the estate comprised 7.7 million sq. ft. of floorspace out of a worldwide inventory of 31 million sq. ft., just over half of which was in the UK. Although the Peerless public house in Buckingham Avenue is held on a 900-year lease - originally granted to Taylor Walker as an inducement to take it over - the group retains the freehold ownership of every building and every square foot of estate land at Slough. According to Nigel Mobbs: "That is the way it is going to stay."

The latest generation of business accommodation at Winnersh, close to Reading.

The trading estate accommodates 430 of the group's 2,100 tenants, a number gradually reducing as the average space occupied by each tenant increases. They are housed in properties which still include basic industrial workspace but which also embrace the latest generation of high-quality accommodation, within which many of the old barriers between office and industrial space have been removed.

A distinctive office development for Coopers & Lybrand at Notting Hill, Melbourne.

The estate's long history has inevitably precluded it from providing the sweeping landscaped surroundings in which some of the latest generation of business parks are set. But a continuing programme of renewal - carried out by a core portfolio operation within the group's development division - has ensured it remains among the most popular business locations in the south east.

By 1990 the controlled programme of rebuilding, modernisation and of careful tenant selection, all orchestrated over the previous decade in a way not previously contemplated, had created a business centre which amounts to a microcosm of British industry.

The days when the estate was crammed with engineering and automotive companies has long since gone; the age of the service industry has arrived and nowhere can it be more readily identified than at Slough, where oily workshops have given way to squeaky-clean distribution centres and computer complexes.

Graeme Elliot emphasises: "We intend to keep the estate as varied as possible, housing all manner of tenants. This is not just for commercial reasons but because we genuinely feel it is important to maintain a good cross-section of industrial and business activities. We never want it to become an office park and will insist on retaining a good mix."

The company acknowledges that not all tenants at Slough are of the highest quality, though the vacancy rates remain consistently low, along with tenant turnover. It believes that it has some obligation to encourage new businesses to get underway.

Nigel Mobbs sums up the Slough estate: "It is a unique investment, nearly 500 acres of income-producing property providing a complete range of buildings, both in terms of size and type. We have companies like Mars, with nearly one million sq. ft., and we also provide start-up space for small businesses. The diversity is so huge that we can accommodate the odd failure - and the small ones often grow very big.

"Every time there is a rent review, it goes straight to the bottom line. It does not make sense to do anything aggressive to a lot of the property other than collect rents as they fall due. Neither are we anxious to acquire a reputation as a landlord who kicks out tenants.

"In some cases we are reviewing leases for another 20 years at rents which do not appear particularly exciting. But they are damned good, considering the sunk cost in the buildings concerned, and we have one hell of a secure rent flow."

The process of regeneration on the estate is set to continue, possibly made easier by the prospect of the creation of a simplified planning zone within its boundaries. Provided the company operates within certain parameters agreed with the council, much of the planning "red tape" which can frustrate development progress will be lifted from specific locations within the estate.

But as its unfolding history shows, Slough Estates is no longer merely the owner of a unique trading estate to the west of London. Its portfolio of warehousing and industrial property, of offices and shops and of development land stretches across Europe and beyond to North America and Australia.

The group's international activities, too, have given rise to criticism along the lines that its experiences abroad have been very mixed and that, having established overseas operations, it has invariably proved tardy in pursuing them.

Some of those who question the group's continuing commitment to overseas markets suggest that the group's resources could be more productively utilised by further improving and expanding its core assets.

Even so, there is no question that Slough Estates intends to maintain a sizeable proportion of its property assets in overseas markets.

By the end of 1990 the overseas assets accounted, in value terms, for about 25 per cent of the portfolio, split between North America (15 per cent), Europe (five per cent) and Australia (five per cent). The group says it is prepared to see its overseas exposure fluctuate, depending on the relative strength of local markets. What is less clear, however, is where the balance of its overseas interests should lie - an issue on which there are differing views within the executive.

The strategy is simple enough. While, for example, the UK market enjoyed a remarkable "bull run" in the late 1980s, renewing questions about the need for groups like Slough Estates to go abroad, the early 1990s looked decidedly less optimistic. The logic is that overseas markets can, providing their economic cycles are not entirely coincidental, offset any deterioration in the domestic outlook.

But overseas markets, as Slough Estates has sometimes found to its cost, rarely offer parallel conditions to those found in the UK. Everything from lease structures to taxation laws mean that any outside operator has to get up very early to beat the locals at their own game.

With some notable exceptions, such as in Brussels during the early 1970s and in Los Angeles in 1990, the group has managed to steer its way safely through the minefield of overseas property development and investment. Patchy returns have invariably had as much to do with the vagaries of exchange rate fluctuations as with local market performance.

Some City observers certainly believed that, by 1990, the group had lost its way in a tough and diverse American market - a situation which the appointment of Marshall Lees was expected to help remedy. The group's continuing involvement in the US is nevertheless likely to come under increasing scrutiny as it ponders whether the weak market justified its continuing presence, whether it might be best to retreat north of the border or to restructure the US operation.

Slough Estates is generally considered to have done well in Canada, establishing a valuable and soundly-based business in tune with local market requirements and active in Toronto, Montreal and Vancouver.

The group is particularly keen on the sort of quality cash flow generated by a Canadian market offering generally higher yields but lower increases in asset values. In markets like the UK, it points out, performance can be too dependent on unrealised appreciation, which can prove vulnerable when conditions deteriorate.

In Australia, finally divested of the Altona estate where the group began its overseas adventures, the business by 1990 looked well bedded-in, although expectations were modest. On a visit to Australia in 1989 Nigel Mobbs engaged in some of his customary plain-talking about prospects for the local economy. He gave a highly critical assessment of its state of health and claimed that conditions for long-term foreign investment in Australia remained very unsatisfactory.

The country, he claimed, was now seen as neither a competitive manufacturing base nor a dynamic customer; its labour costs were high, while the work force managed only low productivity and was known for its awkwardness.

Mobbs also attacked local planning authorities for operating under systems and laws which encouraged them "to be fickle and capricious" in the application of development control. Changes in national attitude, he stressed, were essential if Australia was to become an industrial leader in the 21st Century. Despite his damning indictment, however, Slough Estates seems ready to slog on Down Under.

But it is to Europe, with the 1992 European Single Market on the horizon and ever-closer moves being made towards political and monetary union, that the group's overseas ambitions may now be increasingly directed.

Though Slough Estates does not believe that 1992 will, in itself, do much to change the physical way in which property development and investment is conducted, it does expect changes in the ground rules for doing business.

The group recognises that tremendous scope remains for the development and improvement of Europe's urban infrastructure, though it instinctively hesitates at the prospect of a burgeoning European bureaucracy which threatens to become more intrusive and interventionist - characteristics the property entrepreneur despises.

The group, understandably, is also wary of what it sees as a growing anti-development lobby across Europe, with nations responding to environmental pressures by demanding a halt to the activity which remains an integral part of economic vitality.

According to Nigel Mobbs: "Most countries seem to be adopting a somewhat negative approach to land release for business and it seems inevitable that, without reasonable freedom within the land market, values will increase as will densities of construction which will, in turn, affect environmental values."

The European development industry, he suggests, will have to change some bad habits. In the past, he claims, developers have tended to let down the user by providing an inadequate and poorly specified product, although he emphasises that many "unenlightened" users have been unwilling to pay a fair price for quality design and high specification.

Buildings, Mobbs believes, will have to become increasingly adaptable to change, good for people to work in and efficient to use. He adds: "We will all need to think far more into the future and research into and experiment with more intelligent, loose-fit building solutions."

The prospect, he warns, will lead to "inevitable conflict between enterprise and the negative, reactionary attitudes of the regulators."

While it may have proved a great deal more cautious than many other property companies in joining the rush into Europe in the early 1970s, Slough Estates has at least remained on the Continent, accumulating years of invaluable experience which gives it a headstart on those only just beginning to return to the European scene.

After all the early traumas it is well established in Belgium and slowly expanding in France and Germany, where unification offers vast longer-term opportunities for those businesses with a role to play in welding together Europe's dominant economy. The prospect of developing in Eastern Europe is not yet being taken seriously.

Despite the group's preference for operating in English-speaking countries, the European market will inevitably provide Slough Estates with increasing opportunities, a prospect recognised in its decisions to establish or strengthen local management teams. Progress is expected to be characteristically steady, rather than spectacular, and the next new market to be entered could be Spain.

The outside impression remains, however, of a business still struggling to find the right formula for Europe and, more specifically, to find the proper partners or those companies ripe for acquisition.

Roger Brooke says the group "will need to have a big think about Europe quite soon." He adds: "The Slough Estates style is to experiment a bit, see how it goes and then take another step. In Europe, the time has come to take some more steps."

But the group also has other strategic decisions to make about its future. Wherever it may decide to concentrate its activities, it also has to strike a balance over the type of property it chooses to develop.

Though the group is, and is set to remain, overwhelmingly an industrial property developer, it has begun to establish for itself a capability in retail and office development, generating internally the necessary management skills.

According to Graeme Elliot: "We have become much more opportunist; much less ready to say we will not do it because we have not done it before. We have not yet cracked the old external image, although those within the industry see us as having changed quite significantly."

By the end of 1990 around 65 per cent of the group's worldwide investment portfolio was accounted for by industrial property, with offices taking 20 per cent and the balance in retail accommodation. That, according to Elliot, is where the balance is likely to remain.

To some outsiders the gradual transformation has come about simply because the group felt it was something it should be doing. There was not, they claim, any heartfelt enthusiasm for making the change.

Slough Estates denies the charge, claiming that any company in its position must attempt to spread its activities and, hence, reduce its vulnerability. As Roger Carey puts it: "We are determined to retain our position in the industrial market but we are a property company and not just an industrial property company.

The group cannot claim that its planned diversification into other sectors of the property market has met with universal success. It has faced a tough learning curve which has seen it make mistakes along the way.

Nevertheless, Carey believes the strategy is working well: "Once, no-one would dream of talking to us about taking on a shopping or office scheme. Now that we have proved we can do them, we get asked to do others. But we still have our work cut out in ensuring that people appreciate the breadth of abilities."

The move into offices has been criticised by observers who invariably suggest that the group has not developed the necessary expertise to compete successfully alongside more established office specialists. Despite the scepticism, most of the group's office schemes have proved successful.

In fact the group saw the start of its office developments as a wholly logical step given the narrowing gap between office and industrial accommodation in a "high-tech" property world and the increasing need to blend together both types of floorspace.

The decision to expand into retailing has also drawn critical remarks from those unhappy to see Slough Estates stray from its traditional market. Its experiences at Welwyn Garden City, which has consumed substantial resources and presented the group with numerous problems, may have helped strengthen the case of the detractors.

But the group's link-up with Bredero has been seen in a more positive light, even if the policy of pursuing some retail schemes independently while channelling others through the Bredero partnership is sometimes not always appreciated.

The Bredero deal was indisputably seen as a coup for its 52 per cent owners, bringing into the group overnight a retail development team widely regarded as highly professional, knowledgeable and competent.

But it is common knowledge that the partnership has, at times, been under strain. Given its expertise, the Bredero team has not always been quick to genuflect to its big shareholder and Slough Estates has shown itself nervous at the scale of some of the projects being undertaken.

Nigel Mobbs admits to "moments of tension" but readily praises the skills of a Bredero management motivated by the continuing ownership of a substantial equity stake in their business. The group explains its decision to continue to pursue, without Bredero's involvement, some retail schemes on the grounds that it would otherwise always be depriving its shareholders of 48 per cent of every deal.

"It is conceivable that, one day, Bredero perhaps will grow to the point where it ought to have an even greater degree of independence. We would then want to ensure we had established our own retail presence. It might, however, work the other way round, with us taking full control. Either way, we agreed to do nothing for several years after the acquisition. We will just have to see how it works out," says Mobbs.

At the end of 1990 Slough Estates announced that it was subscribing for up to £10 million of preference shares in Bredero. The move followed concern that Bredero might breach its lending covenants at the end of the year because of a decline in its net asset value brought about by the weakness of the property market.

Slough Estates also revealed that it was reducing its 52 per cent stake in Bredero to 49.5 per cent, a move which meant that it would not have to consolidate the results of Bredero. The Slough Estates board said that, following the new injection of capital, it was rescinding its undertaking not to increase its stake in Bredero.

The group also faces further repeated questioning about its more recent readiness to diversify into non-property activities. Its involvement in US and UK capital funds and in joint ventures to restructure ailing oil and gas businesses in the United States represent a tiny commitment but, quite predictably, leave the analysts, and some people within the group, uncomfortable.

Such ventures, the City claims, do not form part of any clear long-term strategy and do not fulfil any useful function. If they do not understand them, they add, it is because they are never fully explained.

Nigel Mobbs repeatedly stresses that the leveraged buy-out deals do reflect the group's broad investment philosophy and also contribute towards an value-added strategy, something which its critics often claim is missing.

"The sort of deals we are involved in offer an average rate of return of up to 40 per cent per annum. They will never be dominant but to devote a small proportion of resources to this type of investment is perfectly justifiable."

As if to underline its readiness to try pastures new, 1990 saw the group conducting a feasibility study into a proposal to bottle and sell the estate's pure 10,000-year-old water to a public now increasingly prepared to buy drinking water. According to Fergie Wiggin: "Slough does not, it is true, have a mountain stream image but the estate meets all the onerous requirements of a supplier of water.

Ours is of excellent quality and the market is there."

Another source of contention is the group's apparently increasing readiness to participate more actively in property trading, a part of the property market which carries with it considerable risks and which has proved the undoing of many other property companies.

Concern about Slough Estates' trading activities already existed before the disclosure of the 1990 trading losses. The group, however, remains unrepentant about pursuing a trading operation which guarantees a flow of potential projects that may not offer a long-term income stream but which provide good short-term profits. It accepts that the business is left more exposed at times of market weakness and, by the end of 1990, had to face up to the reality that its trading activities had helped provoke the first break in the post-war cycle of ever-increasing profits.

As a result the level of property trading may well be reduced in future. According to one broker: "Slough does not need trading profits of any significance. They have, nevertheless, become a little too important and should never account for more than 20 per cent of profits at most."

One of the most central and intriguing questions remains how Slough Estates intends to maintain the momentum of growth which it has established in recent years.

The group is not acquisitive by nature; there are those who say it is simply not adventurous enough to identify an attractive target and chase it and that when Slough Estates is mentioned in reference to takeovers, the assumption is that it will always be on the receiving end.

In its 70-year history the number of companies the group has acquired remains small and they have usually been relatively insignificant, like Hertford Industrial Estates or Helmlace. The exception was Allnatt, the fruition of a long and unique business relationship. The controlling interest in Bredero came on a plate.

Slough Estates, however, cannot be accused of failing to keep one eye open for possible bid situations. In recent years it has considered links with several major property companies. Nothing has ever materialised.

According to Peter Hardy of S.G. Warburg Securities: "Part of Slough's problem is that it has an industrial portfolio producing very good yields. Whatever it looks at in terms of diversification could easily lead to a dilution of earnings, even if the quality of assets might improve. The group examines quite a lot of things but, much of the time, they do not make any sense. One of the group's great strengths is that management looks at the profit and loss account before it looks at anything else."

Roger Moore, Hardy's colleague at Warburgs, adds: "Some say Slough Estates should be in the market acquiring but there really is no point in it buying up assets just for the sake of it. If they can build up organically, then so much the better."

The group itself denies that it is not interested in acquisition.

Nigel Mobbs concedes that internal growth has accounted for much of the expansion of recent years. Of the company's acquisition record, he adds: "The difference is that we have often acquired real estate rather than companies. We are not against takeovers and marriages but we traditionally resist the dilution of shareholder's interests. If we can secure friendly acquisitions on a broadly matching basis, that is excellent. But a hostile bid means the defence will rely on asset values; the resulting issue of paper is detrimental."

All the indications are, however, that Slough Estates will continue to seek, and intends to secure, major acquisitions. "Given the right opportunities, we will be right in there," says Graeme Elliot. "Portfolios in the £50 million - £100 million range are certain to become available in the medium-term and we will be watching."

But Slough Estates has another constituency besides the City which it needs to please. While analysts and brokers paw over the group's financial performance, it is as a landlord that the business is judged by more than 2,000 tenants.

Companies prepared to endorse the group's philosophy concerning the advantages of leasing or renting over freehold ownership will only do so if they can depend on a landlord who is fair and alive to their changing requirements.

Slough Estates has not always had a reputation as a good landlord although, by its very nature, the role is unlikely ever to win too many friends. It has, at times, been accused of demanding excessive rents, of being an inflexible negotiator and of keeping too tight a rein on tenants.

It has also been criticised for its uncompromising attitude towards dilapidations. When a tenant leaves, a building is expected to be reinstated to the condition in which it was originally found. Nigel Mobbs is uncompromising: "I do not like our buildings being abused."

In more recent years, however, it appears largely to have regained its reputation as a property owner which recognises that its own success rests with the well-being of its tenants.

According to Peter Hardy: "The company's attitude is straightforward enough. It is tough but fair. It will never go for the last penny but it believes in striking a two-way deal in which its tenants also behave reasonably and fairly."

Graeme Elliot concedes that relationships with tenants - now referred to as customers - have not always been good. "Now they all appoint agents to act for them on lease negotiations, so we have fewer opportunities to fall out face to face." He believes, more seriously, that greater efforts to improve liaison between landlord and customer have been made and are paying off.

Wallace Mackenzie concedes that the going will always get tough when rents are up for renegotiation. "Whatever the justification for increases, the tenant will naturally object. Some will always consider what we are asking to be outrageous but all we want is the market value for our property."

Nigel Mobbs has his own views about the group's reputation. "Some think we are nasty and hard. Others think we are fairly tough and difficult when it comes to rent negotiations. Well, I don't mind that. I would be very unhappy if we were known for being soft; that would hardly be good news for our shareholders. And the fact is that tenant turnover remains low."

Mobbs stresses that the room for flexibility in dealing with rents has, in any case, been limited by landlord and tenant legislation. "If we decide to discount rent on review to a tenant, it would be used against us as evidence in every other deal. We are far less able to give special terms. Each tenant is well advised by people sifting all the available evidence and ready to use it to the advantage of their client."

Slough Estates also believes that, as part of its heritage, it has responsibilities which stretch beyond its customers and its shareholders. The community in which it operates remains, as it did during the earliest days of the business, a central and continuing obligation. A social awareness and sense of community still permeates through the group's activities, particularly in Slough, where it all began.

Slough Estates has been careful to maintain links with the organisations which it helped found. Nigel Mobbs is chairman of Corporate Health, formerly the Slough Occupational Health Service, and of the grant-giving Slough Social Fund. The business also operates a community affairs policy intended to ensure a deeper involvement in the life of the local community and to encourage others to follow suit.

By 1990 group charitable donations, the day-to-day responsibility of Neville White, manager, external affairs, had reached nearly £300,000. As a member of the Per Cent Club, Slough Estates undertakes to donate a sum equivalent to at least one per cent of its gross annual dividends to community charities, many of them in the Slough area and extending from the world of business to arts and leisure.

On occasions Slough Estates will also second staff or make available buildings to assist particular charitable causes. Executive directors and some senior managers, who are encouraged by the chairman to develop community interests, are allocated annual budgets to respond to charitable appeals made directly to them. There are also separate trust funds which make contributions to a range of local causes.

Graeme Elliot considers the group's community activities an integral part of its past and of its future. "We are lucky as a company not be based in London but somewhere with a strong sense of local identity. There are plenty of opportunities for us to help. We owe the community."

Nigel Mobbs echoes the same theme of responsibility. "We are part and parcel of the local community. We must have a close relationship with the local council and the local population. Since the inception of the business, it has been encouraged to be aware of its impact on the wider community and never to lose sight of its wider responsibilities. The philosophy will remain in place."

The group's contribution is readily acknowledged and warmly praised by Slough District Council. Arden Bhattacharya, the town clerk, is happy to describe the business as "the backbone of the town."

He explains: "Slough Estates not only provides employment but also commits itself to meeting the wider needs of the town and the community. Co-operation is first class. We have done quite a lot for them and they, in turn, have done a lot for the town. Essentially, we trust each other."

Bhattacharya accepts that relationships over the years, during which the political flavour of the council has changed several times, have not always been easy. At the start of the 1990s the local authority was under Labour control and though its dialogue with a champion of the free-market economy and a reliable contributor to Conservative Party funds might be expected to be less than constructive, the record shows differently.

The town clerk believes that, since the mid-1970s, the council and the property developer have between them provided a consistent example of a mutually beneficial partnership between business and community. "Life is certainly made easier because they control the entire estate and, as the single freeholder, we can work through them and not dozens of individual companies. We have regular discussions on an informal basis at a fairly senior level so that both sides remain well informed. When a major planning application comes in, much of the background work will have already been done."

The town clerk rejects the suggestion that Slough Estates, because of its dominant standing in the town and its influence over the local economy, expects any special treatment. "They would certainly not like a refusal for a planning application and would hope our relationship would always lead to agreement on any aspect of estate development which falls within our remit. They do not, as the biggest centre of employment in the town, throw their weight around."

Bhattacharya adds: "You always get the impression that Slough Estates feels it belongs in Slough. For that reason nothing is too much for them, providing it fits within their corporate strategy. They want to help the people of Slough and their town."

The council, he adds, takes a certain pride from having the name of its town attached to a successful international group with the stature of Slough Estates. A measure of the extent to which the two sides have established a constructive, working bond can be detected in expressions of sadness and regret at the very prospect, however remote, that one day Slough Estates could be taken over.

Bhattacharya reserves a special word of praise for Nigel Mobbs, whom he regards as "amicable and understanding" and intent upon doing his best for his own business and for the town.

Despite the global dimensions to the Slough Estates business, it still manages to retain something of a paternalistic air and approach to its work and Nigel Mobbs remains very much "head of the family."

It is a family which has, until now, made a calculated effort to ensure that the dynasty does not die. Mobbs has been careful to ensure that the group is increasingly capable of regenerating its own management from within.

While people like Roger Carey, Graeme Elliot and Derek Wilson have been brought in from elsewhere, the business now contains within its own ranks managers who will be capable of reaching the top. "We now have very good people coming up through the line which we did not have a decade ago. The succession will appear from within in future," says Mobbs.

As for the chairman himself, he has managed, during his stewardship of the group, to dispel any temptation to suggest that his position owed more to nepotism than to business acumen. According to Roger Brooke: "Nigel may have been born with a silver spoon in his mouth but he has more than proved himself since. He very much runs the show but he is a sufficiently big man to submit his judgements to debate among the other directors."

There are some, however, who still think the business retains something of the air of a private fiefdom, with the chairman retaining the final world on comparatively trivial issues which might not normally justify attention at such a level.

Those people with long enough memories say Mobbs is a full-size replica of his grandfather, displaying the same business skills and instincts. While his tenure at Slough Estates emanated directly from his family connection, he would, they concede, have been successful in whatever he had chosen to do.

His standing in the property world as something of a guru, ready to challenge conventional beliefs, has inevitably given him a high profile. His views may not always have been welcome but they have been valuable; his experience has led government and professional organisations to seek the benefit of his advice.

Apart from his boardroom posts with Barclays Bank and Kingfisher Group, Mobbs is a director of Cookson Group and of Howard de Walden Estates, a major central London landowner. He is also chairman of the Department of Trade and Industry advisory panel on deregulation charged with reducing the amount of "red tape" in government.

His other responsibilities include the chairmanship of the

Groundwork Foundation, a nationwide partnership between public and oprivate sectors to help restore the environmental damage left in the wake of decades of industrial activity, and membership of the Commonwealth War Grave Commission.

Sir Nigel is also chairman of Aims of Industry, the right-wing pressure group for promoting free enterprise, to which Slough Estates first made a subscription in 1943. He is also the inaugural president of the British Council for Offices, formed in 1990 to help promote better quality office space.

According to one City man who knows him well: "He has a very quick brain and always asks the right questions. He has enormous drive and enthusiasm but does not rush his fences. He consults on everything and discusses and deliberates before making decisions." Another remarks: "He has a prodigious knowledge of the property business and, if he has a failing, it is that he dislikes anyone else knowing more than him. It can occasionally cause problems."

Mobbs is often caricatured as the prep school prankster, at heart still the fourth-form schoolboy. It is an image which his ready chuckle and spontaneous sense of fun helps perpetate. But he is also sometimes seen, even by admirers, in a slightly different light. "He can be a bit of a bully. He's a very big guy and there is quite a bit of weight to throw around if he feels like it," according to one old acquaintance.

Any such reservations are, however, overwhelmed by Mobbs' unquestionable contribution to the success and growth of a business which entered the 1990s as Britain's fourth-largest property company, owner of the biggest industrial estate in the country and the nation's largest industrial landlord.

At the end of 1990 the group held assets of more than £2 billion. It was receiving from its worldwide property interests around £100 million in annual rental income. With a global land bank approaching 500 acres, it looked forward to a development programme which, in the medium-term, would cost around £1 billion to complete. The figures provide adequate testimony to the group's progress and offers a scale of achievement which would have proved beyond the comprehension of its far-sighted founders.

Behind the story of Slough Estates' success lies not only a consistent philosophy about the profitable and professional provision of commercial accommodation but an enduring belief in the role of the property entrepreneur.

Back in 1977, when the private property developer was again being told that his day had past, overtaken by the institutional and public agency operator, Nigel Mobbs spelled out the views which have formed the backdrop to his group's progress.

"The role of the real estate company would, to my mind, disappear only if we were to live in a perfect world. In a perfect world there would be no risk; in a perfect world there would be no need, either, for the institutions.

"But we do not live in a perfect world; we live in a world where the enterprise and skill of the individual will always be greater than that of a committee which may be governed by other investment considerations and philosophies."

Sovereign Court, a Georgian-style office development at Wapping in London Docklands.

Mobbs' remarks underline his conviction that, during the previous decade or so, some developers had been motivated more by the needs of the end-investor than of the occupier. The mere fact that there were rich investors willing to buy empty property at inflated prices only created a false market which could never be sustained.

Office/industrial building for Lego in Bentley, an investment property in Toronto, Canada.

"A real estate entrepreneur will recognise and assume the risks; he has the appetite to create investments, the experience to manage the investment effectively and the expertise to provide a service of advice to the customer who, very often, has never before been involved in the creation of new accommodation.

"For these reasons I am confident that there is a role for the property company which is properly managed, conservatively financed, concerned with the wider issues of its business and willing to look forward, rather than backwards."

On top of the estate's 340 ft chimney. It is the summer of 1990 and Sir Nigel Mobbs accepts a presentation trowel from Roger Bierrum, chairman of contractors Bierrums, after the topping out ceremony following the latest modernisation of the power station.

For Slough Estates, occasionally looking back can be a matter of satisfaction and pride. To ensure the story continues, however, it will have to keep its eyes fixed resolutely on the future. The property investor who grows complacent risks all.

The latest Slough Estates board lineup. Standing (left to Right) Joseph Harding, Derek Wilson, John Probert (company secretary). Sitting (left to right) Sir Donald Maitland, Douglas Kramer, Graeme Elliot, Sir Nigel Mobbs, Roger Cary, Wallace Mackenzie, Roger Brooke. Insert Paul Orchard-Lisle.

Slough Estates has championed consistency, security and solid progress in a highly risky business. It may well continue to face accusations of being "boring." But if the alternative is to join the ranks of those "here-today-gone-tomorrow whizz kids," there is no contest over which particular description it will risk.

APPENDIX

Directors Down The Years	Date Appointed	Ceased To Be A Director
Sir Arthur Noel Mobbs KCVO OBE	May 19 1920	Nov 25 1959
Rt. Hon. Lord Perry KBE	May 19 1920	July 1 1952
Commander Redmond Walter McGrath	May 19 1920	Mar 27 1960
Edward Henry Dulley JP	Mar 14 1929	Feb 24 1957
Cecil M. Woodbridge JP	Apr 15 1931	Aug 24 1951
Gerald Aubrey Mobbs DL	Apr 4 1945	Mar 31 1976
Lt. Col. William Henry Kingsmill DSO MC	Apr 4 1945	June 3 1971
Charles William Fairall	Mar 29 1950	Aug 16 1967
Sir Owen Frederick Morshead GCVO KCB DSO MC	Mar 20 1951	May 22 1968
Sir Hubert Nutcombe Hume KBE MC	Oct 5 1954	Dec 22 1967
William Frederick Smith	Oct 5 1954	Feb 5 1958
Ronald William Diggens OBE	Nov 21 1956	Dec 31 1985
Sir Gerald Nigel Mobbs DL	Sept 4 1963	
Christopher Charles Clifford-Kingsmill	Sept 4 1963	May 23 1977
John Godfrey Vaughan	Feb 28 1968	Oct 13 1984
Douglas Lofting	Feb 28 1968	May 20 1981
Sir Roderick Edward Barclay GCVO KCMG	July 2 1969	May 23 1984
Joseph Charles Harding JP	Feb 8 1971	
Wallace John Mackenzie OBE	Mar 22 1972	
Derek Maunsell Millis	May 1 1975	Apr 30 1987
John Barrie Backes	June 29 1977	Jan 31 1980
Robert Anthony Lewis Phipps	May 18 1978	Apr 28 1983
Paul David Orchard-Lisle CBE TD DL	June 25 1980	
Christopher Roger Ettrick Brooke	July 23 1980	
Douglas Kramer	Jan 28 1981	
Sir Donald James Dundas Maitland GCMG OBE	Nov 2 1983	
William Jeremy Baker	Dec 1 1983	Feb 28 1986
Roger William Carey	Dec 1 1983	
Leslie Herbert Smith	Jan 30 1984	Apr 16 1989
Graeme Arthur Elliot	Nov 1 1985	
Derek Robert Wilson	Nov 3 1986	
Peter Handley Johnston	Nov 10 1986	May 31 1989

INDEX